The Bible True, Relevant or a Fairy Tale

Of what relevance is a book, thousands of years old, in our modern times?

Robert J Cottle

Revised and updated revision – 2023.

All scripture quotations are taken from the New King James Version. Copyright © 1982, by Thomas Nelson, Inc. Used by permission. All rights reserved." ™

Scripture quotations marked (NLT) are taken from the Holy Bible, New Living Translation, copyright ©1996, 2004, 2007, 2013, 2015 by Tyndale House Foundation. Used by permission of; Tyndale House Publishers, Inc., Carol Stream, Illinois 60188. All rights reserved.

Scripture quotations marked (KJV) are taken from the King James Version.

Scripture quotations marked (ESV) are taken from the ESV® Bible (The Holy Bible, English Standard Version®), copyright © 2001 by Crossway, a publishing ministry of Good News Publishers. Used by permission. All rights reserved

Unless noted otherwise all scripture quotations in this book (highlighted in italics) are from the New King James, English translation, of the Bible.

Copyright © 2023 by the **Bellbird Trust**

Published by: **Bellbird Books,**
2 Sabine Drive,
Richmond, Nelson, 7020,
New Zealand.

ISBN 978-1-7386150-6-3 (Paperback)
ISBN 978-1-7386150-7-0 (Hardback)

All rights reserved. This book or any part thereof may not be reproduced, stored in a retrieval system, or transmitted in any form or by any means – electronic, mechanical, photocopy, recording, scanning or other – except for brief quotations in critical reviews or articles, without the prior express written permission of the publisher.

Special thanks:

To my Bible study life group leader and Church elder, who asked not to be named, he diligently reviewed this book from a theological perspective helping to ensure my use of scripture was sound.

To my friend Bruce for his time-consuming efforts in editing this book.

Paul tells Timothy (2 Timothy 3:16, ESV); *"all scripture is God breathed"* and in Genesis 2:7 we read; *"God breathed into his nostrils the breath of life, and the man became a living being"*. If the followers of Jesus inhale the God breathed scriptures their souls will truly abound with life. This book sets out to inspire Christians to believe God at his word.

My Life and Family

I once did live, in Can-a-da
Her cousin came there, from afar.
I said my man, she's pretty sweet
Soon we were wed, and then did fleet
To our home, New Zee-a-land
For beaches here, have golden sand

My wife announces, little feet
We have a son, how elite
Work in Scotland, now is best
And soon we were, but further blest
A boy, a girl, together came
Our quiver full, it was no game

But blest we are, and no more roam
And love the place, we do call home
All too soon, our arrows flit
To manage, fly and swim a bit

For further grand ones, we do hope
And pray they too, may learn to cope

So now we have, more time to rest
And truly see, how God has blest
A family, all so versed in Him
Not all battles, did we win
But always He, was near at hand
Walking too, on golden sand

***Dedicated to my wife Julie,
and our arrows Bentley, Joseph and Roberta***

Table of Contents

Special thanks: iii
My Life and Family v
Introduction - What is it about the Bible? ix
Chapter 1 Truth 1
Chapter 2 Fact or Fiction 17
Chapter 3 Fairy Tales 47
Chapter 4 Evidence 80
Chapter 5 Prophecy 100
Chapter 6 History in the Bible 131
Chapter 7 Writing of the Bible 158
Chapter 8 Conflicts within the Bible 182
Chapter 9 History of the Bible 204
Chapter 10 Knowledge 231
Chapter 11 What is the Real Story? 252
Chapter 12 Who is the God of the Bible? 281
Chapter 13 Relevance Today 311
Chapter 14 How to Read It 327
About the Author 337
Notes: 339

Introduction -
What is it about the Bible?

The word 'Bible' comes from the Greek and Latin words which mean 'books' and 'the book'. The Bible is a collection of books as well as a single book. Thousands of other books have been written about the Bible over the years. This book however is not written about the Bible but what is it, about the Bible.

Very few, in any country around the world, would deny having heard of the Bible. Many millions would claim to have read it or at least read a chapter or two, some perhaps when passing time while enduring a seemingly uninteresting sermon. Others have made it their life's work to study every word in it and to delve into the depth of the meaning of each verse. In contrast there are some who have made it their sole ambition to discredit the Bible. While others who perhaps may have never actually held a copy of it, claim it to be a complete work of fiction with zero relevance in today's world.

The statistics around the Bible are staggering; Statistic Brain has compiled the following interesting list of Bible Statistics and facts: [1]

Number of total Bibles printed (mid 2016)	6,001,500,000
Approximate number of languages spoken in the world today	6,900
Number of translations into new languages currently in progress	1,300
Number of languages with a translation of the New Testament	1,185
Number of languages with a translation of the Bible (Protestant Canon)	451
Total Books in the King James Bible	66
Total Number of Authors in the Bible	40
Years it took to write the Bible	1,600
Total Chapters in the King James Bible	1,189
Number of verses in the King James Bible	31,102
Total Words in the King James Bible	788,258

Sales and ownership:

The annual sales figures for the Bible are between $425m and $650m, repeatedly – year after year – it dwarfs the sales of all other books. Gideons International reports it gives away a Bible every second. The Bible is now available all or in part in 2,426 languages, covering 95% of the world's population.

The Economist estimates more than 100m new Bibles are printed every year.[2.] They also point out that in 2005 the number of Bibles sold in the US alone was conservatively estimated at 25 million and Barna Group research indicates that 92% of all American households have at least one Bible and typically own three.[3]

Introduction -
What is it about the Bible?

By comparison the hugely popular Harry Potter seven book series has sold only 400 million copies total. Mao's book of quotations is believed to have sold over 900 million total copies since 1966, and the Koran which became popular in recent years has sold an estimated 800 million copies in total.[3] Saudi Arabia is spearheading the distribution of the Koran and they give away some 30 million Korans each year.

Not only does the Bible continue to enjoy annually increasing sales and distribution totals, it does so strictly without coercion. No one is required to buy, own, read or believe the Bible. In fact, in most Western Countries which are heavily influenced by the Bible, freedom reigns.

In addition to the printed Bible there are numerous electronic versions. The hugely popular Bible App claims to have over 200 million Android and 180 million Apple versions downloaded.

Readership

Availability and access to the Bible today is simply astounding. Yet there follows some very puzzling statistics:

In the earliest years of church history clerics refused to translate the Bible into common languages arguing that only the well trained should read it. Anyone who refused to accept this dictum and made an effort to translate it into any language other than Latin were persecuted and in some cases executed. John Wycliffe was one of the first to translate the Bible from

The Bible – True, Relevant or a Fairy Tale?

Latin into English. Although he died of natural causes, he was persecuted while he lived and pronounced a heretic several years after his death following which his remains were exhumed in 1428, crushed, burned and thrown into the River Swift. William Tyndale was the first to translate the Bible into English directly from Hebrew and Greek. His New Testament was also the first English translation to be printed using the printing press. For his efforts, he was executed by strangling and burned at the stake.

We now fast forward to the twenty first century and according to the Ponce Foundation; despite ownership being at an all-time high, of over 2 billion Christians in the world, less than 30% will ever read through the entire Bible.[4]

A recent survey by LifeWay Research in the USA provided the following interesting results.[5]

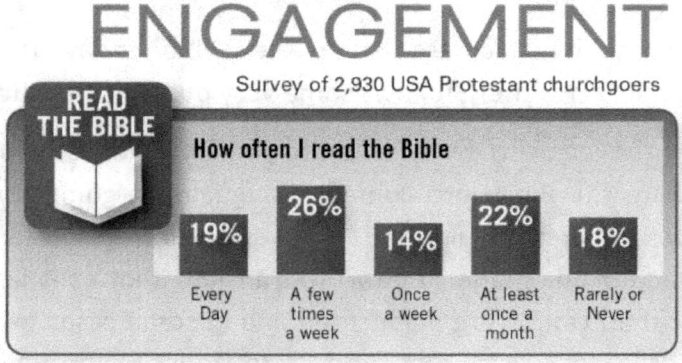

Introduction -
What is it about the Bible?

That's 40% of all Churchgoers who hardly ever read their Bibles!

LifeWay Research and the United Kingdom Bible Society have recently released survey findings on Biblical literacy and found that: [6]

- Only 45% of regular church attendees read their Bible more than once a week.
- Almost 1 in 5 (20%) **churchgoers** say they never read the Bible at all.

It's sad to see that in both the UK and in the USA 18% - 20% of all churchgoers never read their Bibles and only 45% read it more than once a week and a mere 19% of Christians in the USA read their Bibles every day!

Believing and Knowledge

Despite the number of Bibles available in the USA the state of Biblical knowledge is abysmal. A Gallup survey [7] found that less than half of all Americans can name the first book of the Bible (Genesis), only a third know who delivered the Sermon on the Mount (Billy Graham is a popular answer) and a quarter do not know what is celebrated at Easter (the resurrection, the foundational event of Christianity). Sixty per cent cannot name half the Ten Commandments; 12% think Noah was married to Joan of Arc. George Gallup, a leading Evangelical as well as a premier pollster, describes America as "a nation of Biblical illiterates". I suspect it is not just America who is illiterate and that the problem is global – at least in the English speaking regions.

The following is a summary of findings from a 2016 poll on American views on Christian theology. [8] Only the results of American with Evangelical Beliefs are included. Some results are as you would hope but some are astounding – 30% agree they personally choose how to interpret God's Word!

American views on Christian theology from Nashville-based LifeWay Research - 2016	
Results from Americans with Evangelical Beliefs	Agree
God is the author of Scripture.	94%
The Bible alone is the written word of God.	95%
The Bible is 100% accurate in all that it teaches.	95%
The Bible, like all sacred writings, contains helpful accounts of ancient myths but is not literally true.	17%
The Bible was written for each person to interpret as he or she chooses.	30%
Churches that do not preach from the Bible should not be considered a Christian church.	81%
Modern science discredits the claims of Christianity.	56%
God created male and female."	99%
God accepts the worship of all religions, including Christianity, Judaism and Islam.	48%
Even the smallest sin deserves eternal damnation.	47%

Introduction -
What is it about the Bible?

Hell is an eternal place of judgment where God sends all people who do not personally trust in Jesus Christ.	84%

Gallup regularly updates its on-going Values and Beliefs poll [9] and recent results show only 28% of all Americans believe the Bible is the actual word of God and that it should be taken literally. This is somewhat below the 38% to 40% seen in the late 1970s, and near the all-time low of 27% reached in 2001 and 2009. But about half of all Americans continue to say the Bible is the inspired word of God, not to be taken literally -- meaning a combined 75% believe the Bible is in some way connected to God. About one in five (21%) Americans view the Bible in purely secular terms – as ancient fables, legends, history, and precepts written by man – which is up from 13% in 1976.

But in spite this lack of serious readership, knowledge and belief the Bible still enjoys the greatest popularity of any book ever produced in human language in terms of ownership at least.

I have been concerned for some time that many Christians didn't really read or believe the Bible but it wasn't until I began to research for this book that I began to comprehend the magnitude. The Bible itself in says in 2 Timothy 3:16 that *"Every Scripture is God-breathed and profitable for teaching, for reproof, for correction, and for instruction in righteousness."* **"Every Scripture"** is a massively bold statement and the list of what it's profitable for also covers all the bases. Yet the Gallup survey above tells us that 72% of those polled don't actually believe that statement. "Houston we have a problem"!

This book is not intended to debate in depth the existence of God or evolution verses creation. Much has already been very ably written on those subjects.

My intentions are to:

- Demonstrate that the Bible is actually true and factual,
- Discuss what it is really about and determine if it is relevant to our lives today.

A note on Bible verses quoted in this book.

Unless noted otherwise all Bible quotations in this book are taken from the New King James translation of the Bible and used by permission.

Finally, I believe that God has a sense of humour so I have incorporated well-meaning but ambiguous quotes from various church signs around the world at the start of each chapter.

*"Come to Church this Sunday,
It will scare the Hell out of you"*

Chapter 1
Truth

"What is truth"? That's the question Pontus Pilate asked Jesus the same day he ordered his crucifixion. You can almost hear his words breaking off to ponderous thought. Pontus Pilate perhaps for the first time in his life paused to consider what truth actually was. This is a man who at the time was Prefect of the Roman province of Judaea serving under Emperor Tiberius and as such was granted the power of supreme judge. He had the sole authority to determine a criminal's fate and had likely passed numerous judgements involving lengthy prison sentences or the Roman favourite, crucifixion. Yet amazingly here he was trying to figure out what truth actually is. Sounds ridiculous doesn't it? Fortunately today with much better education we all fully understand what "truth" is, - don't we?

The Merriam-Webster's Learner's Dictionary gives the simple definition of truth as: [1]

- The real facts about something: the things that are true.
- The quality or state of being true.

- A statement or idea that is true or accepted as true.

The standout word in those definitions is the word "true" – the real facts. Things are either true or false, it is a binary term. There is no such thing as half-truths or white lies; despite the fact they're common in our vocabulary. The meaning of "I am ok," most will understand, often has little actual truth in it. Merely saying something doesn't make it true.

Based on a Nazi fundamental, one of Hitler's cronies Joseph Goebbels is reported to have infamously said [2] "If you tell a lie big enough and keep repeating it, people will eventually come to believe it."

Jeffrey Herf, a professor of modern German history at the University of Maryland, maintains that [3] Goebbels and the Nazis used the Big Lie to turn long-standing anti-Semitism into mass murder. Herf argues that the Big Lie was a narrative of an innocent, besieged Germany striking back at an "international Jewry", which it said started World War I. The propaganda repeated over and over the conspiracy theory that Jews were the real powers in Britain, Russia and the U.S. It went on to state that the Jews had begun a "war of extermination" against Germany, and so Germany had a duty and a right to "exterminate" and "annihilate" the Jews in self-defence.

Persuasive argument the Nazis used, but not a grain of truth in it.

Chapter 1
Truth

The Internet is a great place to find truth, right? I stumbled across a philosophy blog debating the difference between truth and fact. [4] Here's what one contributor had to say.

"Truths are those things that are not simply acknowledged, but must be discovered, or created. If I say "God exists," and I possess strong reasoning for the affirmative of that statement, then God really does exist, that is a reality. However, if another individual possesses strong reasoning for the negative, and because of this reasoning they believe that God does not exist, then that is also a reality. If we were to debate our ideologies, and my reasoning appeared stronger than theirs, they may choose to adopt my belief that God does exist. If they do, then the existence of God is just as true as the nonexistence of God which they believed a week ago. Truths, as opposed to fact, are much more fluid and malleable than their empirical counterparts."

To express such a statement as a genuine and serious opinion demonstrates just how warped human reasoning has become. So perhaps I extend that argument stating I'm not a human but a cat, and because I also happen to be a powerful debater I'm able to convince others that I actually am a cat, then is that truth? No, I don't think so. In reality it probably means I have stopped taking my psychiatric medication. Sadly such reasoning is the culmination of evolutionary beliefs that holds man as the highest order of developed intelligence. It's the expression of the lie the serpent told the woman in Genesis 3:4 to convince her to eat the forbidden fruit in the Garden of

Eden. *"Your eyes will be opened, and you will be **like God**, knowing good and evil."* (Emphasis added). Man thinks he is "like" God believing his thinking and reasoning creates truth. What utter audacity – man is a created being, and that is truth.

To be very clear, truth is not fluid, nor is it malleable. It is not created; it exists regardless of any human understanding. Adding an "s" to truth (*truths*) does not change the underlying meaning, it does not mean there are many different interpretations, as truth is absolute. Simply because I may not be able to personally verify a truth does not negate the fact that it may be true. God exists even if I haven't verified it personally.

But of course the earth is flat? Influential theologian and philosopher Saint Augustine (354 – 430 AD) objecting to the "fable" of an inhabited Antipodes is reported to have written; [5]

"But as to the fable that there are Antipodes, that is to say, men on the opposite side of the earth, where the sun rises when it sets for us, men who walk with their feet opposite ours that is on no ground credible. And, indeed, it is not affirmed that this has been learned by historical knowledge, but by scientific conjecture, on the ground that the earth is suspended within the concavity of the sky, and that it has as much room on the one side of it as on the other: hence they say that the part that is beneath must also be inhabited. But they do not remark that, although it be supposed or scientifically demonstrated that the world is of a round and spherical form, yet it does not follow that the other side of the earth is bare of

Chapter 1
Truth

water; nor even, though it be bare, does it immediately follow that it is peopled. For Scripture, which proves the truth of its historical statements by the accomplishment of its prophecies, gives no false information; and it is too absurd to say, that some men might have taken ship and traversed the whole wide ocean, and crossed from this side of the world to the other, and that thus even the inhabitants of that distant region are descended from that one first man".

Saint Augustine's rebuttal of a spherical earth is laughable today. However at that time it was the popular belief. Truth is not a matter of belief, it exists whether anybody believes it or not, it is a statement of fact.

Sadly had theologian Augustine looked a bit closer at his Bible he might have noticed a couple of interesting verses:

The Book of Isaiah was written between 701 and 681 B.C. and Isaiah 40:22 states; *"It is he who sits above the circle of the earth."* The Hebrew word translated as "circle" can also be translated spherical.

It's not clear exactly when the Book of Job was written but many scholars place it to the time of the patriarchs at about 1700 to 1900 BC. Job 26:7 states *"He stretches out the north over empty space, He and hangs the earth on nothing."*

The Bible was pretty clear on these facts but yet even a learned theologian such as Saint Augustine didn't really believe the Truth of what he was reading, relying instead on his own reasoning.

A flat earth was a widely held belief by the non-scientific masses to such an extent sailors were afraid to venture too far out towards the horizon at sea in case they dropped off the edge of the world. Today such fear seems ludicrous but to the sailors of those times it was extremely real. A perceived truth is very real to the person believing it regardless of its basis in fact. Just because someone believes something, even with fervent zeal, that does not cause it to be true. Regardless of what these sailors feared, the earth was still round. Truth exists because it is. From a young age we are encouraged and taught to be passionate about what we believe in. On face value there is little wrong with that concept, provided the passion is based on or linked in with truth.

Human reasoning is very creative and a huge variety of beliefs have matured all over the earth and many people are extremely passionate about them, some even to death. A radical Islamic suicide bomber takes his personal belief to the extreme by passionately relying on what he's been told that his entering heaven as a martyr will result in him immediately being allocated 72 virgins for his personal enjoyment. The truth is that, regardless of the terrorist's personal belief, his action is straight-out murder and God says "you shall not murder". No doubt is left of God's statement. The terrorists justify their violent tactics by selectively citing and interpreting their Koran verses according to their own goals and intentions. Coincidently the Koran mentions little of any such a reward for suicide bombers. [6] The 72 virgins promise was originated by one of their terrorist leaders in order to lure new bomb carriers. We

Chapter 1
Truth

call that as brainwashing which, by definition, is diametrically opposed to truth.

The suicide bombers fallacy is crystal clear to most people I expect, but things become considerably murky when one makes an honest review of their personal convictions. Some are passionate about eating only vegetables, while others are adamant meat must be included. In fact there are copious magazine and on-line articles promoting this or that diet and so great is the competition to have their dietary belief promoted there's frequent abandonment of any attempt to determine truth, instead basing theories solely on what the writer passionately believes or prefers. Personally I fully endorse a varied diet, but finding the truth about what we really should or shouldn't eat in this age is nigh-on impossible given the enormous array of dietary advice on offer.

Personal beliefs extend into almost every area of our lives and from one perspective that is what makes us individuals, and after all, God gave us free will. If we are honest though, much of what we personally believe has resulted from what we have been taught, experienced or have a preference for or bias towards. Just because we have been taught the theory of evolution and millions of people around us do believe that somehow through sheer chance man became what he is today, does not mean it's true. God Himself says He created. Who are we going to believe, millions of our peers or the only living God? Truth is truth and truth is binary.

Computer operating software at its most basic levels works solely on a binary principal. Binary code refers to any digital encoding/decoding system in which there are exactly two possible states using the digits 0 and 1 as either off or on. It is mind boggling to me how this simple principal can result in such an incredible array of computer programs that control and influence so many areas of our lives today. Really - my smart phone just counts zeros and ones? I could research for years and perhaps develop an incredibly technical and factual synopsis on how computer software operates but the truth would still remain that at the most basic level any app is only a combination of zeros and ones. Why? Because that is the underlying truth. No matter what words I used or how many for that matter the basic fact would remain 0's and 1's.

At its most basic level there is an amazing bluntness to underlying truth.

"Apparently" during the heart of the industrial revolution at the peak of the coal mining era in Great Britain there was a nasty accident down the mine toward the end of the afternoon shift and unfortunately pick handler Patrick Murphy lost his life. Patrick was part of a strong Irish contingent that had relocated with their wives and families to England to take advantage of the steady employment. Quickly the workmates huddled together to decide how they were to tell poor Patrick's wife and mother of their six youngsters. It was a delicate matter as Patrick had kept them well informed over the years of Mrs Murphy erratic personality. A person of tact was essential and

Chapter 1
Truth

after much debate it was decided that Finn was the most diplomatic and tactful among them, he really had a way with words. Patrick's body was carefully laid into a hand drawn cart and Finn set to his task.

Mrs Murphy was busy preparing the evening meal awaiting the arrival of the breadwinner home for the day when she heard a developing commotion in the street outside. Opening the front door onto the street, along the row of terraced houses she heard a man yelling "Does widow Murphy live here?" "Does widow Murphy live here?" Indigently Mrs Murphy strode from her door exclaiming loudly "I'm Mrs Murphy but I ain't no widow!" Summating all his diplomatic prose Finn replied, "You ain't no widow, ain't you? Well you just come and have a look at what I have in this here cart."

Now nobody could suggest Finn wasn't telling the truth. He certainly was and he left no doubt that he had passed on the truth. I expect few would condone Finn's delivery of the news nowadays nor probably in those days either, but it is a fact that in our culture we have become accustom to things being conveyed to us gently. The underlying news however is still just as raw regardless of how it's presented. Perhaps we have become so accustomed to having negative news bubble wrapped to the extent that what we perceive as truth is not the real truth at all? The Bible does tend to be a little like Finn in getting the word across. I'm not suggesting the Bible is crudely or poorly written, it's exceptionally well written, but when it comes to truth it does not compromise.

The very first line of the first book of the Bible lays all on the line. The words: *"In the beginning, God,"* is simply put as a statement of fact. In a way a little like Finn, no bubble wrapping and simply stated as if it's reiterating an obvious truth.

A padded version of this may read like this;

At the outset of all things, order and sense prevailed allowing it to become apparent that a pre-existing supreme being known as God was the originator of all potential developments.

While that statement is possibly factually correct it has zero impact and blatantly obscures the main point – it's all about God. So just like Finn the Bible begins. No padding, no excuses, this is how it is! *"In the beginning, God."*

Right at this very early point the Bible reader has a decision to make: is this statement true or false? The answer is hugely significant. The Bible itself says whoever comes to Him (God) must believe that He exists, Hebrews 11:6 *"But without faith it is impossible to please Him, for he who comes to God* **must believe that He exists***, and that He is a rewarder of those who diligently seek Him."* [Emphasis added]

The question is not whether the reader understands God; it's simply do they accept God exists. Let's face it, the Bible is a book all about God and if the reader refuses to accept that most basic of statements what's the value in reading on? So does that mean if I'm an atheist I shouldn't read past that point? Of course not. It simply means that the premise of the

Chapter 1
Truth

book "The Bible" is based on the underlying, undeniable, truth that God does exist. That is the foundation for the entire Bible. Deny that truth then the Bible just becomes another book full of history, meaningless stories, numerous genealogies and fairy tales. Accept that truth and suddenly the Book has purpose, it tells me who and what God is, what He has done, what He plans to do, how He relates to people and how I can get to know Him.

The concept of blind acceptance is almost non-existent in the twenty first century. We're all taught from a very early age to question everything. In a secular world that does have some merit, it allows us to expand our knowledge and understanding of many things. Along with this questioning mentality we are also taught facts. 2 + 2 = 4 and sadly for some a lifetime of questioning is never going to change that fact, because it is simply the truth. Truth is truth regardless of our understanding.

A questioning mind when applied to the Bible must be applied in context. Reading the Bible to answer your questions, is what's intended. Questioning everything you read in the Bible will not get you far. So, you're reading along and, bam! there's the answer to your question, what do you do? "Well, I'm not sure I can believe that", or "that just can't be true", "perhaps, maybe." But wait, "if God exists and this book is His handiwork then the answer to my question I have just found should be true too"? 2 Timothy 3:16 states that: *"All Scripture is given by inspiration of God, and is profitable for doctrine, for reproof, for correction, for instruction in righteousness."* Again truth is binary; something is either true or false. If something we are told is not true then it's a lie.

Applying a questioning mentality when reading the Bible initiates an interesting dilemma. If I personally must determine as I read along whether each statement in the Bible is true, then what methodology do I apply to achieve that. How do I substantiate my determination of a true statement? By past experience? What I thought previously? What others tell me? What the majority believe? Or perhaps it just fits best with my world view? Now since the Bible is a book that is telling me about God and how I am to relate to Him, how can I be certain that by picking and choosing what I will believe about Him will help me to understand Him better? It is logical that if I begin reading with a fixed premise then the likely outcome of my Bible reading will be No Change in my understanding.

By believing some statements in the Bible to be true and rejecting others means by extension that the rejected statement must be viewed as a lie. Wait you say, that's a big call, I'm just questioning it. Ok let's just run with that, so you, a created being, are questioning God – remember ALL scripture is given by inspiration of God – and this is the same God that the Bible says in Ephesians 4:6, *"one God and Father of all, who is above all, and through all, and in you all."* God, what you've written here about creation just isn't right. I have studied this methodically and I'm thoroughly convinced that we evolved over billions of years from, well... basically nothing; I just do not accept that you created man and all the animals. Ok so to put it

Chapter 1
Truth

bluntly you're calling God a liar! Bold step. Perhaps Finn's tactful vocabulary is still alive and well after all.

Continuing that argument; if I believe God about some things but that He straight out lied about other things what is my rational for deciding what is true and what is a lie. If God lied about creation what else did He lie to me about? On what basis do I decide? When I finally do find something I agree with, how can I be certain He didn't lie about that too? My eternal salvation through Jesus for example and that I'll go to be with him when I die. Most people really want to believe that because it brings hope of more after death. Just to clarify, of course it is absolutely true, in Jesus we certainly do have eternal life, and I use that to make an obvious example.

Your response may be that the Bible was just written by men and they may have misunderstood God. Ok so you, as a reader of their work in hindsight, have a competent ability to determine what they got right and what they got wrong? Reality is, the same criteria applies, regardless of who you think wrote the Bible, in a way the writer is of no consequence, its either ALL true or its ALL lies. Binary! If we can't believe the writer about creation for example then how can we believe the same writer when he tells us things that resonate with us?

But wait one minute, there were 40 different writers of the Bible! Maybe some of them were better at understanding God than others? Yes, that may possibly be true but despite that all the books of the Bible are completely interconnected and intertwined. In the first book Genesis, we read about Adam and

Eve eating the forbidden fruit which brought about their fall from God and His curse on all mankind. But later in the New Testament we have Jesus coming to give His life to pay the penalty of that curse and restore fully the relationship God fully intended for man.

If these were just random writing by various authors strung together at some much later date it would seem that the author of Genesis had a very fortunate "guess" when he stated that one of the Women's offspring was going to bruise the head of the serpent (Satan). Genesis 3:15 *"And I will put enmity between you and the woman, and between your seed and her Seed; He shall bruise your head, and you shall bruise His heel."* This is a direct prophecy about Jesus and it came to pass when Jesus went to the cross about 4000 years after those words were spoken. Jesus bruised the head of Satan through his death and resurrection. This is just one of many such examples throughout the Bible; clearly someone was overseeing what was written during the extended period when all the books were penned. The Bible itself confirms who that overseer was, none other than God himself.

To suggest the author got some portions of the Bible wrong, by extension means that the untrue portion must be a lie. Since God is the actual author then you're saying God lied? Hebrews 6:17-18 *"In this way God, being determined to show more abundantly to the heirs of the promise the immutability of his counsel, interposed with an oath, that by two immutable things, in which **it is impossible for God to lie**, we may have a*

Chapter 1
Truth

strong encouragement, who have fled for refuge to take hold of the hope set before us." [Emphasis added] Not only is it that God doesn't lie, it's actually impossible for him to do so. We're also told in Numbers 23:19 *"God is not a man, that He should lie, Nor a son of man, that He should repent. Has He said, and will He not do? Or has He spoken, and will He not make it good?"*

The conclusion is that all Scripture therefore must be true. God inspired it regardless of who wrote it down and since it is totally impossible for God to lie then it follows that every single verse in the whole of 66 books of the Bible are totally and completely true and can be fully relied on.

Functioning under that understanding as we read the Bible will put a whole new complexion on it. It is telling the Truth. Everything in it can be relied on 100%. Accepting and fully believing the first four words of the Bible are fundamental to every other word it contains. It bluntly calls those that don't acknowledge God's existence as fools. *"The fool has said in his heart, "There is no God.""* Psalm 14:1. (Part verse). God did give everyone free will but He also gave us reasoning. It is your choice if you wish to have the absolute Supreme Ruler of the universe call you a fool.

Immediately following the statement of the existence of God in Genesis 1:1, it goes on to tells us that God created. Today evolutionary teaching bombards us from every angle. At every opportune moment we are told about billions of years and that somehow through complete random chance man and animals evolved to what we have today. This book is about the Bible and I do not intend to debate the evolution subject as many very competent writers have authored numerous books and papers on the subject. If you have any question regarding creation then I strongly suggest you go to www.creation.com. That independent Christian scientific entity has been around for about 35 years and they have a large vault of information based on physical evidence that strongly supports the Biblical truth of a young earth and an Intelligent Designer.

Given the understanding we have today regarding DNA we know that it is easily degraded yet it is impossible for new information to be added to it randomly without the aid of outside intervention. Despite that we are frequently told, for example, that reptiles randomly found a way to create and add new information to their DNA that allowed them, for example, to develop feathers and take up flight? And that the universe started from a big bang which just randomly occurred out of absolute emptiness. Personally it takes a lot more faith to believe in evolution than it takes to believe in creation and a creator. So why is the theory of evolution so prevalent? Simple: without it you are forced to accept that God created and thereby exists.

Truth - The real facts about something: the things that are true.

Two dangerous negating factors of truth are perceived truth and cotton wool padded truth. "Why let the facts stand in the way of a good story" – anonymous.

*"Need a lifeguard?
Ours walks on water"*

Chapter 2
Fact or Fiction

The darkness was so thick it could be felt and deathly silence was the only atmosphere. Without any precursor suddenly a gigantic thunderous explosion burst out from the centre of this nothingness, simultaneously blasting white hot molten rock and superheated gases in every direction at the speed of light. Darkness was no more, neither was the extreme emptiness. Masses of liquefied rock and gas spewed from the epicentre like continuously erupting popcorn.

Smaller globules of molten rock crashed into larger ones as they screamed outwards into the deep darkness of outer space. For years, centuries and many millennia these molten rocks journeyed onwards to unknown destinations frequently colliding and merging with larger cooling masses of rock and huge gas clouds.

It took a few billion years but eventually some form of organised chaos prevailed. No longer were these rocks hurtling in every which direction. In one particular corner of space several, now much cooler gigantic rocks and enormous gas balls had organised themselves into a group dominated by a colossal gaseous fiery mass which became known as Helios. A gravitation effect held the spherical masses in a trance like orbit around Helios even though there were millions of miles between them. One particular rock sphere had fortuitously gained an orbit about 93 million miles from Helios. This resulted in near optimum temperature zones allowing liquid water to flow freely and water now covered almost its entire surface. This utopia rock eventually became known as Gaea.

Over millions and millions of ensuing years Gaea completely transformed itself through a series of incredible coincidences. The dry land increased, mountains and valleys formed which enabled plant like material to develop and grow, eventually covering all the land. Creatures propelled by their own energy and will, miraculously appeared and evolved to mass produce in the oceans which in time became exceptionally overcrowded forcing some of them to seek habitat on the dry land. Finding no natural predators there, they flourished. Through a process of environmental and natural selection some of these land creatures evolved to become unbelievably large animals while others chose to morph into tiny creatures able to invade the lowest strata of the giant forests. This process continued for many hundreds of thousands of years and eventually one animal, homo erectus, quite by chance developed super intelligence and quickly became dominant over all the other creatures. Because of its naturally developed cunning, extreme

Chapter 2
Fact or Fiction

curiosity together with its ability to farm an abundant food source man thrived and multiplied.

That, my friends is a work of fiction. It's completely the words of my own imagination – but of course loosely based around the prevailing theory of evolution. While it does contain interesting word pictures which paint a particular bias, what I have written is not based on any fact which I have personally researched or proven. It therefore is completely untrue and quite rightly classified as fiction.

The opposite of fiction is non-fiction. Non-fiction deals with facts. The Webster's Dictionary defines fact as: [1]

- something that truly exists or happens: something that has actual existence,
- a true piece of information.

Facts are concrete realities that no amount of reasoning will change. When I acknowledge a fact, I'm doing just that. Facts are not discovered, facts are not created, facts are simply acknowledged as observed.

So what then is the difference between truth and fact? Here's how Jason Hodge put it in his blog: [2]

Truth is, by definition, the extent of all truisms. Everything that is true is part of truth. In every trial the man is either guilty or innocent, never both, never neither. Despite what the fallible court may rule, a truth exists, hidden from all human knowledge, perhaps, but true nonetheless. The thing that is true is also a fact. Fact, in scientific terms is something that is "observably" true, but not different in substance from truth.

All books have a category which allows us to understand in advance a little of the author's bias. In-keeping with the binary truth principal there are only two categories, non-fiction or fiction.

- Non-fiction books contain factual information, such as biographies and history books etc.
- Fiction books always contain a story which was made up by the author.

The Bible has always been placed firmly in the non-fiction category which indicates it is generally accepted to contain factual information. For this to be true it must therefore contain facts. So what are these known facts in the bible? Possibly they are far more numerous than many people realise. Let's take a look at a few;

Creation of the heavens and the earth is the first obvious one. Regardless of your personal belief nobody can deny that the sun, all the stars in the universe, the earth and all the plants and animals on it do actually exist. Somehow they arrived to be where and what they are today. The Bible presents God the creator as an indisputable truth. It gives us clear details on how and what he created and the resulting evidence is plain for all to see.

Chapter 2
Fact or Fiction

Noah's Flood

A little further into Genesis a global flood is recorded. Interestingly several indigenous nations such as the Australian Aborigines and the North American Indians have stories of a global flood passed down by word of mouth through their generations. These stories have an uncanny resemblance to the narrative of the global flood in the Bible, and why not? These nations are the post flood descendants of Noah but only lacked a written language.

Most modern day geologists interpret various rocks strata and formations based on the premise that there never was a global flood, perhaps a large local flood but definitely not a global one. Eliminating a global flood, even as a possibility, in their interpretations of how things came to be, only serves to reinforce a well-developed worldview bias. Other geologists and scientists who *do* take into account the global flood generally arrive at an entirely different interpretation regarding how various canyons formed and pockets of well-preserved fossils originated. Again it's not my place in this book to argue evolution vs. creation and I refer you to www.creation.com for substantial evidence of a global flood.

Be sure to check out on that website the outstanding article [4] by John Baumgardner who has a PhD in Geophysics and Space Physics. He has undertaken a tremendous amount of secular work modelling catastrophic plate tectonics and provides very strong evidence that a breakup of the Earth's tectonic plates caused the movement of various land masses which created the continents we see today. It is widely accepted that the movement of the earth's tectonic plates did create the shape and locations the land masses we now have, except most hold that this could only have occurred over a very long time period. John Baumgartner demonstrates however that these plates moved rapidly, in relative terms, causing catastrophic upheaval. The Bible completely supports this fact, when it states in Genesis 7:11 *"the fountains of the great deep were broken up"*. (part verse) Even for those of us without a PhD its relatively easy to visualise that if huge landmasses were violently broken apart beneath the oceans over a relatively short period then this would likely force fast moving tectonic plates down under others, resulting in a massive change to the level of the seabed together with the thrusting up of the land to fashion massive mountains and valleys then yes, it probably did cause an enormous flood and it certainly doesn't take a great leap of faith from there to accept that those floodwaters covered the entire planet.

Once a global flood is accepted then the reason we find so many well preserved fossils becomes understandable. The flood rapidly buried millions of plants and animals, creating the right conditions for fossils to form. Typically when an animal dies, it decomposes or is scattered by scavengers over time. However, most of the fossils found in sedimentary layers were buried rapidly and some instantaneously. Fossils such as fish eating or giving birth appear to have been frozen in time without warning. Fossilized jellyfish must be rapidly buried to form a fossil because their soft bodies float and decay within

Chapter 2
Fact or Fiction

hours of death. The Earth's surface is covered with sedimentary layers full of fossils that could not possibly have formed by a slow and gradual process as demonstrated in the photo of a fossil below showing a fish eating another. Fish generally are not slow eaters therefore for such a fossil to occur the event must have been catastrophic and extremely rapid.

A fossilised fish eating another fish [5]

Countries and regions

The Bible references many countries that are still in existence and well known to us today; Lebanon, Syria Persia (Iran), Egypt, Ethiopia, India, Greece, Rome, Spain, Crete, Macedonia and of course Israel, to name just some of them. These are all clearly defined in the Bible, often describing their location and geography, mountains, rivers, seas and general features in considerable details. It goes into specific detail, describing the vegetation of some lands, mentioning the cedars that grow in Lebanon used by King Solomon in his vast building campaigns, and the papyrus plants along the river Nile where the baby Moses was hidden at 3 months old. It also defines various ethnic groups; their languages, cultures and traditions. I ask you, how many of these are disputed as fact.

The land of Israel

Israel is an incredible example of Biblical accuracy. Israel today is a powerful modern nation yet its religion and culture are exactly as described in the Bible. The towns around the Sea of Galilee where Jesus lived and taught during his public teaching years are real places and in many cases still inhabited as modern villages. Jerusalem of course exists as a large city, as does the Temple Mount the location of the Israelite Temple of God. The Temple Mount area is still known as Mount Moriah which is documented as the location where Abraham was told to sacrifice his son Isaac, until God intervened. The Kidron Valley (also known as the Valley of Josaphat) is the valley on the eastern side of The Old City of Jerusalem, separating the Temple Mount from the Mount of Olives. King David mentions that valley and Jesus crossed it many times with his disciples on his way to the Mount of Olives and the Garden of Gethsemane.

The Mount of Olives or Mount Olivet is a literal mountain ridge east of and adjacent to the old city of Jerusalem down which is the route from Bethany to Jerusalem. It is named for the olive groves that once covered its slopes and it still has numerous pockets of these groves today. The Mount has been used as a Jewish cemetery for over 3,000 years and holds

Chapter 2
Fact or Fiction

approximately 150,000 graves. Next to the central summit, on the southern side is the singular catacomb known as the "Tombs of the Prophets," which Jesus alluded to in Matthew 23:29 " *Woe to you, scribes and Pharisees, hypocrites! Because you build the tombs of the prophets and adorn the monuments of the righteous."*

The Prophet Zechariah names the Mount of Olives "which faces Jerusalem on the East" – its accurate geographic location today – as the place where Jesus will stand when he returns at the end of time. The Mount of Olives is a real place and the return of Jesus is just as real although it has not yet occurred. Zechariah 14:4 *"And in that day His feet will stand on the Mount of Olives, which faces Jerusalem on the east. And the Mount of Olives shall be split in two, from east to west, making a very large valley; Half of the mountain shall move toward the north and half of it toward the south."*

The book of Acts 1:9–12 *"Now when He had spoken these things, while they watched, He was taken up, and a cloud received Him out of their sight. 10And while they looked steadfastly toward heaven as He went up, behold, two men stood by them in white apparel, 11who also said, "Men of Galilee, why do you stand gazing up into heaven? This same Jesus, who was taken up from you into heaven, will so come in like manner as you saw Him go into heaven."*

Then they returned to Jerusalem **from the mount called Olivet, which is near Jerusalem**, a Sabbath day's journey away." [Emphasis added] This scripture names the mountain called Olivet (the Mount of Olives) as the very spot from which Jesus ascended to heaven and the men dressed in white also confirm Zechariah's prophecy of where Jesus will return to.

Descending down from the Mount of Olives is the road that Jesus took riding the donkey for His triumphant entry into Jerusalem a few days before his death on the cross. This event is still celebrated today by many Christians as Palm Sunday. Luke 19:35-37 *"Then they brought him to Jesus. And they threw their own clothes on the colt, and they set Jesus on him. And as He went, many spread their clothes on the road. Then, as He was now drawing near* **the descent of the Mount of Olives**, *the whole multitude of the disciples began to rejoice and praise God with a loud voice for all the mighty works they had seen."* [Emphasis added] I personally travelled down that narrow descent road just a few years ago and can assure you it definitely exists still. The Mount is also the place where Jesus wept as he looked over Jerusalem. Luke 19:41 *"When He drew near, He saw the city and wept over it."* Sitting there on the side of that Mount does provide an excellent vantage point to view the old part of the city and the Temple Mount.

At the foot of the Mount of Olives just up from the Kidron brook or stream lies the Garden of Gethsemane (from the Hebrew words "gat shemanim" or olive press) where Jesus was betrayed and seized Mark 14:32 *"Then they came to a place which was named Gethsemane; and He said to His disciples, "Sit here while I pray.""* and Mark 14:45-46 *"As soon as he had come, immediately he went up to Him and said to Him, "Rabbi,*

Chapter 2
Fact or Fiction

Rabbi!" and kissed Him. Then they laid their hands on Him and took Him." This garden still exists today and interestingly it contains several gnarly old olive trees which are reported to be at least 2000 years old, and which, if correct, likely witnessed the arrest of Jesus.

One very old olive tree in the Garden of Gethsemane - 2006

The Apostle Paul in Romans 11:17 makes reference to branches being grafted into an olive tree. There's an extremely interesting fact, unique to the olive tree. Provided the roots of the olive tree remain undisturbed then the stump and trunk of the tree remains alive even though it may be devoid of any branches and leaves. If it is cut down completely it will sprout new branches. If a branch or cutting from a live olive tree is grafted into the old dead looking trunk then it will heal-in and flourish due to the well-nourished extensive root structure of the stump. The photo above demonstrates this beautifully, showing branches grafted and thriving in this very old stump. In truth every green branch on that old stump had been grafted in relatively recently (within the past 50 years). This seemingly casual reference to olive tree grafting by the Apostle Paul increases significantly in meaning when the full facts relating to this special factual characteristic of olive trees is more fully understood.

Babylon

Babylon is a well-documented city and region referenced in the Bible in particular relating to the destruction of Jerusalem and captivity of the survivors. Today extensive archaeological works have been undertaken at the desolate Babylonian ruins in modern day Iraq and this has provided direct historical evidence of the destruction of Jerusalem and the fate of the king of Judah at that time. Eighteen ostraca (clay tablets with writing in ink) written in an ancient cursive script belonging to the seventh century B.C were discovered in 1935 and these completely confirm the Biblical account.

One of Babylonian tablets records: [6]

"In the seventh month (of Nebuchadnezzar-599 BC.) in the month Chislev (Nov/Dec) the king of Babylon assembled his army, and after he had invaded the land of Hatti (Syria/Israel)

Chapter 2
Fact or Fiction

he laid siege to the city of Judah. On the second day of the month of Adara (16th of March) he conquered the city and took the king (Jehoiachin) prisoner. He installed in his place a king (Zedekiah) of his own choice, and after he had received rich tribute, he sent (them) forth to Babylon."

Compare this text from ancient Babylon with the record of the Babylonian invasion in 2 Kings 24:10-17.

"At that time the servants of Nebuchadnezzar king of Babylon came up against Jerusalem, and the city was besieged. And Nebuchadnezzar king of Babylon came against the city, as his servants were besieging it. Then Jehoiachin king of Judah, his mother, his servants, his princes, and his officers went out to the king of Babylon; and the king of Babylon, in the eighth year of his reign, took him prisoner.

And he carried out from there all the treasures of the house of the Lord and the treasures of the king's house, and he cut in pieces all the articles of gold which Solomon king of Israel had made in the temple of the Lord, as the Lord had said. Also he carried into captivity all Jerusalem: all the captains and all the mighty men of valor, ten thousand captives, and all the craftsmen and smiths. None remained except the poorest people of the land. And he carried Jehoiachin captive to Babylon. The king's mother, the king's wives, his officers, and the mighty of the land he carried into captivity from Jerusalem to Babylon. All the valiant men, seven thousand, and craftsmen and smiths, one thousand, all who were strong and fit for war, these the king of Babylon brought captive to Babylon.

> Then the king of Babylon made Mattaniah, Jehoiachin's uncle, king in his place, and changed his name to Zedekiah."

Esther

The modern Iranian town of Shush, the administrative capital of the Shush County of Iran's Khuzestan province, is located at the site of the ancient city of Susa an important capital of the First Persian Empire. The book of Esther gives an account of her becoming the wife of King Xerxes (Ahasuerus) who ruled his Kingdom from Susa. Esther 1:1 states *"Now it came to pass in the days of Ahasuerus (this was the Ahasuerus who reigned over one hundred and twenty-seven provinces, **from India to Ethiopia**)."* [emphasis added], clearly Xerxes was a super power of his time.

Three stele (stone slabs), called the "Daiva Inscription," were found during archaeological excavations at the royal compound of Persepolis [7] (a later Persian capital). The Old Persian text from these slabs gives a description of countries which Xerxes conquered: [8] "King Xerxes says: "the countries of which I was king apart from Persia. I had lordship over them. They bore me tribute. What was said to them by me, that they did. My law that upheld them: **Media, Elam, India, Nubians (Ethiopia)."** This archaeological evidence gives direct confirmation of the same account of King Xerxes in the book of Esther.

Chapter 2
Fact or Fiction

Daniel

A tomb understood to be that of Daniel, a prophet and writer of the book of Daniel, is located in the area near the town of Shush and today is still known as Shush-Daniel tomb. Daniel is recorded in the Bible as being appointed as one of three Governors over the whole kingdom of Darius the Mede and that he later prospered during the reign of Cyrus the Persian. Daniel was in the city of Shushan – Daniel 8:2 "*I saw in the vision, and it so happened while I was looking, that I was in Shushan, the citadel, which is in the province of Elam; and I saw in the vision that I was by the River Ulai.*" Although the Bible doesn't actually record where Daniel died or was buried it does record he was in Shushan and it is conceivable that since he was active during the First Persian Empire and that Empire was centred in Shushan and because of his importance in the Empire that when he died he was buried there, prominently. Jewish tradition also supports this.

There is an interesting aside recorded in history regarding Daniel's tomb. Benjamin of Tudela who visited Asia between 1160 and 1163 mentions Daniel's Tomb in his writings:[9]

"In the facade of one of its many synagogues I was shown the tomb assigned by tradition to Daniel. However the tomb does not hold Daniel's remains. His remains were believed to bring good fortune and bitter quarrels arose between the inhabitants of the two banks of the Choaspes River. Those living on the side on which Daniel's grave was situated were rich and happy, while those on the opposite side were poor and in want.

The latter, therefore, wished the bier of Daniel be transferred to their side of the river. After much hostility they agreed that the bier should rest alternately one year on each side. This agreement was practiced successfully for many years, until the Persian shah Sanjar (AD 1185 – 1187), on visiting the city, stopped the practice, asserting that the continual removal of the bier was disrespectful to the prophet. He ordered the bier to be securely hung by chains directly under the middle of the Choaspes River Bridge. He then erected a chapel on the spot that previously housed Daniel's remains for use by both Jews and non-Jews alike. The king also forbade fishing in the river within a mile of Daniel's bier stating that the place was a dangerous one for navigation, since godless persons will perish immediately on passing it and because the water under the bier is distinguished by the presence of goldfish."

A couple of things are very clear from that non-Biblical account; clearly Daniel did exist and was well known as a revered prophet by both Jews and non-Jews and also that not much has changed in politics over the centuries!

Pontius Pilate

Well known as the one who authorised the crucifixion of Jesus, Pontius Pilate as the Prefect of Rome and ruler of Israel is also clearly documented by independent non-Biblical sources.

The principal source for Pilate's existence comes from an inscription known as the Pilate Stone which is currently located at the Israel Museum in Jerusalem. The Pilate stone [10] is a

Chapter 2
Fact or Fiction

damaged block (82 cm x 65 cm) of carved limestone with a partially intact inscription attributed to, and mentioning, Pontius Pilate, a prefect of the Roman province of Judaea from AD 26–36. It was discovered at the archaeological site of Caesarea Marittima in 1961. The artefact is particularly significant because it is an archaeological find, of an authentic 1st-century Roman inscription mentioning the name "Pontius Pilatus". It is contemporary to Pilate's lifetime, and accords with what is known of his reported career.

Jesus

Of course we cannot list the main facts mentioned in the Bible without including Jesus.

Jesus Christ in Hebrew is "Yeshua ha Mashiah". Yeshua" is how Jesus' name is pronounced in Hebrew and ha Mashiah is Hebrew for "the Messiah". Hebrew ha Mashiah and Greek the Christós (Christ) both mean "the anointed one." Christ is his title or position and certainly not a surname as surprisingly many people today believe. In terms of early non-Christian history Jesus Christ is often referred to simply as Yeshua or Yeshua of Nazareth.

One non-Christian who provides non-Biblical evidence of Jesus is Josephus, [11] a Jewish priest who grew up as an aristocrat in first-century Israel and ended up living in Rome, supported by the patronage of three successive emperors. In the early days of the first Jewish Revolt against Rome (66–70 A.D.), Josephus was a commander in Galilee but soon surrendered and became a prisoner of war. He then prophesied that his conqueror, the Roman commander Vespasian, would become emperor, and when this actually happened, Vespasian freed him. From then on Josephus lived in Rome under the protection of the Flavians (a Roman imperial dynasty) and there composed his historical and apologetic writings. [12]

"Now, there was about this time, Jesus, a wise man, if it be lawful to call him a man, for he was a doer of wonderful works, a teacher of such men as received the truth with pleasure. He drew over to him both many of the Jews and many of the gentiles. He was the Christ; and when Pilate, at the suggestion of the principal men amongst us, had condemned him to the cross, those that loved him at the first did not forsake him, for he appeared to them alive again the third day, as the divine prophets had foretold these and ten thousand other wonderful things concerning him; and the tribe of Christians, so named from him, are not extinct at this day."

Critics have claimed that parts of this passage are a Christian insertion – particularly "He was the Christ". However, there is strong evidence from the ancient manuscripts that this passage was in the original. It is present in all of the extant ancient manuscripts and was quoted by early church fathers, such as Eusebius, as early as 325 C.E.

Another of the writings of Josephus gives the following account; [13]

Chapter 2
Fact or Fiction

"Festus was now dead, and Albinus was but upon the road; so he assembled the Sanhedrim of judges, and brought before them the brother of Jesus, who was called Christ, whose name was James, and some others, [or, some of his companions]; and when he had formed an accusation against them as breakers of the law, he delivered them to be stoned: but as for those who seemed the most equitable of the citizens, and such as were the most uneasy at the breach of the laws, they disliked what was done; they also sent to the king Agrippa, desiring him to send to Ananus that he should act so no more, for that what he had already done was not to be justified;"

A Roman named Tacitus also makes a mention of Jesus (*Christos*) in his writings. Cornelius Tacitus, born circa 52-55 A.D., was a Roman senator, orator and ethnographer, and is a great source for Roman history. His name is based on the Latin word *tacitus*, "silent," from which we get the English word *tacit*.

Writing in the year 116 C.E., in his Annals, he writes of the burning of Rome in 64 A.D. and how Caesar Nero had tried to stop the rumour that he (Nero) was behind the destruction.

"Therefore, to scotch the rumour that Nero had burned Rome] Nero substituted as culprits, and punished with the utmost refinements of cruelty, a class of men, loathed for their vices, whom the crowd styled Christians. **Christos, the founder of the name, had undergone the death penalty in the reign of Tiberius, by sentence of the procurator Pontius Pilatus,** and the pernicious superstition was checked for a moment, only to break out once more, not merely in Judea, the home of the disease, but in the capital itself, where all things horrible or shameful in the world collect and find a vogue...They the Christians were covered with wild beasts' skins and torn to death by dogs; or they were fastened on crosses, and, when daylight failed were burned to serve as lamps by night. Nero had offered his gardens for the spectacle, and gave an exhibition in his circus, mixing with the crowd in the habit of a charioteer, or mounted on his car. Hence, in spite of a guilt which had earned the most exemplary punishment, there arose a sentiment of pity, due to the impression that they were being sacrificed not for the welfare of the state but to the ferocity of a single man."

This amazing writing verifies that Jesus, or Christos, was a true historical figure that he lived and was killed during the reign of Caesar Tiberius, that he was sentenced under Pontius Pilate and that by about 64 A.D. Christianity had spread rapidly throughout the Roman Empire. Tacitus verifies that Christians were viciously tortured by Nero only 32 years after the death of Jesus of Nazareth. The historical validity of this letter by Tacitus is doubted by very few scholars. According to some scholars, Tacitus is: "Universally considered the most reliable of historians, a man in whom sensibility and imagination, though lively, could never spoil a critical sense, rare in his time and a great honesty in the examination of the documents."

Another important source of evidence about Jesus and early Christianity can be found in the letters of Pliny the

Chapter 2
Fact or Fiction

Younger to Emperor Trajan. Pliny was the Roman governor of Bithynia in Asia Minor. n one of his letters, dated around A.D. 112, he asks Trajan's advice about the appropriate way to conduct legal proceedings against those accused of being Christians. Pliny says that he needed to consult the emperor about this issue because a great multitude of every age, class, and sex stood accused of Christianity.

Pliny's letter to the Emperor Trajan [15]

It is my practice, my lord, to refer to you all matters concerning which I am in doubt. For who can better give guidance to my hesitation or inform my ignorance? I have never participated in trials of Christians. I therefore do not know what offences it is the practice to punish or investigate, and to what extent. And I have been not a little hesitant as to whether there should be any distinction on account of age or no difference between the very young and the more mature; whether pardon is to be granted for repentance, or, if a man has once been a Christian, it does him no good to have ceased to be one; whether the name itself, even without offences, or only the offences associated with the name are to be punished.

Meanwhile, in the case of those who were denounced to me as Christians, I have observed the following procedure: I interrogated these as to whether they were Christians; those who confessed I interrogated a second and a third time, threatening them with punishment; those who persisted I ordered executed. For I had no doubt that, whatever the nature of their creed, stubbornness and inflexible obstinacy surely deserve to be punished. There were others possessed of the same folly; but because they were Roman citizens, I signed an order for them to be transferred to Rome.

Soon accusations spread, as usually happens, because of the proceedings going on, and several incidents occurred. An anonymous document was published containing the names of many persons. Those who denied that they were or had been Christians, when they invoked the gods in words dictated by me, offered prayer with incense and wine to your image, which I had ordered to be brought for this purpose together with statues of the gods, and moreover cursed Christ--none of which those who are really Christians, it is said, can be forced to do – these I thought should be discharged. Others named by the informer declared that they were Christians, but then denied it, asserting that they had been but had ceased to be, some three years before, others many years, some as much as twenty-five years. They all worshipped your image and the statues of the gods, and cursed Christ.

They asserted, however, that the sum and substance of their fault or error had been that **they were accustomed to meet on a fixed day before dawn and sing responsively a hymn to Christ as to a god**, and to bind themselves by oath, not to some crime, but not to commit fraud, theft, or adultery, not falsify their trust, nor to refuse to return a trust when called upon to do so. When this was over, it was their custom to depart and to assemble again to partake of food--but ordinary and innocent food. Even this, they affirmed, they had ceased to

Chapter 2
Fact or Fiction

do after my edict by which, in accordance with your instructions, I had forbidden political associations. Accordingly, I judged it all the more necessary to find out what the truth was by torturing two female slaves who were called deaconesses. But I discovered nothing else but depraved, excessive superstition.

I therefore postponed the investigation and hastened to consult you. For the matter seemed to me to warrant consulting you, especially because of the number involved. For many persons of every age, every rank, and also of both sexes are and will be endangered. For the contagion of this superstition has spread not only to the cities but also to the villages and farms. But it seems possible to check and cure it. It is certainly quite clear that the temples, which had been almost deserted, have begun to be frequented, that the established religious rites, long neglected, are being resumed, and that from everywhere sacrificial animals are coming, for which until now very few purchasers could be found. Hence it is easy to imagine what a multitude of people can be reformed if an opportunity for repentance is afforded.

Emperor Trajan's reply to Pliny [16]

You observed proper procedure, my dear Pliny, in sifting the cases of those who had been denounced to you as Christians. For it is not possible to lay down any general rule to serve as a kind of fixed standard. They are not to be sought out; if they are denounced and proved guilty, they are to be punished, with this reservation, that whoever denies that he is a Christian and really proves it--that is, by worshiping our gods--even though he was under suspicion in the past, shall obtain pardon through repentance. But anonymously posted accusations ought to have no place in any prosecution. For this is both a dangerous kind of precedent and out of keeping with the spirit of our age.

An interesting question arises when considering these Roman government documents. Why would the Roman government brutally persecute peaceful followers of a non-historical figure? Why would tens of thousands of first century Christians, almost exclusively Jewish believers in Jesus, who lived within forty years of a "mythical event," willingly suffer the loss of all possessions and status, and be murdered for a myth? Why would Saul of Tarsus, a Jewish Pharisee, a leader of the Jews, be willing to give up everything and join the crowd that he had admittedly been persecuting? The obvious conclusion is that Jesus was clearly a real historical figure and the accounts about his life and resurrection are completely true.

Gregorian calendar

Our Gregorian calendar, on which we base our everyday lives, counts the years since Jesus was born. That alone fact is undeniable evidence that something very major occurred at that juncture in history to cause every person on earth today to mark their progress through time by it.

Chapter 2
Fact or Fiction

The Gregorian calendar, also called the Western calendar and the Christian calendar, is internationally the most widely used civil calendar. It is named for Pope Gregory XIII, who introduced it in October 1582. The calendar was a refinement to the Julian calendar amounted to a 0.002% correction in the length of the year. The motivation for the reform was to bring the date for the celebration of Easter to the time of the year in which it was celebrated when it was introduced by the early Church. Because the celebration of Easter was tied to the spring equinox, the Roman Catholic Church considered the steady drift in the date of Easter caused by the year being slightly too long to be undesirable. The reform was adopted initially by the Catholic countries of Europe. Protestants and Eastern Orthodox countries continued to use the traditional Julian calendar and adopted the Gregorian reform after a time, for the sake of convenience in international trade. Interestingly the last European country to adopt the reform was Greece, in 1923.

Catholic Church

The history of the papacy, the office held by the pope as head of the Roman Catholic Church, according to Catholic doctrine, spans from the time of Peter, as its founding father, to the present day. When visiting the Vatican in Rome you can see on public display a historic record of every (Catholic) leader of the church from the time of the Apostle Peter right through to the current Pope today. This is the same Peter that was recorded as a fisherman disciple of Jesus.

Protestants (non-Catholics) tend to deny that Peter and those claimed to be his immediate successors had universally recognized supreme authority over all the early churches and that Rome's prominence may be seen as only moral, not ecclesiastical, and that emergence of the Roman pontiff to supreme power and prominence happened by natural circumstance rather than divine appointment.

Book of Job

So far we have been considering mostly historic facts. However the Bible also contains a huge array of other facts, particularly given by the writer of Job whose recorded discourse between God and Job is believed to have been written about 1900 to 1700 BC. The list of things given is clearly a supernatural utterance as many are seemingly beyond the general knowledge of one man from that age but all undisputable and proven facts today. The list is nothing short of amazing;

- Job 38:16. The sea is described as having springs. Only in recent times has that fact been confirmed through the development of submarines that have allowed cameras to film such springs at depth on the sea floor.

- The constellations of the stars are recorded defining Pleiades chain and Orion's belt and informing that different season (summer winter etc.) reveal different constellations. Job 38:31-32.

Chapter 2
Fact or Fiction

- Job 38:39 says that the female Lions do the hunting but that the male lions hunger is satisfied first.

- The ox has great strength and that it is used in agriculture Job 39:9-11. Still a fact in some regions today.

- It confirms that even though the ostrich has wings it can't fly. It lays its eggs in the sand but doesn't sit on them and then disowns her young, Job 39:13-16. Anyone that has watched a David Attenborough series on Southern Africa has most likely witnessed these facts first hand.

- A horse is strong and fierce and great for warfare, charging into the fray, snorting at the scent of battle, Job 39;19-25

- It goes on to tell of the eagles building its nest up high and that it has incredible eyesight and can see its prey from afar, Job 39:27-30.

- It describes in detail a Behemoth which matches the profile of the Diplodocids dinosaur. Job 40:15-24 says *"He eats grass like an ox. See now, his strength is in his hips, and his power is in his stomach muscles. He moves his tail like a cedar."* While the verse clearly doesn't confirm that this is a Diplodocids a recent description found on Wikipedia certainly sounds like one. Interestingly as late as 2001 an expedition into Cameroon was initiated by the BBC to study reports of living Diplodocids. [17] Led by Canadians Brian Sass and Peter Beach they discovered an island in the Dja River which contained nesting caves and they actually had a brief encounter with the elusive monster of Cameroon as it swam past their dugout canoe toward its lair. While they were unable to formally identify the creature, based on many accounts from locals they strongly believe it to be a living Diplodocids. A living dinosaur – but they all died out 65million years ago! Yet another question against the man-made theory of evolution.

- Then God goes on to the Leviathan with a whole chapter (Job 41) devoted to it. The Leviathan is described in great detail and is an amazing creature. Only recently has it been determined that a possible candidate for this creature is the dinosaur Sarcosuchus. At www.creation.com the Sarcosuchus is discussed in detail in their chapter on "Dragons of the Deep" by Carl Wieland. [18] It was a monstrous armour plated crocodile like creature that breathed flames out of its nostrils. We know this animal existed because fossils of it have been found and are well documented. Interestingly the Sarcosuchus has an unusual bulbous cavity at the end of its snout that could conceivably have been used for mixing fire-generating chemicals.

What is interesting regarding both the Behemoth and the Leviathan is that God fully expected Job to have totally understood and appreciated what those creatures were. This

Chapter 2
Fact or Fiction

again questions the theory the dinosaurs died out 65 million years ago, especially given a possible sighting of one less than two decades ago.

Minor Facts

In addition to all these interesting fact the Bible divulges a huge array of minor facts. The Book of Leviticus is full of detail that the writer gives us relating to marriage, sleeping with close relative, identifying various skin diseases and what to do about them, healthy foods to eat, what kind of animals we should or should not eat - those that are good for our bodies and those that are not so good. The moral creed which many Nations today still base their laws upon is all found in the book of Leviticus and Deuteronomy. These books give great detail regarding non-discrimination; how to treat people, how to look after the poor, the widows, the orphans, foreigners and how to treat your employees. Surprisingly it makes no reference to discrimination by racial skin colour. It does talk about foreigners, defining these simply as someone who is not from your country. Sadly, it seems that racism based on skin colour is a relatively recent invention by man.

The detail and description of the numerous Biblical facts are absolutely amazing. It is abundantly clear that the originator of these facts was certainly someone in the know. The extent and number of the facts, many of which were not completely understood for centuries after being written down, means we can definitely rule out a fortunate guess by the writer. The Bible as a whole is full of historic factual information from start to finish, hardly a page that goes by where we're not presented with something that is either known history or a well-known fact.

Of course some will point to the parables of Jesus to make the point that there are "stories" in the Bible. And of course parables are not true stories. I have used stories in this book to better explain things and likewise a parable is just a story used to illustrate a point.

Chapter 3
Fairy Tales

*"God is rich,
because Jesus saves"*

Chapter 3
Fairy Tales

Start a paragraph with "Once upon a time" and generally our minds will flip to fairy tale mode. Since the Bible is the inspired word of God it may be surprising to some that these actual words are found in the Bible. Judges 9:8 reads: *"Once upon a time the trees decided to choose a king. First they said to the olive tree, 'Be our king!'...."* (NLT). Other versions use slightly different wording, the New King James reads *"The trees once went forth to anoint a king over them. And they said to the olive tree, 'Reign over us."* The basic meaning is the same; it's the start of a fairy tale. Yes, the Bible does contain fairy tales with this one in Judges being the obvious example.

This story in Judges was recited by a man named Jotham the youngest son of Gideon (Gideon was also called Jerubbaal), one of the great Judges of Israel before it became a Kingdom. Gideon had a total of seventy sons – one would hope through multiple wives. He also had a mistress (concubine) who gave birth to his son Abimelech. When his father died, Abimelech went to Shechem, the city of his mother, and sweet-talked his relatives into appointing him their ruler. The elders of the city gave him some money from the idol temple of Baal and Abimelech hired a rebel gang which gave him the power to slaughter his seventy brothers; however, the youngest Jotham managed to escape. Impressed with his murderous feat the people of Shechem made him their king. Naturally Jotham wasn't terribly delighted with the situation or with the people of Shechem for their support so he went nearby and shouted out his interesting fairy tale to make his point. Judges 9:6-15 (NLT).

"*Then all the leading citizens of Shechem and Beth-millo called a meeting under the oak beside the pillar at Shechem and made Abimelech their king. When Jotham heard about this, he climbed to the top of Mount Gerizim and shouted, "Listen to me, citizens of Shechem! Listen to me if you want God to listen to you!*

Once upon a time the trees decided to choose a king.

First they said to the olive tree,

'Be our king!'

But the olive tree refused, saying, 'Should I quit producing the olive oil that blesses both God and people, just to wave back and forth over the trees?'

"Then they said to the fig tree,

'You be our king!'

But the fig tree also refused, saying, 'Should I quit producing my sweet fruit just to wave back and forth over the trees?'

"Then they said to the grapevine,

'You be our king!'

Chapter 3
Fairy Tales

But the grapevine also refused, saying, 'Should I quit producing the wine that cheers both God and people, just to wave back and forth over the trees?'
"Then all the trees finally turned to the thorn bush and said, 'Come, you be our king!'
And the thorn bush replied to the trees, 'If you truly want to make me your king, come and take shelter in my shade. If not, let fire come out from me and devour the cedars of Lebanon.'"

Fairy tales generally have some sort of a moral interwoven into the fabric of the story and mostly the moral revolves around good overcoming evil or the underdog succeeding against all the odds. Jotham's story is no different in that it contains a very clear moral; all choices have consequences. So even though the Bible does contain a fairy tale, the Bible itself is not a fairy tale as the facts surrounding this record of life in ancient Israel demonstrate.

After telling this tale Jotham told the people of Shechem in no uncertain terms what he thought of them rewarding his step-brother Abimelech, just after he had slaughter all his own family, by making him their king. Jotham concludes by binding the city with a curse and having delivered his message, raced into hiding.

Abimelech continued on for three murderous years as king. The people of Shechem however soon turned on him, causing Abimelech to attack their city and burn 1,000 men and women alive in the fortified compound of the temple of their god Berith. He went on and threatened the city of Thebez but the residents locked themselves into their strong tower and when Abimelech attacked it, a woman in the tower dropped a mill stone on him, crushing his skull.

Judges 9:56-57 added a footnote regarding the death of this terrible blood thirsty man. *"Thus God repaid the wickedness of Abimelech, which he had done to his father by killing his seventy brothers. And all the evil of the men of Shechem God returned on their own heads, and on them came the curse of Jotham the son of Jerubbaal."*

While this historic event demonstrates that God sees everything and does bring about divine justice, to be honest, if I were the writer trying to demonstrate the love of God, based on my human reasoning, I doubt I would have used such a murderous example to make my point. The Bible nevertheless tells everything including history just like it is. It uses everyday happenings and circumstances as its base.

So why include this gruesome happening in the Bible? The event was not of God's making nor was it His plan. It was one hundred per cent man created and inspired by evil. At every step a decision was made by people and every decision had a consequence. If the time is taken to deeply study this small episode in history there is a large amount of understanding that would result. Choices are extremely important regardless of how small, as are actions – things may have ended differently if Abimelech hadn't come so close to the tower at Thebez. That words spoken are very powerful - Jotham's curse matured completely. Greed and insecurity together with pride and

Chapter 3
Fairy Tales

arrogance are all included. Most importantly it demonstrates that even though we live in an evil, fallen, world, God sees all things; He is in overall charge and what He wills does happen in the end.

If I read this Judges account simply as a story that is what it will always be for me. Just a murderous, crue account of man's suffering at the hand of another. As we mentioned in an early chapter, the first line of the Bible gives the premise for the book – it's all about God, what He has done, what He is like and what He does. With every verse we read that main premise must be foremost in our thinking. Failure to do this will certainly result in a very different conclusion of God and what the Bible is all about.

Reading the Bible purely in human terms precludes an understanding of what its really about. If I were to read Genesis chapter 1 with a fixed belief in the man-made theory of evolution then it is understandable that my likely conclusion will be that the six day creation account is just an interesting fairy tale. This would no doubt be further reinforced when a talking snake is introduced in chapter 3 or a first murder in Chapter 4 followed by a massive global flood in chapter 7 which covered all the mountains by 15 cubits (about 7 meters or 22½ feet) destroying every living thing except the eight people and numerous animals and creatures in Noah's homemade ark.

Viewed solely in human terms, by Genesis chapter 7 the Bible could pass for a very well-thought-out work of fantasy fiction or fairy tales. So what is the basis to think differently? Let's take a look at some of these in a little more detail.

If a truly unbiased look is taken at the theory of evolution it should quickly become clear that there are some very large gaps in the theory – the missing link is extremely real. Evolution is claimed to be based on "science", which in broad terms it is. Mention science and most people assume formal science such as chemistry or physics which are founded on the principle that the underlying result of something can be proven through a repeatable experiment e.g. two hydrogen atoms when combined with one oxygen atom, will produce water. There are many such examples. Creation (or earth) science cannot be proven or repeated as it already exists; therefore the only way to increase understanding of it is through observation. Observations by nature are subject to conjecture and interpretation. If an interpretation is based on a flawed or biased premise then the results cannot be accurate. Evolutionists point to numerous examples of fossils which they have evaluated aligned to their beliefs, as being proof that nature has evolved over time. Based almost entirely on similar skeletons and features the evolutionary ascent of man icon below is taught in most western culture schools today. [1]

Chapter 3
Fairy Tales

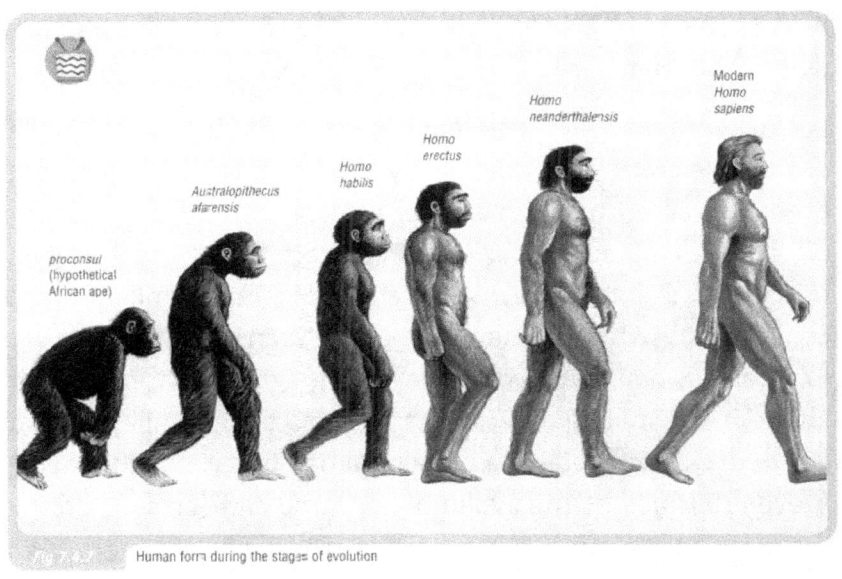

Human form during the stages of evolution

Apart from the small detail that the man-figures 2 – 5 have never been found to exist, one standout feature of this man generated artwork is that supposedly the progression also goes from dark skin to white. What utter boloney! Skin colour is nothing to do with development! All men are the same regardless of their skin colour or ethnic background. Yet our children are taught exclusively that this is exactly how we came about – no discussion tolerated. Is there any wonder that racism is rampant and that fans are heard to chant ape like hoots of abuse at a player of dark skin on opposing teams at some sporting matches! No, God created man and He didn't make him black or white. Skin colour is primarily due to difference in amounts of the pigment melanin in the skin and is inherited from a parent in a similar way to eye or hair colour.

Psalm 139:14 *"I will praise You, for I am fearfully and wonderfully made; Marvelous are Your works."*

Further fallacy in the ascent of man icon is that if man really did evolve from apes, then why do the internal organs and other characteristics of man more closely resemble those of a pig and not of a chimpanzee? Pig heart valves are routinely transplanted into humans because of their similarity and compatibility with the human body. Human reasoning has led to a conclusion by an evolutionary fringe group that man came about by the mating of a chimpanzee and a pig. While this may go some way to explaining certain human behaviour the theory is even ridiculed by the evolutionary camp and certainly on this the creationist concur. It is total man-made rubbish.

Evolution science is **completely** dependent upon the interpretation of observations. If a particular bias or a flawed hypothesis is used then naturally the observed becomes absurd. On this basis any theory could potentially result. Man has adhered strictly to the development of the theory of evolution because it negates God. If man evolved then God didn't create him. The decision is simple, did God create or not? The Bible clearly says He did.

Creation.com has an abundance of extremely useful and accurate articles on the creation account in Genesis 1, and debating evolution is not the focus of this book. To help us comprehend that God did create everything in six literal days we first need to take into account exactly who God actually is. Man tends to consider God strictly in human terms, which is

Chapter 3
Fairy Tales

incredibly limiting. The whole of the Bible is about God, but even so it realistically only covers the basics. God is wonderful, mighty, absolute sovereign, immortal, over all things, omnipresent (present all the time or everywhere), omnipotent (possessing complete, unlimited, or universal power and authority). 1 Timothy 6:15-16 *"which He will manifest in His own time, He who is the blessed and only Potentate, the King of kings and Lord of lords, who alone has immortality, dwelling in unapproachable light, whom no man has seen or can see, to whom be honor and everlasting power. Amen."*

That's just a few of the basic characteristics of the one and only God. Regardless of man's opinion He definitely is not a fantasy figure in a fairy tale. He's absolutely real and has complete, unlimited, or universal power and authority.

Imagine for a moment an ant that had lived its entire life in a large city building together with a vast colony of fellow ants finding all their food and resources within the various floors of the structure spreading back over copious generations. One day, his ant companion tells him that he has read somewhere that the structure they live within was actually built by man only a few decades ago and their colony moved in a short time later. The ant, having never actually seen a man, scoffs at his friend suggesting he has been chewing on the vinyl again. "How could anyone possibly create such a vast structure?" he replies, "Moving all the components into its exact place is completely impossible for any creature to achieve. Of course it's always been here – idiot!"

We could go on with my fictitious ant story, but I'm sure you see the point. To an ant the thought any one could create something so massive would be completely beyond his level of comprehension. The magnitude of difference between God and man is many times the difference between man and an ant. The concept of someone living outside the realm of time for instance is mind boggling. Describe eternity for me – it never ends, ever! God created time. Genesis 1:3-5. *"Then God said, "Let there be light"; and there was light. And God saw the light, that it was good; and God divided the light from the darkness. God called the light Day, and the darkness He called Night. So the evening and the morning were* **the first day***."* [Emphasis added].

The Hebrew word for day in this instance is yō-wm. The literal translated meaning of that word is a day as defined by an evening and a morning. Simply put, it is a 24 hour period starting at the evening, a physical day just as we still know it. Right at that point God created time. To the natural human mind that does not compute, the concept of how it could be done is way beyond our reasoning or comprehension. However to God it was accomplished by His word only. He **spoke** the words "let there be light" and then there was light. Again how does that happen just with words? Folks, let's just call it supernatural! Ephesians 3:20-21 *"Now to Him who is able to do exceedingly abundantly above all that we ask or think, according to the power that works in us, to Him be glory in the church by Christ Jesus to all generations, forever and ever. Amen."* Not sure exactly how to define exceeding abundantly

Chapter 3
Fairy Tales

myself, all I can say is that it's clearly a massive amount. And that's above what we can think or imagine, and I have met some people with a very wild imagination.

So here's the formula: God's greatness = your wildest imaginations of magnificence multiplied by exceeding abundantly. Gg = (wi x ea).

A humanistic world view finds it impossible to accept or believe that there exists a power so vastly superior. It says that if there is a God then He must only be different to me, not necessarily better, as in the humanist world man is the highest order. Sorry, but God made the rules and His rules stand. Man is a created being; God is almighty, powerful and over all things. The apostle Paul when writing to the Romans says, Romans 9:20 *"But indeed, O man, who are you to reply against God? Will the thing formed say to him who formed it, "Why have you made me like this?"*

Viewed in this context it's very simple to accept that God created all things and that He did it just like He said He did. Every word in Genesis is one hundred per cent true. God also was pleased with His handiwork and frequently says that He saw that it was good. When He finished making everything at the end of the sixth day He said: Genesis 1:31 *"Then God saw everything that He had made, and indeed it was **very good**. Then God saw everything that He had made, and indeed."* [Emphasis added.] At this point there was no evil present, no death, no sickness or disease, nothing of the sort, everything that God created and put man into was very good. Negative things appeared later through the actions of the created being man.

When God made man He also gave him power and authority over everything on the earth. Genesis 1:26 *"Then God said, "Let Us make man in Our image, according to Our likeness; let them have dominion over the fish of the sea, over the birds of the air, and over the cattle, over all the earth and over every creeping thing that creeps on the earth."* Verse 28 continues *"Then God blessed them, and God said to them, "Be fruitful and multiply; fill the earth and subdue it; have dominion over the fish of the sea, over the birds of the air, and over every living thing that moves on the earth."* God gave Man undisputed authority over every creature on the earth and in the air, telling him to fill the earth and subdue it. Today it's clear to see man has actually been very successful in this God given task.

Some point to the "man" wording of verse 26 suggesting God may have made hundreds of people at that time to allow marriage, colonies etc. Verse 27 clarifies this: *"So God created man in His own image; in the image of God He created him; male and female He created them."* The male and female are definitely in the singular. Genesis chapter 2 provides the specific detail of how God created this male and this female and even though this detail is provided after the account of God resting on the seventh day, in context it's very clear mankind was created on day six. Man was the purpose of the creation: God gave man a very interesting and detailed world to

Chapter 3
Fairy Tales

live in and explore. His plan was, and very much still is, to have a full, intimate and personal relationship with man.

Death was not part of God's creation plan. Man caused death to be introduced through his disobedience. Animals weren't created to attack and devour each other. The idea of the hunted or fear by man or beast simply didn't exist. We're given clear details of God's dietary plans for the creatures he'd created. Genesis 1:29-30 *"And God said, "See, I have given you **every herb that yields seed** which is on the face of all the earth, and **whose fruit yields seed; to you it shall be for food.** Also to **every beast** of the earth, to **every bird** of the air, and to **everything that creeps** on the earth, in which there is life, **I have given every green herb for food**;" and it was so."* [Emphasis added.] God spoke to Man first then to everything that had the breath of life in it and advised them they were created to be vegetarians. No need for animals to eat each other. It finishes by reinforcing the fact by saying "and it was so".

Does this mean we should all abstain from eating meat? No, the disobedience of man in the Garden of Eden brought in death and following the global flood God told Noah and his family to revise their diet. Genesis 9:2-4 *"And the fear of you and the dread of you shall be on every beast of the earth, on every bird of the air, on all that move on the earth, and on all the fish of the sea. They are given into your hand. **Every moving thing that lives shall be food for you. I have given you all things, even as the green herbs.** But you shall not eat flesh with* *its life, that is, its blood."* [Emphasis added.] God told Man it was okay to eat meat in addition to his greens.

Genesis 9:26 also introduces fear between mankind and animals and this is still fully existent today for all non-domesticated creatures. Fear itself was created immediately when Adam and Eve disobeyed God in Eden. Genesis 3:10 *"And he said, "I heard your voice in the garden, and I was afraid, because I was naked; and I hid myself.""* Fear resulted from a broken relationship with God not because of nakedness. Man created fear, not God. 1 John 4:18 *"There is no fear in love; but perfect love casts out fear, because fear involves torment. But he who fears has not been made perfect in love."*

Alright, so God created, what about a talking snake, that must be a fairy tale? Today there's no such thing as a talking snake (or serpent) yet in Genesis 3:1 *"Now **the serpent** was more cunning than any beast of the field which the Lord God had made. And **he said to the woman**, "Has God indeed said, 'You shall not eat of every tree of the garden'?""* [Emphasis added.] The woman obviously recognised that the serpent was actually talking to her because she answers him and carried out a conversation with him. This was a real event, but how could it be?

Let's take a step back and understand a little more about what's really going on here. The Bible is clear in that this wasn't some scheme concocted by the serpent to deceive Eve; Satan was the underlying factor at play in this historic event. Who is

Chapter 3
Fairy Tales

Satan and why was he so determined to disrupt God's relationship with Man?

The Bible tells us that Satan, also called Lucifer, was a guardian cherub (a type of angel). The angels were created beings and it tells us so in Colossians 1:16 *"For by Him all things were created that are in heaven and that are on earth, visible and invisible, whether thrones or dominions or principalities or powers. All things were created through Him and for Him."* "In heaven" includes angels.

The Bible does not specifically say when God created the angels but when speaking to Job God says; Job 38: 4-7 *""Where were you when I laid the foundations of the earth? Tell me, if you know so much. Who determined its dimensions and stretched out the surveying line? What supports its foundations, and who laid its cornerstone as the morning stars sang together **and all the angels shouted for joy?*** [Emphasis added.] (NLT) It is apparent that the angels were there on the first day of creation but we are not told if God created them on that day or some other time. The fact is they were there then.

In Ezekiel 28 the prophet takes up a lament against the King of Tyre. Ezekiel 28:12-17

*"Son of man, take up a lamentation for the king of Tyre, and say to him, 'Thus says the Lord God: "You were the seal of perfection, full of wisdom and perfect in beauty. **You were in Eden, the garden of God**. Every precious stone was your covering: The sardius, topaz, and diamond, beryl, onyx, and*

*jasper, sapphire, turquoise, and emerald with gold. The workmanship of your timbrels and pipes was prepared for you on the day **you were created**. You were the **anointed cherub** who covers. I established you; You were on the holy mountain of God; You walked back and forth in the midst of fiery stones. You were perfect in your ways from the day that **you were created**, till iniquity was found in you. By the abundance of your trading you became filled with violence within, and you sinned; Therefore I cast you as a profane thing out of the mountain of God; And I have destroyed **you, O covering cherub**, from the midst of the fiery stones.*

*"Your heart was lifted up because of your beauty; you corrupted your wisdom for the sake of your splendor. **I have cast you to the ground**. I laid you before kings, that they may gaze at you."* [Emphasis added.]

The start this is referenced to the King of Tyre, who was a real king living in the day of Ezekiel, however, further on it tells us that he was there in Eden, the garden of God. Twice later God calls him a cherub. Clearly this isn't describing the actual king of Tyre. This is a description of Lucifer.

In Isaiah 14:12–15 the same event is recorded which expands on what his sin was.

*"How you have fallen from heaven, **O Lucifer, son of the morning!** How you are cut down to the ground, you who weakened the nations! For you have said in your heart: 'I will ascend into heaven, I will exalt my throne above the stars of*

Chapter 3
Fairy Tales

God; I will also sit on the mount of the congregation on the farthest sides of the north; I will ascend above the heights of the clouds, **I will be like the Most High.***" Yet you shall be brought down to Sheol, to the lowest depths of the Pit."* [Emphasis added.]

This description clarifies exactly who the person is "Lucifer," "son of the morning." The name Lucifer means "Day Star," or "shining star."

Jesus himself says in Luke 10:18 *"And He said to them, "I saw Satan fall like lightning from heaven."* This is the referencing that Jesus saw the account above in Isaiah or Ezekiel. Lucifer and Satan are one in the same person.

All these scriptures mesh together completely. We are told that Satan was created blameless but that he decided he would like to usurp God and become the boss *"I will be like the Most High!"* God acted quickly against the wickedness and *"cast"* Satan out of heaven – to the ground (the earth). This was both physical and literal. Ezekiel 28 also confirms that Satan was in the Garden of Eden. *"You were in Eden, the garden of God;"*

So when did his fall from grace take place. Genesis 1:30 tells us that when God had finished creating, at the end of the sixth day, God saw **all** that He had made, and it was **very good**. Since it uses the word "all" it's safe to include the created angels. It tells us that God saw everything as "very good". If Satan had risen up against God before the sixth day then God wouldn't have considered that "very good", clearly his discharge from heaven took place after the seventh day when God rested.

We're not told of the time lapse between that sixth day, until Eve was deceived in Chapter 3. Conceivably it could have been several years. What is certain is that Satan did rebel at some point after the sixth day of creation but before the revolt in the Garden of Eden. I suggest that after being cast out Satan would have been hopping mad and the top of his agenda would have been to attempt to destroy the special relationship Adam and Eve had with God.

So, back to our talking snake. The serpent wasn't Satan impersonating it because when God passed judgement He cursed the reptile directly. Genesis 3:14-15 *"So the Lord God said to the serpent: "Because you have done this, you are cursed more than all cattle, and more than every beast of the field; On your belly you shall go, and you shall eat dust all the days of your life. And I will put enmity between you and the woman, and between your seed and her Seed; He shall bruise your head, and you shall bruise His heel."* There was no miscarriage of justice here, God knew exactly who did what, after all these are His created beings and He is omnipresent. The serpent was a willing participant, but why?

The serpent was an agent of Satan's. The Bible doesn't tell us but somehow Satan had deceived the snake, promising it goodness knows what. Judas Iscariot sheds light on how this can happen. Just before Judas left the Upper Room to go and betray Jesus, John 13:27 says *"Satan entered him."* Even though

Chapter 3
Fairy Tales

Satan was in him the Bible still records it was Judas who betrayed Jesus.

Demons (Satan's helper angels) can indwell either human bodies or animal bodies. Jesus cast out a legion of devils from a man in Mark 5:11- 13 it tells us *"Now a large herd of swine was feeding there near the mountains. So all the demons begged Him, saying, "Send us to the swine, that we may enter them." And at once Jesus gave them permission. Then the unclean spirits went out and entered the swine (there were about two thousand); and the herd ran violently down the steep place into the sea, and drowned in the sea."* We can safely conclude then that Satan appropriated and used the body of a serpent on this occasion to cunningly carry out his purpose of tempting Eve to sin.

What the serpent was like before God cursed it we're not told. The Bible tells us it talked to Eve. It was therefore certainly able to talk. Had it been Satan talking through the reptile perhaps Eve may have been less susceptible to being deceived by a creature that had unexpectedly learned speech. The situation suggests Eve may have chatted to the serpent previously; that's pure speculation on my part but, what is clear is that Eve was not alarmed when the serpent spoke to her as she focused only on considering what it had to say.

We all know how things unfolded from this point. Eve was deceived by the smooth talking serpent which had been demonically possessed by Satan. Adam never questioned his wife's offer to eat the forbidden fruit so being a willing participant he also disobeyed God. Because of this disobedience to what God had expressly told them not to do, God cursed Adam, Eve and the serpent and banished them from the Garden of Eden and told them they would return to dust from whence they were made – they would eventually die. This real life event at the very start of the human race is known as the Fall. The special relationship man had with God was broken with no avenue open to him at that time for it ever to be restored. Truly a very dark point in human history.

Why was God's punishment so harsh? God cursed them all; he cursed the earth and blocked the way to this early paradise. Just for a single sin of disobedience? In human terms you may wonder if perhaps He had experienced a bad day and was taking it out on His subjects or that He was just naturally angry. God is not human, He doesn't behave like humans do and other passages of scripture clearly confirm He does not have an angry nature. Again, why so harsh? What Adam and Eve did was massive, much more than just disobedience.

God told man in Genesis 2:16-17 *"And the Lord God commanded the man, saying, "Of every tree of the garden you may freely eat; but of the tree of the knowledge of good and evil you shall not eat, for in the day that you eat of it you shall surely die."* God clearly set the ground rules in advance, the penalty for eating it was death. On that man had a choice. Fast forward to the silver-tongued serpent in Genesis 3:4-5 *"Then the serpent said to the woman, "You will not surely die. For God knows that in the day you eat of it your eyes will be opened,*

Chapter 3
Fairy Tales

and you will be like God, knowing good and evil." Satan through the serpent straight out lied about dying. He knew they would die because, as we read earlier, he was there when man was placed in the Garden of Eden and had heard what God told them. Adam and Eve both fully understood what God had instructed them so now they had an easy choice believe God or believe Satan. One said they would die if they ate the fruit and the other said they would not. Someone was lying, who to choose? Sadly they elected to believe Satan thereby aligning with him and rejecting God. By their actions they told God we believe Satan's words hold greater truth then yours. The very same Satan that God had recently banished from heaven because he wanted to take over from God! Wow, Adam and Eve had **chosen** to align with this evil angel. Notice also the words Satan throws in when talking to Eve *"and you will be like God"* Firstly, no they wouldn't and second wasn't that the very reason why Satan no longer called heaven home? Satan's plan was that since he couldn't be the boss in heaven he'd be the boss on the earth. Man had been given God's authority to subdue the earth so if Satan got man onto his side then he'd commandeer that authority for his own use.

That's the reason why God reacted so emphatically. This Man he had created in his image and likeness, to have a close personal relationship with, had fully aligned himself with a wicked angel who, possibly quite recently, had blasphemously declared that he was as great as God. God couldn't react in any other way; He had no choice but to honour the decision of Adam and Eve who had chosen to introduce death and thereby suffering and grief into this very good world that God had created. A cursed world containing death and man in rebellion to Him was no longer "very good". At that point nothing on the earth was pleasing to God and everything was doomed to eventual destruction.

There's little wonder God was upset and in my opinion His resulting curse on mankind was extremely measured given the magnitude of what man did. What an incredibly merciful God we have!

Satan, I'm sure, was delighted with the result; however, God being God foreknew man was going to be deceived and had already devised an incredible loving plan to fully restore and enhance His relationship with man through Jesus the Christ. This restoration program wasn't God's plan 'B' it was His master plan all along. God created man with free will for a very good reason; He wanted man to choose to have a relationship with Him. The sweetness of being chosen is much greater than an ordered relationship and that is absolutely what God is yearning for from each one of us still today. Choose God.

By stealth Satan had wrestled Man's God given authority over the earth away from Him and taken it for himself. Exactly as God told man in advance, the earth now had death in it. Controlled by Satan the world is full of everything that God is not – fear, hate, anger, death, disease, suffering, war, malice, envy, pride, the list is almost endless. When God finished making the earth He described it as very good, now it was anything but.

Chapter 3
Fairy Tales

This same earth still remains today, under the authority of Satan. When Jesus died on the cross He paid the full price of the redemption of Man back to God and through Jesus Christ our relationship is completely restored. Thank you Jesus! Jesus annihilated the power of the curse and the authority of Satan over man by going to the Cross. The earth, however, is not yet physically restored and continues for now under the control of Satan and still today sickness, death and misery abound. God is not the cause of any of the bad stuff that happens on the earth every day, no, that blame still sits squarely on Satan, Lucifer the Devil. When Jesus returns to take up his kingdom Satan will be bound and removed from the earth. Be still, God's plan will succeed.

In conclusion, yes it was a talking snake but it's definitely not a fairy tale. It was absolutely God's plan and the second most significant event in human history. The most significant was when Jesus went to the Cross, fully and permanently restoring that relationship.

Satan, the Devil, is frequently portrayed as some sort of gruesome mythical character with red horns ruling over his dominion hell with his fellow demons. Is such a description accurate or even real? Is this not just another fairy tale character?

As we've demonstrated previously the only way to find out the real answers is to search the Bible. Firstly as we have discussed already he is very real. He definitely exists and lives on this same earth we call home. Ezekiel 28 confirms that Satan was banished from heaven to the ground.

John 12:31 *"The time for judging this world has come, when Satan, the ruler of this world, will be cast out."* (NLT) Here Jesus calls him the ruler of this world.

John 16:11 *"of judgment, because the ruler of this world is judged."* here Jesus calls him the ruler of this world.

Ephesians 2:2, *"in which you once walked according to the course of this world, according to the prince of the power of the air, the spirit who now works in the sons of disobedience."* The apostle Paul here calls him the prince of the power of the air. He also confirms that he (Satan) still works through those who do not obey God.

Not much doubt with these verses. Yes sadly Satan is still very much in charge on the earth but definitely his days are numbered. He also has fewer operatives. He can only work through those who remain in rebellion against God. Because of the work of Jesus on the Cross he cannot operate through those who have surrendered their lives (and authority) to Jesus. Unfortunately all the death and destruction brought about by the fall in the Garden of Eden is still in full sway on the earth today. Satan may not be able to touch a believer's soul but because we still physically live in a fallen world Christians are very much affected by its powers. Sickness, death, accident and the evil of man can afflict Christian or non-Christian alike. It's a result of the dangerous neighbourhood we're currently residing

Chapter 3
Fairy Tales

in. The big difference for the believer in Jesus is that we have divine hope. In Jesus our eternal salvation is assured and nobody can take that from us. Soon Jesus is returning and Satan will be swiftly dealt to. What Christians must remember is that when things do strike us down, and they will, then it is just the world we live in, not God's hand against us. Can't our loving God protect us from these things, I hear you ask? Of course, he certainly can and frequently does provide divine protection in many situations, but not from everything and if He doesn't it's not because we have failed or haven't got close enough to Him.

God allows negative things to happen to us for a myriad of reasons, but rest assured He will always have just cause. Mostly it helps us experience His strength and love better but sometimes our suffering is for the benefit of others. Numerous Christians over the ages have been martyred for their belief in Jesus. Why does God allow that? It's hard to imagine it being for the benefit of the one dying, so it must be for the profit of others. Such a benefit resulted from the stoning of Stephen in Acts 7: this caused a massive expansion in the spread of the gospel of Jesus. It goes on to tell us that because of the resulting persecution Christians were scattered throughout the regions of Judea and Samaria, no doubt telling all and sundry the good news.

Jesus Himself tells us in Luke 21:12-13 *"But before all these things, they will lay their hands on you and persecute you, delivering you up to the synagogues and prisons. You will be* brought before kings and rulers for My name's sake. **But it will turn out for you as an occasion for testimony.**" [Emphasis added]. God therefore allows persecution in order to further the spread of the gospel.

The apostle Paul could easily be described as a model Christian, yet he suffered incredibly for the gospel of Jesus. He wrote Philippians while in prison: Philippians 1:12-14 *"But I want you to know, brethren, that the things which happened to me have actually turned out for the furtherance of the gospel, so that it has become evident to the whole palace guard, and to all the rest, that my chains are in Christ; and most of the brethren in the Lord, having become confident by my chains, are much more bold to speak the word without fear."*

Suffering and persecution has little to do with your standing with God and God never initiates it. He may allow it to happen to us but it's not God doing it. We live in a broken, Satan-controlled world, stuff happens.

Satan is the source of all evil and most Christians readily accept that description of him. The mythical presentation of a red horned evil tailed devil is easy to imagine given what he is capable of. But is he really like that? Actually quite the opposite is true of his outward appearance.

Ezekiel 28:12-14 speaking of Lucifer says; *"'Thus says the Lord God:*

"You were the seal of perfection, full of wisdom and perfect in beauty. You were in Eden, the garden of God; Every precious

Chapter 3
Fairy Tales

stone was your covering: the sardius, topaz, and diamond, beryl, onyx, and jasper, sapphire, turquoise, and emerald with gold. The workmanship of your timbrels and pipes was prepared for you on the day you were created." The seal of perfection? Perfect in beauty? That doesn't sound like one that's inherently evil, no; the verse is describing the outward appearance only. Verse 17 tells us; *"**Your heart was lifted up** because of your beauty.*

You have corrupted your wisdom by reason of your splendour." [Emphasis added] The problem wasn't external it was internal, he had a heart problem. Basically he fell in love with himself. Incredibly his outward magnificence has never changed despite his being cast out of heaven. His appearance today is just as Ezekiel 28 records it.

To a Christian this aspect of Satan is most dangerous. Because of all the evil that the devil lathers over the earth our focus is more naturally on his negative side. Evil satanic occurrences are relatively easy for a Christian to recognise. Satan, though, is not averse to using the full force of his outward appearance when he wants to. The apostle Paul speaks about this in 2 Corinthians 11:14-15 *"And no wonder! For Satan himself transforms himself into an angel of light. Therefore it is no great thing if his ministers also transform themselves into ministers of righteousness, whose end will be according to their works."* Detecting the evil or deception in something appearing as angelic in brilliant flaunts of light and splendour is not clear cut. Such a creature will not coming spewing evil but rather with a pleasant style and slight twist on the word of God. *"Has God really said?"* That's his old trick with Eve way back in Genesis 3:1. It's called the thin edge of the wedge. The devil is so desperate to disrupt God's plan he will do absolutely anything to achieve that. The subtle side of evil comes up with statements like "going to church is more important than reading your Bible". No, actually **both** are extremely important.

Over the years the devil has tried all sorts of tricks to deceive and discourage believers. Church schisms through the centuries have been frequent and often well documented. The majority of these have occurred when man's reasoning had been applied to the interruptions of scripture regarding the best way to worship or relate to God etc. God is not divided therefore any such divisions within a church are inspired by something not of God – the devil.

How have these supposed men of God been brought to such deep disagreement so as to divide whole congregations of Christians? The devil "masquerading as an angel of light" could effortlessly allow a leader to believe he has received a divine revelation involving the interpretation of scripture. So strong is the belief of this seemingly celestial impartation that some church fathers stifled all contrary opinion by clinging to a particular extension of one segment of God's word in isolation to the rest of the Bible. Once such a devoted opinion sets in, blindness to all other clarifying verses results. Sadly, strong leaders have sometimes persuaded large numbers of

Chapter 3
Fairy Tales

parishioners to side with them resulting in the opposing sides demonstrating anything but godly love to each other. The Bible is intended to be read and understood as a whole; to stand on a human translation of just one or two verses is very shaky ground.

Today because of the vast number of non-denominational churches schisms are less common but sadly do still occur. The devil's tools today are much more subtle. The basic intent, however, is the same – to deceive and discourage as many Christians as possible. There are many examples and they usually result when one aspect of scripture is overemphasized. The so called teaching of the "prosperity gospel" is one such example. It has many facets but the basic principal is that once you have given your life to Jesus Christ and become born again that you will enter the full blessings of God and you will live life to the full. That's absolutely Biblically correct from one perspective as Jesus himself said in John 10:10 *"The thief comes only to steal and kill and destroy. I came that they may have life and have it abundantly."* (ESV). The words of Jesus are clear that in Him we have an abundant life but does this mean that if negative things were to happen to me (and they will) disrupting this abundant life that somehow I'm not living close enough to Jesus? This is the lie that naturally the "angel of light" promotes. Because you're not living this abundant life somehow you haven't quite made it with Jesus yet therefore you must try harder, do better, tithe more, excel in good works, something, anything. This falsehood only ends in discouragement, which is the devils objective. Once discouraged he has greater scope to come at us with more serious misrepresentations, perhaps enticing us back into sin and away from God.

The apostle Paul was a mighty man of God but he had a continuous assortment of terrible things happen to him. Did he need to have God continually chastise him in order to keep him close to Jesus? Absolutely not, he tells us in Philippians 4:12-13 *"I know how to be abased, and I know how to abound. Everywhere and in all things I have learned both to be full and to be hungry, both to abound and to suffer need. I can do all things through Christ who strengthens me."* His strength and power had no relationship to, or connection with, his external circumstances. He possessed a very deep understanding of the power of God (the Holy Spirit) at work within him which no person or negative experience could ever take away.

Paul goes on in Philippians 4:19 *"And my God shall supply all your need according to His riches in glory by Christ Jesus."* Every need, not necessarily all our wants, – big difference. Yes, God has richly blessed every person that has given their life to the Lord Jesus Christ and made Him the Lord, the King, the boss of their lives. He has named us sons and co-heirs with King Jesus and we will live with him forever and ever. In the meantime we still abide in a fallen world and in that world we are still subject to the same laws of physics as all other earth-dwellers. Stuff happens but when it afflicts you that it does not mean God loves you any less. Through all things He is always there.

Chapter 3
Fairy Tales

Godly favour upon Christians certainly is a very real thing; however, founding our Christian walk solely on prosperous living, using our blessing experiences as a barometer of our relationship with God is especially dangerous territory that will undoubtedly only end in discouragement and opportunity for full-on demonic attack.

Humanism is an extreme example of the clever lies of the "angel of light" but that is a whole new subject we'll take a look at later. Throughout your Christian life always be on your guard against the deceptive and subtle lies of the devil as he is extremely desperate to turn you away from God. Not because he wants to have you on his team (he doesn't even have a team) but because he doesn't want God to enjoy spending eternity with you. Whatever you come across in life, regardless of who tells you – even your church pastor, – always check it against what the Bible says and always consider any verse in the full context of which it was written.

And just to clarify, Satan is not the boss of hell where he and his demons sit around enjoying tormenting those condemned there. Satan is the temporary ruler on this earth but when he is cast into hell he suffers the same horrific fate of all other non-believer. No hierarchy in hell, everybody shares the same terrible destiny. Every human being has a choice to go there or not, my very strong recommendation is – don't choose hell. Satan on the other hand has no choice as God has already decreed that's where he's going as foretold in the book of Revelation.

The red horned image of the devil is mythical, but Satan himself is very real. Hell is a very real place but absolutely not a Satan presided over competitive opposite to heaven.

Miracles are another bone of contention by Bible sceptics. There are numerous miraculous happenings throughout the Bible, from the animals coming to Noah's ark to the events of Jesus' life and the work of the apostles. Surely they're just a writer with a vivid imagination. Well, who is the main enduring character in the Bible? It's God Himself. It's all about God, folks. God is not human, He is great and the formula for His greatness is given above. He is **extremely** great.

So what is a miracle? The Webster dictionary describes it as: [2]

An extraordinary and welcome event that is not explicable by natural or scientific laws and is therefore attributed to a divine agency.

Oh, so something that God does then? Miracles cannot be confined to human understanding yet that is precisely what so many sceptics do. I can't see how that could happen, therefore someone invented the story. Sorry to prick that overinflated bubble of human ego but a miracle is only a miracle to mankind. To God it's just what He does.

If a car owner goes to a car mechanic with a problem in the engine and he repairs, it the owner rarely comes away exclaiming "it's a miracle!" No, the owner fully appreciates the repair is wholly within the mechanic's capabilities and isn't the

Chapter 3
Fairy Tales

least bit amazed when he does what is required. The same scenario applies when for example Jesus (the Son of God) heals a blind man. The Creator simply made some adjustments to one of His created beings whose light receptors were malfunctioning. Not spectacular from God's perspective but from Man's point of view, simply speaking to a blind man's problem appears ludicrous. All the miracles in the Bible are the work of God, not man. Yes God frequently operates through men, even today, to carry out these miraculous acts, nevertheless it is always God's power behind them.

Miracles then are just things that God does in man's realm for the benefit of man.

A friend of mine had a humorous extension to the miracle Jesus did at Cana of Galilee when he turned the water into wine.

"Joseph had immensely enjoyed the fantastic wine the groom served during the latter half of the Cana wedding feast and unfortunately rather over imbibed. Next morning his hangover was unbearable. Mary hovered about offering assistance but poor Joseph only wanted to be left alone to sleep things off. Finally Mary said "Is there anything I can get you Joseph, anything at all?" "Well" mumbled Joseph, "perhaps a nice glass of water then – but don't let your Boy touch it!""

While that is an extremely unlikely rendition of events following the Cana wedding it does loosely demonstrate that when God is involved the miraculous becomes the everyday.

"Experts made the Titanic, Amateurs made the ark"

Chapter 4
Evidence

The word "Bible" comes from bíblia in Latin and bíblos in Greek. The term means book, or books. The word probably originated from the ancient Egyptian port of Byblos (in modern-day Lebanon), where papyrus was used for making books and scrolls then exported to Greece. Genesis, the first book of the Bible was written about 1400 BC and the last book of Revelation about 96 AD. So, essentially it's a very old book! But just because it's ancient, does that make it untrustworthy?

What other aged documents are of a similar age? The earliest known written non-Biblical literature, the classical Sumerian, dates from about 2600 BC. The earliest literary author known by name is Enheduanna, dated to around 2400 BC. Some literary texts, such as the Book of the Dead, ancient Egyptian funerary texts, were recorded in the Papyrus of Ani around 1240 BC, but other versions of the book date from about 1800 BC.

In fact today there are 33 known writings which are believed to predate the 1400 BC writing date of Genesis and a couple that, we're told, predate Noah's flood of about 2300 BC.

Chapter 4
Evidence

What's interesting is that very little controversy surrounds any of these writings. Generally they're accepted as what probably did occur at that period. Clearly some writings are mythical or poetic but most in their own way do provide a tiny window to life in that era. So why then is it only the Bible that has to prove its authenticity at every turn? The answer is in fact uncomplicated; the Bible says of itself that it is the Word of God. Man, still in his rebellion against God, responds to that statement by saying either, "it's just a load of unreliable ramblings" or "Since it's true I had better fully comprehend every word." With this later assertion, what is written becomes crucial; how can I know what I'm reading today is the same as the original writer intended?

If something is copied over and over, surely through time, numerous errors will inadvertently occur. You've probably experienced as a kid the game of Chinese whispers. One person whispers a message to another, passing along a line of people until the last player announces the message to the entire group. Errors typically accumulate in the retellings, so much so that the statement announced by the last player differs significantly, and often amusingly, from the one uttered by the first. Sceptics will point to this factor and dismiss the Bible as unreliable. How do we prove if what I'm reading today is original?

Firstly it's important to appreciate just how these ancient texts were reproduced without the aid of the modern-day photocopy machine. When replicating the Old Testament, trained Jewish scribes would duplicate portions of Scripture by hand, initially onto animal skins until about 100 B.C. when they began to use papyrus or paper. They took extreme care to ensure the precision of their scribal copying to such extent that if there was one error between a copy and the original, the copy was burned.

Fortunately, the Bible has been subjected to extremely vigorous literary and historical criticism, probably more than any other ancient work, and the good news is it's emerged unscathed and the answer is derived by historical science. To determine the reliability of ancient documents secular and non-secular historians alike use the historiography test. This test has three parts; the bibliographical test, the internal test and the external test.

Bibliographical test.

The bibliographic test looks at the ancient manuscripts of the Bible and asks whether the text of the Bible we have today is the same as the original. There are thousands of ancient manuscripts of the Bible, dating from the early second century down to the middle ages.

Let's look first at the Old Testament's textual history and compare it to other documents of antiquity. With most ancient documents, generally there is about a thousand year gap between the writing of the document and the first available copy that archaeologists have found. Tacitus is a well-known Roman historian and the first known manuscript copy of his

Chapter 4
Evidence

work dates to around 1100 A.D. but Tacitus actually wrote his works around 100 A.D. Interestingly, very few historians doubt that we have a clear reproduction of what Tacitus really wrote, even though only about 20 total partial or complete, manuscripts exist and the earliest manuscript dates to about 1,000 years after his original writing. In comparison, the oldest manuscript copy of the Old Testament dates from 250 B.C. only 150 years after the original book of Malachi was written around 400 B.C.

When comparing the number of manuscripts available for the Bible with the manuscripts that exist for other important works such as Plato or Thucydides — it's striking. For the Bible, there are 5,000 Greek manuscripts, hundreds of papyri, almost 350 Syriac copies with most dating to about 400AD. In addition, virtually the entire New Testament could be reproduced from quotations by the early church fathers 32,000 such quotations existed before the Council of Nicaea in AD325.

Prior to 1948, some of the earliest complete manuscripts of various books of the Old Testament dated to around 900 to 1000 A.D. Over last 70 years however that has changed dramatically.

About the time of Christ, the Jewish Essenes community hid their valuable scrolls in sealed pottery jars in several caves along the Dead Sea to protect them from the occupying Roman conquers. Their community was eventually overrun by the Roman army in about 70AD and the scrolls remained hidden and forgotten. However, in 1947, Bedouin shepherds while looking for some lost sheep in the hills surrounding the Dead Sea, threw a rock into a darkened cave and heard the sound of breaking pottery. In the pottery was perhaps the greatest archaeological discovery of modern times. [1]

Learning of the report, scholars explored the cave and eleven others nearby ones. Their work uncovered nearly 1,100 ancient documents which included several complete scrolls and more than 100,000 fragments from every Old Testament book, except for the book of Esther, together with various commentaries on Old Testament books, and other extra-Biblical literature. The majority of the texts were written in the Hebrew language, but there were also manuscripts written in Aramaic and Greek.

Scholars were anxious to confirm if these Dead Sea Scrolls were the most ancient of all Old Testament manuscripts in the Hebrew language. They used three types of dating tools: archaeology and palaeography orthography (the study of ancient languages) and the carbon-14 dating method.

Archaeologists studied the pottery, coins, graves, and garments at Khirbet Qumran, where the Essenes community lived. From their deduction they concluded the scrolls dated between the second century B.C. and the first century A.D. Palaeographers studied the style of writing and arrived at dates raging from the third century B.C. to the first century A.D. Scientists, using the radiocarbon dating method, dated the scrolls to range from the fourth century B.C. to the first century A.D. Since all the methods came to a similar conclusion,

Chapter 4
Evidence

scholars are very confident of their assigned date for the texts. Some scrolls date as early as the third century B.C. and other up to the first century A.D.

Following years of careful study by various experts, they have concluded that the Dead Sea Scrolls give precise confirmation that the Old Testament text has been very accurately preserved. The scrolls were found to be almost identical with the Masoretic text. [2] (The Old Testament that we use today is translated from what is called the Masoretic Text. It's so named because of the Masoretes Jewish scholars who worked between 500 and 1000 A.D. These scholars compiled a system of pronunciation and grammatical guides in the form of diacritical notes on the external form of the Biblical text in order to standardize the pronunciation, paragraph and verse divisions of the Bible).

Without doubt the most significant discovery was an almost complete scroll of the book of Isaiah which was verified to have been written around 100 B.C. A major comparison study was conducted on the Dead Sea Scroll of Isaiah and the text of Isaiah found in the Masoretic copy from about 900AD. After much research, scholars found that the two texts were practically identical. Most variants were minor spelling differences, and none affected the meaning of the text. This finding is momentous as Isaiah contains numerous prophecies regarding the coming Messiah, Jesus Christ. Critics had previously claimed that since Isaiah's prophecies were so specific, and since they were all fulfilled by Jesus, they must have been written after the fact. Exact copies written 100 years before his birth certainly shows the fallacy of that point.

The Isaiah scroll, as well as many other scrolls and fragments from the Dead Sea, are currently stored and are on display in Jerusalem at the Shrine of the Book. [3]

The New Testament's reliability and accuracy is constantly under attack by critics. However, to disregard the New Testament, then one must also disregard other ancient writings such as Plato, Aristotle, and Homer. This is because the New Testament documents are better-preserved and more numerous than any other ancient writings. Simply since they are so numerous, the various New Testament books can be easily cross-checked for accuracy.

There are presently 5,686 Greek manuscripts in existence today for the New Testament. Compared to other manuscripts of ancient writings, the New Testament manuscripts far outweigh the others in terms of quantity which the table following illustrates. [4]

This table demonstrates there is a magnitude of thousands between the number of New Testament Greek manuscripts and any other ancient writing. In addition to the 5,600 number in the table above, there are over 19,000 copies in the Syriac, Latin, Coptic, and Aramaic languages. The total number of New Testament manuscripts available is over 24,000. Compared to the undisputed writings of Homer the authenticity of the whole New Testament is, without a doubt, beyond dispute.

Chapter 4
Evidence

Author	Date Written	Earliest Copy	Approximate Time Span between original & copy	Number of Copies	Accuracy of Copies
Lucretius	died 55 or 53 B.C.		1100 yrs	2	----
Pliny	A.D. 61-113	A.D. 850	750 yrs	7	----
Plato	427-347 B.C.	A.D. 900	1200 yrs	7	
Demosthenes	4th Cent. B.C.	A.D. 1100	800 yrs	8	----
Herodotus	480-425 B.C.	A.D. 900	1300 yrs	8	----
Suetonius	A.D. 75-160	A.D. 950	800 yrs	8	----
Thucydides	460-400 B.C.	A.D. 900	1300 yrs	8	----
Euripides	480-406 B.C.	A.D. 1100	1300 yrs	9	----
Aristophanes	450-385 B.C.	A.D. 900	1200 yrs	10	----
Caesar	100-44 B.C.	A.D. 900	1000 yrs	10	----
Livy	59 BC-AD 17	----	???	20	----
Tacitus	circa A.D. 100	A.D. 1100	1000 yrs	20	----
Aristotle	384-322 B.C.	A.D. 1100	1400 yrs	49	----
Sophocles	496-406 B.C.	A.D. 1000	1400 yrs	193	----
Homer (Iliad)	900 B.C.	400 B.C.	500 yrs	643	95%
New Testament	1st Cent. A.D. (A.D. 50-100)	2nd Cent. A.D.(c. A.D. 130)	less than 100 years	5600	99.50%

87

Internal test

This test asks whether we can determine if the document we have was written by eyewitnesses. The New Testament especially is very significant in this regard.

As we saw in our table above the internal consistency of the Old and New Testament manuscripts is 99.5% textually pure – an amazing accuracy. Few Biblical scholars dispute that the New Testament books were all written before the close of the 1st Century AD. History records that Jesus was crucified between the years 30 and 33 AD. Therefore the entire New Testament was completed within 70 years of His death and resurrection. This is significant as it means there were ample people around when the New Testament books were written who could have easily contested the writings were they incorrect or fictitious. Clearly the authors knew that if they were inaccurate, plenty of people would have pointed it out. But there is not a single document contemporary with the First Century that contests any of the New Testament texts.

Law professor and historian, John Warwick Montgomery, gives the following four 'fundamental principles of laws of evidence' to the New Testament documents: [5]

The ancient documents rule

In order to establish the credibility of a document, Aristotle's dictum is to be followed by the literary critic. This dictum states: "The benefit of the doubt is to be given to the document itself, and not arrogated by the critic to himself." In

Chapter 4
Evidence

other words, one must listen to the claims of the New Testament under analysis, and not assume fraud or error unless the authors disqualify themselves by contradictions or known factual inaccuracies.

The parole evidence rule

External, oral testimony or tradition will not be received in evidence to add to, subtract from, vary, or contradict an executed written instrument such as a will. This rule insists that the New Testament documents should be allowed to 'interpret itself' and not be twisted to external, extra-Biblical data. In other words, we should not interpret the documents in the light of our own - or other's - preconceived assumptions. For example, we should not simply dismiss the New Testament as unreliable because we feel that miracles cannot happen. We should not make up our minds before we have examined the evidence.

The hearsay rule

"A witness must testify 'of his own knowledge', not on the basis of what has come to him indirectly from others i.e. hearsay. Were the writers on the New Testament documents eyewitnesses of the events that they recorded?

The cross-examination principle

The more a witness is subjected to close and searching cross examination, the more confidence we can place in their testimony. Were the witnesses of Jesus and His life subjected to severe opposition - hostile cross-examiners who would destroy the case of Christianity if the early Christian's testimony had been contradicted by the facts?

When these four legal principles are considered, with regards to the credibility and accuracy of the New Testament documents, we find that the documents should be unequivocally pronounced valid and reliable as evidence about Jesus Christ.

Clearly The New Testament passes the Internal Test with flying colours. What then of the Old Testament?

The majority of the Old Testament authors were eyewitnesses of — or interviewed eyewitnesses of — the majority of the events they described. Moses participated in and was an eyewitness of the remarkable events of the Egyptian captivity, the Exodus, the forty years in the desert, and Israel's final encampment before entering the Promised Land. These events he chronicled in the first five books of the Old Testament.

Josh McDowell put it well when he wrote; [6]

"The Bible was composed over a period of roughly 1500 years. It's the work of more than 40 authors from every walk of life, including kings, peasants, philosophers, fishermen, poets, statesmen, and scholars. Portions of the Bible were written in the wilderness, in a dungeon, in a palace, in exile, in wartime, and in peace time. Written on 2 continents in 3 languages, yet this astounding diverse book speaks with astonishing

Chapter 4
Evidence

continuity. There is one unfolding story from page one to "The End".

External test

Time and time again, archaeology has confirmed that the writers of the Biblical texts knew what they were talking about. Along with the writings of non-Christian historians from the first century such as the Jewish historian Josephus, archaeology endorses the Biblical text at many points. So what is some of this Archaeology evidence from the Bible?

Archaeology and the Old Testament [7]

- Ebla tablets—discovered in 1970s in Northern Syria. Documents written on clay tablets from around 2300 B.C. demonstrate that personal and place names in the Patriarchal accounts are genuine. In use in Ebla was the name "Canaan," a name critics once said was not used at that time and was used incorrectly in the early chapters of the Bible. The tablets refer to all five "cities of the plain" mentioned in Genesis 14, previously assumed to have been mere legends.

- Egyptian words in the Pentateuch (first five Bible books). Accurate Egyptian names: Potiphar (Gen.39), Zaphenath-Paneah (Joseph's Egyptian name, Gen. 41:45), Asenath (Gen.41:45), On (Gen. 41:45), Rameses (Gen. 47:11), Oithom (Exodus 1:11).

- Finds in Egypt are consistent with the time, place, and other details of Biblical accounts of the Israelites in

Egypt. These include housing and tombs that most likely belonged to the Israelites, as well as a villa and tomb that is believed to have been built for Joseph.

- Confounding earlier sceptics, but confirming the Bible, an important discovery was made in Egypt in 1896. A tablet — the Merneptah Stela — was found that mentions Israel. (Merneptah was the Pharaoh that ruled Egypt in 1212-1202 B.C.) The context of the stela indicates that Israel was a significant entity in the late 13th century B.C.

- The Hittites were once thought to be a Biblical legend, until their capital and records were discovered in Turkey in 1906.

- A crucial find in Nuzi (north-eastern Iraq), an entire cache of Hittite legal documents from 1400 B.C. confirms many details of Genesis, Deuteronomy, such as:
  - a: Siring of legitimate children through handmaidens,
  - b: Oral deathbed will as binding,
  - c: The power to sell one's birth-right for relatively trivial property (Jacob & Esau),
  - d: Need for family idols, such as Rachel stole from Laban, to secure inheritance,
  - e: Form of the covenant in Deuteronomy exactly matches the form of suzerainty treaties between Hittite emperors and vassal kings.

Chapter 4
Evidence

- Walls of Jericho—discovery in 1930s by John Garstang. The walls fell suddenly, and outwardly (unique), so the Israelites could clamber over the ruins into the city (Joshua 6:20).

- In 1986, scholars identified an ancient seal belonging to Baruch, son of Neriah, a scribe who recorded the prophecies of Jeremiah (Jer. 45:1).

- In 1990, Harvard researchers unearthed a silver-plated bronze calf figurine reminiscent of the Aaron's golden calf mentioned in the book of Exodus.

- In 1993, archaeologists uncovered a 9th century B.C. inscription at Tel Dan in northern Israel. The words carved into a chunk of basalt refer to the "House of David" and the "King of Israel." Also, the Bible's version of Israelite history after the reign of David's son, Solomon, is believed to be based on historical fact since it is corroborated by independent accounts of Egyptian and Assyrian inscriptions.

- It was once claimed there was no Assyrian king named Sargon as recorded in Isaiah 20:1, because this name was not known in any other record. Then, Sargon's palace was discovered in Iraq. The very event mentioned in Isaiah 20, his capture of Ashdod, was recorded on the palace walls! Even more, fragments of a stela (a poetic eulogy) memorializing the victory was found at Ashdod itself.

- Another king who was in doubt was Belshazzar, king of Babylon, named in Daniel 5. The last king of Babylon was Nabonidus according to recorded history. A tablet was found showing that Belshazzar was Nabonidus' son.

- The ruins of Sodom and Gomorrah have been discovered southeast of the Dead Sea. Evidence at the site seems consistent with the Biblical account: Genesis 19:24 *("Then God rained on Sodom and on Gomorrah sulphur and fire from God out of the sky.")* The destruction debris was about 3 feet thick and buildings were burned from fires that started on the rooftops. Geologist Frederick Clapp theorizes that that pressure from an earthquake could have spewed out sulphur-laden bitumen (similar to asphalt) known to be in the area through the fault line upon which the cities rest. The dense smoke reported by Abraham is consistent with a fire from such material, which could have ignited by a spark or ground fire.

Archaeology and the New Testament [8]

- The New Testament mentions specific individuals, places, and various official titles of local authorities, confirmed by recent archaeology. Luke addressed his Gospel and the book of Acts to "most excellent Theophilus," and although it is assumed he was a Christian Roman official, his true identity remains unknown. Luke, however, does mention exact titles of several other proven officials. (Titles varied from city to

Chapter 4
Evidence

city therefore the following finds demonstrate Luke's incredible accuracy.)
- o Lysanias the Tetrarch in Abilene (Luke 3:1) — verified by inscription dated 14-29 A.D.
- o Erastus, city treasurer of Corinth (Romans 16:23)—verified by pavement inscription.
- o Gallio—proconsul of Achaia (Greece) in A.D. 51 (Acts 18:12).
- o Stone Pavement at Pilate's headquarters (John 19:13) —discovered recently.
- o Pool at Bethesda— discovered in 1888.
- o Many examples of silver shrines to Artem have been found (Acts 19:28). One inscription confirms the title of the city as "Temple Warden of Artemis".
- o The detailed navigation provided on the account of Paul's sea voyage in Acts is one of the most instructive documents for the understanding of ancient seamanship."

- Census of Luke 1. These began under Augustus and occurred approximately every 14 years: 23-22 B.C., 9-8 B.C. and 6 A.D. There is evidence of enrolment in 11-8 B.C. in Egyptian papyri. There was previously wide scepticism surrounding this census however the critics have been silenced by recent findings. The following is a list of sceptic's questions and what has been answered:
    - o Problem: Historian Josephus puts Quirinius as Governor in Syria at 6 A.D. Solution: Recent

inscription confirms that Quirinius was governing in Syria in 7 B. C. (in an extraordinary, military capacity but not necessarily as Governor).
- Problem: Herod's kingdom was not part of the Roman Empire at the time, so there would not have been a census. Solution: it was a client kingdom. Augustus treated Herod as a subject (Josephus). Parallel—a census took place in the client kingdom of Antiochus in eastern Asia Minor under Tiberius.
- Problem: Enrolment in home town? Solution: This was confirmed by edict of Vibius Maximus, Roman prefect of Egypt in 104 A.D. "...it is necessary for all who are for any cause whatsoever away from their administrative divisions to return home to comply with the customary ordinance of enrolment."

• Opinion of Sir William Ramsay, one of the outstanding Near Eastern archaeologists: "Luke is a historian of the first rank; not merely are his statements of fact trustworthy; he is possessed of the true historic sense; he fixes his mind on the idea and plan that rules in the evolution of history, and proportions the scale of his treatment to the importance of each incident. He seizes the important and critical events and shows their true nature at greater length. In short, this author should be placed among the very greatest of historians."

Chapter 4
Evidence

- Diggers recently uncovered an ossuary (repository for bones) with the inscription "Joseph Son of Caiaphas." This marked the first archaeological evidence that the high priest Caiaphas was a real person. The gospels show Caiaphas presided at the Sanhedrin's trial of Jesus.

- [9] In Acts 17:6-8, Luke uses the Greek word politarchs to describe the city officials in Thessalonica. That word doesn't appear in classical Greek literature so for many years, critics accused Luke of making a mistake. Then archaeologists discovered a first-century arch in the town that used this very term — showing that the term was in use for government officials at the very time Luke was writing.

- Similarly in Acts 18:12, Luke uses the term "proconsul" to describe a gentleman called Gallio. That word didn't appear in classical literature either so; again, scholars questioned Luke's accuracy. Then an inscription was found at Delphi, dating to AD51, using the same term — and amazingly, to describe the very same official, Gallio.

- In John 5:1-2, it mentions "a pool in Jerusalem, by the Sheep Gate, called in Hebrew 'Bethesda', which has five porticoes". Until the 20th century, there was no evidence outside of John's Gospel for such a place and, again, critics questioned John's reliability. Then in the 1930s, the pool was uncovered by archaeologists — complete with four colonnades around the edges and one across the middle.

- One final example will suffice and it's perhaps the most intriguing — the so-called "James ossuary" which according to the Gospels, and to the Jewish historian Josephus, James was the brother of Jesus and was killed in AD62. In 2002, a mid-first century bone box, or ossuary, was discovered in Jerusalem, bearing the Aramaic inscription "James, son of Joseph, brother of Jesus". There is very strong evidence that the box and its inscription are authentic. Ed Keall, of the Royal Ontario Museum in Toronto, has said "we stand by our opinion that the James Ossuary is not a forgery". As New Testament historian Ben Witherington put it: "If, as seems probable, the ossuary found in the vicinity of Jerusalem and dated to about AD 63 is indeed the burial box of James, the brother of Jesus, this inscription is the most important extra-Biblical evidence of its kind."

The key point is this: archaeology doesn't prove the New Testament is true. What it does do is endorse the narratives by showing that the Biblical writings are historical and geographical in character — and thus deserve to be weighed and treated as seriously as any other texts from antiquity.

Millar Burrows, former professor of archaeology at Yale wrote: [10]

"On the whole archaeological work has unquestionably strengthened confidence in the reliability of the Scriptural record. More than one archaeologist has found his respect for the Bible increased by the experience of excavation in Israel.

Chapter 4
Evidence

Archaeology has in many cases refuted the views of modern critics."

In addition to this Bibliographical test is the extensive evidence of prophecy given and prophecy fulfilled throughout the Bible. Many such prophetic fulfilments didn't occur until centuries after they were given and in the time of a different writer, yet every prophetic realization has occurred with 100% accuracy. Only a writer inspired by a supernatural God could predict precisely an event many years in the future.

*"Tomorrows forecast,
God reigns and
The Son shines"*

Chapter 5
Prophecy

Time – we measure time, keep time, meet and greet in time and our daily lives are completely wrapped around the onward lunge of time. We perceive time as past present and future. Mankind in his natural state is locked in time with no means of escape. How many occasions have you expressed; if only I had a little more time? From a kid being told to go to bed at night, to relationships, to learning, to playing, family, friends, everything eventually comes to an end. The well know verses of Ecclesiastes 3:1-8 says it all.

> *"To everything there is a season,*
> *A time for every purpose under heaven:*
> *A time to be born,*
> *And a time to die;*
> *A time to plant,*
> *And a time to pluck what is planted;*
> *A time to kill,*
> *And a time to heal;*
> *A time to break down,*
> *And a time to build up;*

Chapter 5
Prophecy

A time to weep,
And a time to laugh;
A time to mourn,
And a time to dance;
A time to cast away stones,
And a time to gather stones;
A time to embrace,
And a time to refrain from embracing;
A time to gain,
And a time to lose;
A time to keep,
And a time to throw away;
A time to tear,
And a time to sew;
A time to keep silence,
And a time to speak;
A time to love,
And a time to hate;
A time of war,
And a time of peace."

Time's most serious consequence is that we are all locked in the present. We can look back on the past but solely through memories or recorded history. Once the moment has passed it is etched as in granite and no amount of desire, or will, on our part can ever change the occurrence of it. The past stands a perpetual memorial of every single instant of time. Things can be done to appease past occurrences, but to change what occurred in the past is impossible for man.

The future is equally outside our control. We may have a strong vision of the future with well-developed plans to accomplish them. We frequently succeed in implementing them but never is there a cast iron guarantee of success. Even our life is fickle in terms of future events; we don't know for certain if we'll even be alive tomorrow. "He was hit by a bus on the way to collect his lottery prize!" How many times have you heard, or used, the expression; if I only knew **that** was going to happen, then I would have done…." Man only has control of the moment, which sadly is not too much in the greater picture of life.

A comprehensive realisation of that fact can be very frustrating and frankly downright depressing. A natural attribute of man is a desire to control, however the truth is we're just achieving life step by step, reflecting on the past and hoping for the future. Hope is an inherent characteristic of mankind, control is not. The desire to control was a side effect of the rebellion in the Garden of Eden. *"You'll be like God"* was part of the lie the serpent told Eve. Hope is extremely powerful; with it we become creative and filled with such positive emotions as happiness, joy, peace, love, courage, and empowerment. It opens the door of possible fulfilment and to the desire to attempt to achieve. Remove hope and all you have is negativity, death and darkness.

Clearly hope is fundamentally vital, so what then are the feeders of hope? What draws it out and what develops it? The short answer is: an expectation for the future. Whatever I'm experiencing at this very moment can, with different

Chapter 5
Prophecy

circumstances or environment, be better in a time yet to come. Life necessitates that we all should make plans for the future and set up programs and structures to achieve them. Thankfully God also gave us wisdom. Wisdom will help us evaluate the most productive actions to create the future we hope for. Once these actions are initiated they must be constantly monitored and tweaked in real time to achieve the future we desire. Regrettably even with great wisdom, skill, hope and enthusiasm nothing in life is guaranteed. Hope remains as our driver to the future.

Hope is not a facet of our physical body, in that it can be materially identified, it's a trait of our soul. Our soul, or more correctly our heart, is an integral part of us as much as our arm or eye. The fact that man is made in the image of God with spirit (soul), heart and body is something we'll explore later in this book. For now hope abides and springs from the heart.

God placed the essence of hope within us on the day we were created and since hope is an expectation of the future, understanding of, or about, the future is paramount. As we've said, man in his natural state has very little control over the future outside his immediate area of influence simply because man is confined within the boundaries of time. Even the wisest man on earth cannot with any certainty define precise future events; the best he can predict is a calculated guess. One human being may set up a certain chain of events which should determine a particular outcome, only at a later date to have another person manipulate them allowing an alternative result.

Time is linear, like an unstoppable juggernaut traversing a continuous line. Man is an embedded player on that ever-progressing route and therefore unable to observe it from any other viewpoint. If that were possible then the future could be clearly seen, together with all the points leading up to it. If man could achieve that vantage angle then predicting the future could become a certainty. So is there such a time viewing platform and who gets to see it? Yes there is, and naturally the creator of it. God created time at the same time He made the heavens and the earth. God cannot be confined by something he created; He lives, moves and exists in His normal state outside of it. Jesus entered time when He became a man and lived on this earth. After His resurrection Jesus returned to His Father in heaven and now resides outside of time again.

Everything that God does and says therefore is from outside any constraint of time. God is the controller of His created time. The flow of time is directed by God who appoints particular "times" within His unfolding purposes. God ordered the children of Israel to hold His feasts at their appointed time. Leviticus 23:4 *"These are the feasts of the LORD, holy convocations, which you shall proclaim in their **appointed times**."* [Emphasis added]. God has divided time into seasons Deuteronomy 11:14 *"then I will give you the rain for your land **in its season**, the early rain and the latter rain, that you may gather in your grain, your new wine, and your oil."* [Emphasis added]. God is fully in control of time, He is its director and He sees the entire line of time from His throne.

Chapter 5
Prophecy

It should come as no surprise then when God tells us of something occurring in the near or distant future. He can clearly observe, and is in control of, every detail of every single event from this day until the end of time. To our natural mind that's "difficult" to comprehend but from His viewpoint it's actually quite unremarkable. Imagine you're reading a non-fictional diary of someone's life. You can freely flip over to page 215, to the end, or to any other page and read that day's events. You have a complete overview of any time in that person's life. In the same way God has that ability even though to us our book has not yet been completed.

With this perspective of God why are we surprised when things predicted in the Bible come to pass? And not just occur but will be fulfilled in precise detail. Critics of God's Word have claimed that since some of the prophecies in the Bible have come to pass in such detail that they must have been written after the fact. This is particularly enunciated with the book of Daniel and Isaiah. Awkwardly for these critics, manuscripts of both these books available today are proven to have existed prior to the fulfilment of their prophecies.

Prophecies are not confined to just those two books; the Bible contains an enormous volume of the foretelling of future happenings. It accurately accounts numerous specific events - in detail - many years, sometimes centuries, before they occur. Approximately 2,500 clear prophecies are found in its pages. About 2,000 of which already have been fulfilled to the letter — with absolutely zero errors. The remaining 500 or so reach into the future and will be seen unfolding as days go by.

Mathematically speaking the probability of **any one** of these 2,000 prophecies having been fulfilled by chance is conservatively figured at one in ten. Since the prophecies are for the most part independent of one another, the odds for all these prophecies having been fulfilled by chance without error is less than one in $10^{2,000}$ (that is 10 with 2,000 zeros written after it)! [1] Basically in layman's terms – not at all likely! Using this level of accuracy when applied to yet-to-be-fulfilled prophecies we can be absolutely certain the named happenings will occur and not just transpire but will do so, exactly as they are described.

The word prophecy comes from the Greek verb, προφημι (prophemi), which means "to say beforehand, foretell"; it is a combination of the Greek words, προ and φημι. The Greek prefix προ also means "before," "in front of," so etymologically προφημι means to speak in front of, as a spokesperson.

Prophecy involves a process in which messages are communicated to a prophet by God and then communicated to other people in either written or oral form. Prophetic messages can involve inspiration, interpretation, or revelation of events to come as compared to imparting divine knowledge.

The Hebrew term for prophet is Navi; it literally means "spokesperson". It infers a two way conversation, in that he also speaks to God on behalf of the people.

Bible prophecy is not just a prediction of future events, as the term "prediction" conveys doubt, suggesting a probability, however small, that it may not occur. God's word spoken

Chapter 5
Prophecy

through His prophets is identical to the telling of history. God knows all things; good, bad, past, present, future and everything is under His control. He is not the originator of evil or negative things that occur on our timeline but knows about all of them and He allows them to happen (or not) in order to bring about His Will. Because God observes all events outside of time, everything on our timeline is as history to Him. God is in effect recounting the event to a prophet exactly as He has planned, allowed and observed it. For this reason God's prophetic word can be relied on 100% and will come to pass in complete detail exactly as He spoke it. By His word alone He created the heavens and the earth which to our human understanding is a foreign concept, never-the-less it is a fact. When God the Creator speaks what He says never fails to come to pass.

Future tellers come in many forms, some of which are Godly and others not so. Many have claimed to be able to tell the future but have only faked it for personal enrichment. Even if their initial message was somehow inspired they've been tempted to expand it using their own cunning.

Sadon was a medieval astrologer who foretold to the king that his favourite wife would soon die.

Sure enough, the woman died a short time later. The king was outraged at Sadon, certain that his prediction had brought about the woman's death. He summoned Sadon and gave him this command: "Clairvoyant, tell me when you will die!" Sadon suspected that the king was planning to kill him, immediately, no matter what answer he gave. After pondering for a time he finally answered, "I do not know when I will die. I only know that whenever I die, you will die three days later."

I suspect Sadon was faking his later prediction but could the king be sure? In the same way Satan uses false prophets. His sole purpose in doing so is to deceive. Satan however is only a created being; he is not God nor is he any sort of rival. His methods of deception rely on trickery. Generally his utterances are so vague that numerous outcomes are possible and if through sheer fluke one actually comes to pass he uses that to claim credibility. Satan does not observe future events as God does therefore his only knowledge of them is through what he has learned. He fully comprehends the Bible and understands his fate together with all the events leading up to it.

False prophets inspired by the devil are very real, but his utterances are always lies. That is Satan's nature and Jesus makes it clear in John 8:44 *"You are of your father the devil, and the desires of your father you want to do. He was a murderer from the beginning, and does not stand in the truth, because there is no truth in him. When he speaks a lie, he speaks from his own resources, for he is a liar and the father of it."*

The Bible tells of false prophets and warns us of them. We must always be on our guard as Satan can be very persuasive and can transform himself into an angel of light. So how do we detect false prophets – those not of God? The epistle of John tells us 1 John 4:1-3 *"Beloved, don't believe every spirit, but test the spirits, whether they are of God, because many false*

Chapter 5
Prophecy

prophets have gone out into the world. By this you know the Spirit of God: every spirit who confesses that Jesus Christ has come in the flesh is of God, and every spirit who doesn't confess that Jesus Christ has come in the flesh is not of God, and this is the spirit of the Antichrist, of whom you have heard that it comes. Now it is in the world already." The Bible emphatically testifies "that Jesus Christ has come in the flesh".

Now that's we've established what prophecy is and who it comes from and that there is so much of it in the Bible, why is it there? Simple, because man is unable to see with any certainty past his immediate moment in time, God in His mercy has explained to us the main points of the future in advance. Yet another amazing characteristic of the loving God we have. Glory to God!

From our vantage point today in the progression of time much of what God spoke about in the Bible has already transpired. We have a distinct advantage over our forefathers who, being in the thick of it, couldn't easily distinguish light and darkness when the prophets spoke. The prophet Jeremiah for example was only a young lad when the Lord called him: Jeremiah 1:6. He made his complaint to God who flatly told him not to talk like that because He (God) was sending him. Imagine the reaction of the residents of Jerusalem when this young kid on his first assignment told the city and its king that God was bringing charges against them because they had rejected God and turned to idols. I can almost hear the crowd's reactions; what do you know? Who sent you? On what authority do you speak?

Later by the end of the book much of what Jeremiah had prophesied about had come to pass to such an extent that Nebuzaradan, the captain of the guard of the invading Babylonian armies, had heard of his accurate foresights. He was so impressed that he sent some of his King's chief officers to take Jeremiah from the court of the Jerusalem prison where he was confined and release him to his home town.

Witnessing after the fact brings assurance. The ultimate proof that God has sent a prophet is when his words come true. Recall the odds we spoke about above; once a critical mass of correctly fulfilled God-given prophecies has occurred, you can literally stake your life on all the remaining ones being fully realised. Taking the Bible as a whole, and considering about 2,000 recorded prophecies have already come to pass, we are therefore entirely without excuse when it comes to accepting the remaining 500 prophecies will likewise transpire.

So what are some of these 2000 fulfilled prophecies in the Bible and what's their reason for being there? The short answer for us is credibility. For those to whom they were given at the time it was often literal life and death. God has not changed and still points us to the way to life.

There are distinct categories of **fulfilled** prophecies in the Old Testament.

- The establishment and nurturing of the nation of Israel.
- The fall of the nation of Israel and its reestablishment and ultimate demise

Chapter 5
Prophecy

- The rise and fall of Gentile nations surrounding Israel.

- The coming of Jesus the Messiah.

- The creation of Israel as a nation again in the last days (1948 AD)

This is a very simplified list as there are numerous prophecies on a vast array of subjects. What should be glaringly obvious to us at this juncture in time is that given the copious volume of confirmed prophetic utterances throughout the Bible there can be little doubt, on that foundation alone, the Bible is the inspired word of God. Detailed prophecies or prophetic utterances can be found in almost every book of the Old Testament beginning from the third chapter Genesis when God himself told the serpent that one from the woman's offspring would bruise his head. The Testament ends with the book of Zechariah detailing in the last chapter the, yet to occur, events relating to the second coming of the Messiah to this earth. The consistent theme God uses with these prophecies is to reveal events occurring in the future and to warn man to repent and change his ways.

Critics of prophecy claim some prophetic utterances are worded so vaguely they can be applied to anything. Let's consider that then.

The prophet Daniel is often seen as being full of description and difficult to understand. The prophecy of Daniel 11 includes amazing details about great empires, political developments and end-time powers that would affect the Jewish people. [2]

Daniel 11:2 begins with the statement that *"three more kings will arise in Persia"* followed by a fourth who would *"stir up all against the realm of Greece."* History records that the next three Persian kings after Cyrus were:

1. His son, Cambyses II (530 - 522 BC)
2. Gaumata the Magian (also known as the pseudo-Smerdis – 522 BC)
3. The Persian Darius I (the Great – 522 - 486 BC)the forth Persian king who invaded Greece was Xerxes, who reigned – 485-464 B.C.

Daniel 11:3-4 speaks of the appearance of *"a mighty king,"* whose kingdom *"shall be broken, and will be divided toward the four winds of heaven"* Think Alexander the Great. In about eight years Alexander accomplished the most dazzling military conquest in human history. But in 323BC after one of his drunken bouts, he died of a fever (or possibly was poisoned) in the imperial capital of Babylon. His empire was divided among his generals and became four separate kingdoms, Macedonia-Greece under Antipater and his son, Thrace–Asia Minor under Lysimachus, the rest of Asia except lower Syria and Northern Israel under Seleucus Nicator, and Egypt and Southern Israel under Ptolemy.

The remainder of Daniel 11:5-39 documents the actions of the last two of these kingdoms—Egypt to the south of Jerusalem and Syria to the north of Jerusalem. These rulers are simply referred to as the *"king of the North"* and the *"king of the South."* Jerusalem is the centre in God's view and specific compass points in the Bible generally are referenced from that centre-point.

Daniel 11:5-39 outlines a very detailed blow by blow account of what was to come and the accuracy of its historical fulfilment is amazing.

Verse 5: *"Also the king of the South shall become strong, as well as one of his princes; and he shall gain power over him and have dominion. His dominion shall be a great dominion.."* The king of the South was Ptolemy I (Soter), son of Lagus, whose ambitions extended far beyond the borders of Egypt to Israel and the rest of Asia. The prince under Ptolemy I who became stronger than him was Seleucus Nicator of the Selucid Empire.

Verse 6: *"And at the end of some years they shall join forces, for the daughter of the king of the South shall go to the king of the North to make an agreement; but she shall not retain the power of her authority, and neither he nor his authority shall stand; but she shall be given up, with those who brought her, and with him who begot her, and with him who strengthened her in those times."* The agreement was a proposed peace treaty that called for Antiochus II to marry Berenice, the daughter of Ptolemy II. But Antiochus already had a wife, a powerful and influential woman named Laodice. She didn't take kindly to being divorced therefore she organized a successful conspiracy. She managed to have both Berenice and her infant son, whom she had borne to Antiochus, assassinated. Not long after that Antiochus was poisoned to death (247 B.C.), and the queen (Antiochus's wife Laodice) assumed power until her son, Seleucus II became of age. Daniel's prophecy was fulfilled concerning Berenice, saying she would be betrayed, (or given up) along with the nobles who supported her.

Verse 7: *"But from a branch of her roots one shall arise in his place, who shall come with an army, enter the fortress of the king of the North, and deal with them and prevail."* Ptolemy III organized a great expeditionary force against Syria, in order to avenge the death of his sister, the widow of the Seleucid king Antiochus II. Ptolemy's armies waged war against Seleucus II's forces from 246 to 241 BC. Finally he returned to Egypt laden with spoil.

Verse 8: *"And he shall also carry their gods captive to Egypt, with their princes and their precious articles of silver and gold; and he shall continue more years than the king of the North."* Ptolemy III recovered the idols of Egypt taken by Cambyses in 524 B.C.

Verse 9: *"Also the king of the North shall come to the kingdom of the king of the South, but shall return to his own land."* Seleucus II regained control of northern Syria and Phoenicia which belonged to Ptolemy III but he didn't have the courage to enter Egypt itself and returned to his home country.

Verses 10-12: *"However his sons shall stir up strife, and assemble a multitude of great forces; and one shall certainly come and overwhelm and pass through; then he shall return to his fortress and stir up strife. And the king of the South shall be moved with rage, and go out and fight with him, with the king*

Chapter 5
Prophecy

of the North, who shall muster a great multitude; but the multitude shall be given into the hand of his enemy. When he has taken away the multitude, his heart will be lifted up; and he will cast down tens of thousands, but he will not prevail." Antiochus III (a son of Seleucus II) launched an expedition against Phoenicia and Israel (219-218 BC) that ended in a serious setback at the Battle of Raphia, where he was soundly beaten by the smaller army of Ptolemy IV. But finally in 203 BC, Antiochus III saw his opportunity to strike at Egypt again, since Ptolemy IV had just died and had been succeeded by Ptolemy V, who was just a four year old boy.

Verses 13-16: *"For the king of the North will return and muster a multitude greater than the former, and shall certainly come at the end of some years with a great army and much equipment. Now in those times many shall rise up against the king of the South. Also, violent men of your people shall exalt themselves in fulfillment of the vision, but they shall fall. So the king of the North shall come and build a siege mound, and take a fortified city; and the forces of the South shall not withstand him. Even his choice troops shall have no strength to resist. But he who comes against him shall do according to his own will, and no one shall stand against him. He shall stand in the Glorious Land with destruction in his power."* These verses document the eventual wresting of the land of Israel from Egypt's control by Antiochus the Great. In 205/204 BC the infant Ptolemy V succeeded to the Egyptian throne, and Antiochus is said to have concluded a secret pact with Philip V of Macedon for the partition of the Ptolemaic possessions.

Under the terms of this pact, Macedon was to receive the Ptolemaic possessions around the Aegean Sea and Cyrene, while Antiochus would annex Cyprus and Egypt. Once more Antiochus attacked the Ptolemaic province of Coele Syria and Phoenicia, and by 199 BC he had possession of it before the Aetolian leader Scopas recovered it for Ptolemy. But that recovery proved brief, for in 198 BC Antiochus defeated Scopas at the Battle of Panium, near the sources of the Jordan, a battle which marks the end of Ptolemaic rule in Judea. Israel was now under the control of the king of the North.

Verses 17-19: *"He shall also set his face to enter with the strength of his whole kingdom, and upright ones with him; thus shall he do. And he shall give him the daughter of women to destroy it; but she shall not stand with him, or be for him. After this he shall turn his face to the coastlands, and shall take many. But a ruler shall bring the reproach against them to an end; and with the reproach removed, he shall turn back on him. Then he shall turn his face toward the fortress of his own land; but he shall stumble and fall, and not be found."* Hoping to gain advantage over Egypt, Antiochus the Great gave his daughter, Cleopatra, in marriage to Ptolemy V in 195 B.C. But Antiochus' daughter sided with her husband and no advantage was gained. Antiochus then lost a battle against Roman forces. After his defeat, Antiochus had to surrender his entire elephant brigade, all his navy, and twenty selected hostages and pay an indemnity of twenty thousand talents over a period of several years. Being unable to make his indemnity payments, Antiochus the Great was killed while trying to pillage a temple in Elymais.

Chapter 5
Prophecy

A footnote belongs to that saga; Antiochus's second son was among the twenty hostages taken to Rome, where he spent the formative years of his life. He later became the dreaded persecutor of the Jews, Antiochus Epiphanies.

Verse 20: *"There shall arise in his place one who imposes taxes on the glorious kingdom; but within a few days he shall be destroyed, but not in anger or in battle."* The 12-year reign of Antiochus III's eldest son, Seleucus IV, was marked by heavy taxes throughout Israel. Unpopular Seleucus was poisoned to death by his minister, Heliodorus.

Verses 21-39: These verses document the tyrannical oppression of the Jewish people by Antiochus Epiphanies, who by force tried to make the Jewish people forgo their religion in favour of all things Greek. This was the time of the Maccabees, who resisted this Hellenistic influence. A meticulous account of this period is well documented in Jewish history and every detail of Daniel's account was fulfilled. The Roman Empire defeated Seleucid Syria in 65 B.C. and then Egypt in 30 B.C. Thus the identities of the king of the North and the king of the South came to an end.

The actual history relating to each of these verses is well documented in recorded history therefore I have only included a very brief account here. Daniel 11 contains extremely detailed prophecies which have all been fulfilled exactly as they were revealed to Daniel. The detail of the prophecy and the accuracy of every step of fulfilment is astonishing leading to the claim by some that it could only have been written after the fact. Alexander the Great however was fascinated to find details of his exploits outlined in Daniel's prophecy. Historian Josephus provides an account of Alexander the Great having a detailed dream, of meeting an important priest, while in Dion, Macedonia and still planning his conquering campaign. While battling in Gaza Alexander met a Jewish priest who matched his dream exactly. Believing the Jewish priest to be significant he went with him to Jerusalem where the Jewish teachers explained to him about Daniel's dreams and visions pertaining to the rise of a third kingdom that would quickly conquer the world. Alexander recognised the description of his kingdom by Daniel and being enthused about the prophecy he allowed the laws about Jerusalem that were established by the Persians to remain in place and gave the Jews some special privileges, such as not paying tribute every seven years. Not the normal actions of an invading conqueror.

It is believed that the prophet Daniel died somewhere about 530 BC. Alexander visited Jerusalem around 332 BC just over two hundred years after Daniel's prophecy about him. Daniel's writings were for the most part written while he was in Babylon and in only two hundred years they had become widely known and were in common use in Jerusalem. Definitely the book of Daniel is history written in advance.

Even more detailed than Daniel's prophecies were those relating to the coming on the Messiah Jesus Son of God. The books of the Old Testament contain numerous passages about the Messiah—every single prophecy about Jesus Christ was fulfilled in complete detail. The crucifixion of Jesus for example

Chapter 5
Prophecy

was mentioned in Psalm 22:16 (*"They have pierced my hands and feet."*) approximately 900 years before Jesus was born, long before this method of execution was even practiced. In fact there are more than 300 prophetic Scriptures completed during the life of Jesus.

The following is a table of just 44 messianic prophecies clearly fulfilled by Jesus Christ. [3] The prophecy reference from the Old Testament is given along with its fulfilment in the New Testament This list is by no means exhaustive it is given as a conclusive example.

	44 Prophecies About Jesus		
	Prophecy Given	**Prophecy Scripture**	**Fulfilment Scripture**
1	Messiah would be born of a woman.	Genesis 3:15	Matthew 1:20 Galatians 4:4
2	Messiah would be born in Bethlehem.	Micah 5:2	Matthew 2:1 Luke 2:4-6
3	Messiah would be born of a virgin.	Isaiah 7:14	Matthew 1:22-23 Luke 1:26-31
4	Messiah from line of Abraham.	Genesis 12:3 Genesis 22:18	Matthew 1:1 Romans 9:5
5	A descendant of Isaac.	Genesis 17:19 Genesis 21:12	Luke 3:34
6	Messiah to be a descendant of Jacob.	Numbers 24:17	Matthew 1:2
7	Messiah would come from the	Genesis 49:10	Luke 3:33 Hebrews 7:14

	tribe of Judah.		
8	Messiah would be heir to King David's throne.	2 Samuel 7:12-13 Isaiah 9:7	Luke 1:32-33 Romans 1:3
9	Messiah's throne will be anointed and eternal.	Psalm 45:6-7 Daniel 2:44	Luke 1:33 Hebrews 1:8-12
10	Messiah would be called Immanuel.	Isaiah 7:14	Matthew 1:23
11	Messiah would spend a season in Egypt.	Hosea 11:1	Matthew 2:14-15
12	A massacre of children would happen at Messiah's birthplace.	Jeremiah 31:15	Matthew 2:16-18
13	A messenger would prepare the way for Messiah	Isaiah 40:3-5	Luke 3:3-6
14	Messiah would be rejected by his own people.	Psalm 69:8 Isaiah 53:3	John 1:11 John 7:5
15	Messiah would be a prophet.	Deuteronomy 18:15	Acts 3:20-22
16	Messiah would be preceded by Elijah.	Malachi 4:5-6	Matthew 11:13-14
17	Messiah declared the Son of God.	Psalm 2:7	Matthew 3:16-17

Chapter 5
Prophecy

18	Messiah would be called a Nazarene (Branch?).	Isaiah 11:1	Matthew 2:23
19	Messiah would bring light to Galilee.	Isaiah 9:1-2	Matthew 4:13-16
20	Messiah would speak in parables.	Psalm 78:2-4 Isaiah 6:9-10	Matthew 13:10-15 Matthew 13:34-35
21	Messiah would be sent to heal the broken-hearted.	Isaiah 61:1-2	Luke 4:18-21
22	Messiah would be a priest after the order of Melchizedek.	Psalm 110:4	Hebrews 5:5-6
23	Messiah would be called King.	Psalm 2:6 Zechariah 9:9	Matthew 27:37 Mark 11:7-11
24	Messiah would be praised by little children.	Psalm 8:2	Matthew 21:16
25	Messiah would be betrayed.	Psalm 41:9	Luke 22:47-48
26	Messiah's price money would be used to buy a Potter's field.	Zechariah 11:12-13	Matthew 26:14-16 Matthew 27:9-10
27	Messiah would be falsely accused.	Psalm 35:11	Mark 14:57-58
28	Messiah silent before accusers.	Isaiah 53:7	Mark 15:4-5

#	Prophecy	Old Testament	New Testament
29	Messiah would be spat upon and struck.	Isaiah 50:6	Matthew 26:67
30	Messiah would be hated without cause.	Psalm 35:19 Psalm 69:4	John 15:24-25
31	Messiah would be crucified with criminals.	Isaiah 53:12	Matthew 27:38
			Mark 15:27-28
32	Messiah would be given vinegar to drink.	Psalm 69:21	Matthew 27:34 John 19:28-30
33	Messiah's hands and feet would be pierced.	Psalm 22:16 Zechariah 12:10	John 20:25-27
34	Messiah would be mocked and ridiculed.	Psalm 22:7-8	Luke 23:35
35	Soldiers would gamble for Messiah's garments.	Psalm 22:18	Luke 23:34 Matthew 27:35-36
36	Messiah's bones would not be broken.	Exodus 12:46 Psalm 34:20	John 19:33-36
37	Messiah would be forsaken by God.	Psalm 22:1	Matthew 27:46
38	Messiah to pray for his enemies.	Psalm 109:4	Luke 23:34

Chapter 5
Prophecy

39	Soldiers would pierce Messiah's side.	Zechariah 12:10	John 19:34
40	Messiah would be buried with the rich.	Isaiah 53:9	Matthew 27:57-60
41	Messiah would resurrect from the dead.	Psalm 16:10 Psalm 49:15	Matthew 28:2-7 Acts 2:22-32
42	Messiah would ascend to heaven.	Psalm 24:7-10	Mark 16:19 Luke 24:51
43	Messiah would be seated at God's right hand.	Psalm 68:18 Psalm 110:1	Mark 16:19 Matthew 22:44
44	Messiah would be a sacrifice for sin.	Isaiah 53:5-12	Romans 5:6-8

The number of prophecies fulfilled by Jesus is staggering. The odds of any one man in all of history fulfilling even only eight of these 44 major prophecies (let alone the total of well over 300) are mind blowing. [4] Mathematicians calculate the probability that Jesus of Nazareth could have fulfilled just eight of the prophecies given about him would be only 1 in 10^{17}. That's 1 in 100,000,000,000,000,000. Pure chance – I think not!

The critics will point to those odds and suggest that the prophecies must clearly have been written after the fact. Two problems with that; the Dead Sea scrolls date prior to the time of Christ and Jesus himself quoted from some of the scriptures which critics question. Jesus read from the book of Isaiah and quoted from the Psalms. Given the extent of prophecy in the Bible as a whole which has come to pass, the only conclusion can be the "it **is** divinely inspired".

You may say, "Those are all old prophecies, aren't there any that have been fulfilled more recently, in our time?" As it happens, quite a number have been realised in just the last 70 years. These prophecies relate to the establishment of the modern state of Israel and the return of the Jews to their homeland.

Several distinct prophecies have been fulfilled in recent time by the rebirth of the nation of Israel and the following are 10 of them: [5]

1. Israel's rebirth after nearly 1,900 years (70AD - 1948AD)-
Bible passage: Amos 9:14-15
Written: 750 BC
Fulfilled: Since 1948

2. Israel would be brought back to life -
Bible passage: Ezekiel 37: 10-14
Written: between 593-571 BC
Fulfilled: 1948

3. Isaiah spoke of Israel being reborn in one day -
Bible passage: Isaiah 66: 7-8
Written: Between 701-681 BC
Fulfilled: 1948

4. Israel would be re-established as a united nation -
Bible passage: Ezekiel 37: 21-22

Chapter 5
Prophecy

Written: between 593-571 BC
Fulfilled: 1948

5. The Reborn Israel to be more impressive than the first -
Bible passage: Jeremiah 16: 14-15
Written: Between 626 - 586 BC
Fulfilled: 1948

6. Ezekiel foretold when Israel would be re-established -
Bible passage: Ezekiel 4: 3-6
Written: Between 593-571 BC
Fulfilled: 1948

7. The people of Israel would return to "their own land" -
Bible passage: Ezekiel 39:28
Written: Between 593-571 BC
Fulfilled: after May 14, 1948

8. God would watch over the people of Israel -
Bible passage: Jeremiah 31:10
Written: Between 626 - 586 BC
Fulfilled: 1948, and ongoing.

9. Israel's army would be disproportionately powerful -
Bible passage: Leviticus 26:3, 7-8
Written: Around 1400 BC
Fulfilled: 1948-49, 1967 - on-going.

10. The fortunes of the people of Israel would be restored -
Bible passage: Deuteronomy 30:3-5
Written: Around 1400 BC
Fulfilled: 1948, etc.

Let's take a more detailed look at a couple of these.

Israel was reborn in one day. (#3 above)

Isaiah 66: 7-10 *"Before she was in labor, she gave birth; Before her pain came, she delivered a male child. Who has heard such a thing? Who has seen such things? Shall the earth be made to give birth in one day? Or shall a nation be born at once? For as soon as Zion was in labor, she gave birth to her children. Shall I bring to the time of birth, and not cause delivery?" says the Lord. "Shall I who cause delivery shut up the womb?" says your God. "Rejoice with Jerusalem, and be glad with her, all you who love her; Rejoice for joy with her, all you who mourn for her;"*

This literally describes what happened.

On May 14, 1948, David Ben-Gurion, the head of the Jewish Agency in Israel, proclaimed the establishment of the State of Israel. U.S. President Harry S. Truman recognized the new nation on the same day and the Soviet Union soon followed suit. The British mandate over the Palestine territory officially terminated at midnight on that same May 14 day. During a 24-hour span of time, foreign control of the land of Israel had formally ceased, and Israel had declared its independence, and its independence was acknowledged by other nations. Modern Israel was literally was born in a single day.

Within hours of the declaration of independence in 1948, Israel was attacked by the surrounding countries of Egypt, Jordan, Syria, Lebanon, Iraq and Saudi Arabia. This war of which

Chapter 5
Prophecy

the new born nation was victorious did indeed cause Israel much distress likened to labour pains exactly as Isaiah foretold.

Israel's status as a sovereign nation was established and reaffirmed during the course of a single day, and that its declaration of independence was not the result of a war but rather the cause of one.

The date when Israel would be re-established (#6 above).

Ezekiel 4:3-6 "*Moreover take for yourself an iron plate, and set it as an iron wall between you and the city. Set your face against it, and it shall be besieged, and you shall lay siege against it. This will be a sign to the house of Israel. Lie also on your left side, and lay the iniquity of the house of Israel upon it.* **According to the number of the days that you shall lie on it, you shall bear their iniquity.** *For I have laid on you the years of their iniquity, according to the number of the days,* **three hundred ninety days.** *So you shall bear the iniquity of the house of Israel. And when you have completed them, lie again on your right side; then you shall bear the iniquity of the house of Judah* **forty days.** *I have laid on you a day for each year.*" [Emphasis added]

The total number of days Ezekiel says Israel would be punished was 430 years (390 plus 40). This prophecy, according to Bible scholar Grant Jeffrey, exactly pinpoints the 1948 rebirth of Israel. Here's a summary of Jeffrey's theory: [6]

- Ezekiel said the Jews were to be punished for 430 years because they had turned away from God. As part of the punishment, the Jews lost control of their homeland to Babylon. Many Jews were taken as captives to Babylon.

- Babylon was later conquered by Cyrus in 539 BC. Cyrus allowed the Jews to leave Babylon and to return to their homeland but, only a small number returned. The return took place in 536 BC, 70 years after Judah lost independence to Babylon.

- Because most of the exiles chose to stay in pagan Babylon rather than return to their God given land of Israel, the remaining 360 years (430 minus the 70 served in Babylon) of their punishment was multiplied by seven. The reason is explained in Bible's book of Leviticus 26:14-18 "*'But if you do not obey Me, and do not observe all these commandments, and if you despise My statutes, or if your soul abhors My judgments, so that you do not perform all My commandments, but break My covenant, I also will do this to you: I will even appoint terror over you, wasting disease and fever which shall consume the eyes and cause sorrow of heart. And you shall sow your seed in vain, for your enemies shall eat it. I will set My face against you, and you shall be defeated by your enemies. Those who hate you shall reign over you, and you shall flee when no one pursues you. And after all this, if you do not obey Me, then **I will punish you seven times more for your sins.**"* [Emphasis added] By staying in pagan Babylon, most exiles were refusing to repent.

Chapter 5
Prophecy

- If you take the remaining 360 years of punishment and multiply by 7, you get 2,520 years. But, Jeffrey says those years are based on the ancient 360-day lunar calendar. If those years are adjusted to the modern solar calendar, the result is 2,484 years (in accordance with the calculation made by Grant Jeffrey).
- There were exactly 2,484 years from 536 BC (the year a remnant returned to Judea) to 1948, which is the year that Israel regained independence.

What a remarkably precise prophecy and fulfilled to the day. Do you agree? Before researching for this book I had never heard of this particular prophesy fulfilment but the scripture references are correct and according to my calculations the maths appear about right. The Books of Ezra and Nehemiah both tell us that a total of 42,300 Israelites left Babylon to return to Israel in 536 BC. However history also records that most chose to remain there. Esther became the wife of Persian king Ahasuerus in 478 B.C and as recorded in the book of Esther there were still a large number of Jews disbursed and settled through the various provinces at that time.

Given the sheer volume of fulfilled prophecy throughout the Bible that has so accurately come to pass we are well advised to seriously consider all, as yet, unfulfilled prophecy. And there are at least 500 of those. The majority of these 500 relate to the second coming of our Lord Jesus Christ and the setting up of his kingdom on this earth with Jerusalem as its centre. Collectively these prophecies are termed as end-times prophecy. Many have tried to claim fulfilment of this or that particular prophecy only to have their claim fall over on closer examination. It's not necessary to try and date these prophecies prior to their fulfilment but there two things we can be absolutely certain of: They will most definitely come to pass – every single one of them will categorically occur. In addition they will all happen exactly as they've been described. Furthermore when they do occur we will definitely know, provided we have Godly sense. An obsession with Biblical prophecy, however, such as trying to pin down a date for Jesus' return, can easily lead a person into doctrinal error or to following false prophets.

Prophecy throughout the Bible is a major proof of God's existence and that "all scripture" is divinely inspired. The continual fulfilment of it also shows that his word can be categorically relied upon. This realisation catapults our hope into great faith. We are absolutely assured of salvation through Jesus Christ and thereby eternal life. Why? Because Jesus himself said in John 14:6 "*I am the way, the truth, and the life. No one comes to the Father, except through me.*" This unequivocally assures us of two things:

- Through Jesus we have life.
- Jesus is the only way to get this life.

*"Don't have worry kill you,
Let the Church help"*

Chapter 6
History in the Bible

God is a meticulous book keeper and He tells us so:

Exodus 32:32 "*Yet now, if You will, forgive their sin—but if not, I pray, blot me out of Your **book which You have written**.*" [Emphasis added]

Daniel 7:10 "*A fiery stream issued and came forth from before him. A thousand thousands ministered to Him; Ten thousand times ten thousand stood before Him. The court was seated, and **the books were opened**.*" [Emphasis added]

Revelation 20:12 "*And I saw the dead, small and great, standing before God, **and books were opened. And another book was opened**, which is **the Book of Life**. And the dead were judged according to their works, by the things which were written in the books.*" [Emphasis added]

Revelation 13:8 "*All who dwell on the earth will worship him, whose names have not been written in **the Book of Life of the Lamb** slain from the foundation of the world.*" [Emphasis added]

Revelation 20:15 *"And anyone not found written in* ***the book of life****, was cast into the lake of fire."* [Emphasis added]

He also has a book of our tears. Psalm 56:8 *"You keep track of all my sorrows. You have collected all my tears in your bottle.* ***You have recorded each one in your book****."* [NLT Version] [Emphasis added]

Strangely God also keeps track of the hair on our head, Matthew 10:30 *"but the very hairs of your head are all numbered."* Jesus mentions the sheer detail of what he keeps account of in Matthew 12:36 *"But I say to you* ***that for every idle word that men may speak****, they will give account of it in the day of judgment."* [Emphasis added] Might be a rather long account for some!

He also has a book of memory relating to what God hears about those that honour him Malachi 3:16 *"Then those who feared the LORD spoke one with another; and the LORD heard them; So a book of remembrance was written before Him for those who fear the Lord and who meditate on His name."*

It seems God truly is a prolific author and a stickler for detail. One book in particular is named; the "Book of Life". It is imperative we pay close regard to this book as the Bible is very unambiguous about the fate of those not found written in it.

In addition to ***His*** books, God also directly instructed His servants to record the words He's giving them into books. He gave this command to Moses, Habakkuk, Ezekiel, Jeremiah, Isaiah and John in Revelation.

Chapter 6
History in the Bible

Ok so we get it. God records just about everything. Why? Isn't He ever-knowing and all powerful so why does He need to be reminded, His memory is perfect isn't it? All good questions but the answer is simple. He keeps the records for our benefit and for others to see. Most military establishments have honour rolls of those that have fallen in battle or have fought heroically. These are of no benefit to the fallen soldiers; they're there to remind the living.

Our God is infinitely fair. The Bible plainly states that a judgement day for all mankind is coming. On that day God's books will be opened for all to see. Before any single person, from all generations that have ever lived, can be judged that person will be shown their written record. Revelation 20:12, *"And the dead were judged according to their works, by the things which were written in the books. "* [Part of verse.] You can imagine an atheist being shown their copious denials of God's existence, then God saying "Well here I am!" What answer could possibly follow that. Likewise visualise an unbeliever being shown a comprehensive list of every time they rejected what they had heard or seen that Jesus was the only way to life. Following which God the Father simply turns and points to Jesus – alive.

In that day of judgement there will be no argument, every unbeliever will be exposed and their recorded actions will be self-incriminating. I for one certainly do not wish to be among that number. Yet another reason why it's imperative we read our Bible now as it lays out very clearly how we have been redeemed by the death and resurrection of our Lord Jesus the Christ and are saved from all judgement if we submit ourselves to Him and His Lordship. The youth pastor of the church my children were bought up in reckoned that the word Bible was actually an acronym B.I.B.L.E - Basic Instructions Before Leaving Earth. Lot of truth in that!

So what about the believers? Most of them did plenty wrong before, or even after, they received salvation. Are their actions still on record? We're told about that in the book of Isaiah 43:25 *"I, even I, am He who blots out your transgressions for My own sake; and I will not remember your sins."* This states that our actions were all recorded but that God Himself blots out our transgressions (sins). When and how does that happen and under what circumstance? It's all there in 1 John 1:7 *"But if we walk in the light as He is in the light, we have fellowship with one another, and the blood of Jesus Christ His Son **cleanses us from all sin.**"* [Emphasis added] Walk in the light, what does that mean? Jesus Himself tells us in John 12:46 *"I have come as a light into the world, that whoever believes in Me should not abide in darkness."* All very clear-cut then, put your trust in Jesus, then God will blot **all** your sins out of His book. Incredible grace on God's part – on judgement day the page where our detail was will just be blank. Not one single negative entry. But what's more remarkable is that God transfers our name to another of His books the "Book of Life" and starts a new record of our life.

Chapter 6
History in the Bible

What is the purpose of this book of life then? Firstly, we're told who owns it. We're told in Revelation 13:8 *"And all the people who belong to this world worshiped the beast. They are the ones whose names were not written in the Book of Life before the world was made--the Book that belongs to the Lamb who was slaughtered."* [NLT version] The book belongs to the Lamb – Jesus Christ is frequently referred to as the Lamb in scripture because He became the lamb in a literal fulfilment of the Passover celebrated by the Children of Israel since their departure from slavery in the land of Egypt.

This verse also brings up a controversial subject in Christian history from the sixteenth-century, which almost brought theologians to blows. It's the subject of predestination. Many books have been written on this issue so I don't intend to go into great detail but it is a necessary topic to understand as critics have pointed to this to suggest God has been selective in His love towards man. Such a concept is completely foreign to God and just not possible for Him. So what does He mean when He says *"he wrote the names in the Book of Life before the world was made"*? A book that does not include all of mankind!

In order to understand this let's take a look, as usual, at what other scriptures say about this. Here are some of them:

Ephesians 1:11 *"In him we have obtained an inheritance, having been predestined according to the purpose of him who works all things according to the counsel of his will"* [ESV]

Ephesians 1:4-5 *"just as He chose us in Him before the foundation of the world, that we should be holy and without blame before Him in love, having predestined us to adoption as sons by Jesus Christ to Himself, according to the good pleasure of His will,"*

Romans 8:29-30 *"For whom He foreknew, He also predestined to be conformed to the image of His Son, that He might be the firstborn among many brethren. Moreover whom He predestined, these He also called; whom He called, these He also justified; and whom He justified, these He also glorified."*

The verses seem to be clear enough so why is there this controversy regarding predestination

In very simple terms the controversy arises over the question of whether God's gift of saving grace to man depends to any degree on some action--or even decision--by man to accept (or at least not to reject) that gift. If man does anything at all, salvation is arguably not by grace alone; man contributes to it, if only a little bit. But if man does nothing at all, man is arguably predestined by God.

Let's look at the dictionary meaning of this word predestined; it simply means "to decide or decree in advance what is going to happen". [1]

Westminster Confession of Faith from 1646 explains that predestination in its broadest conception is the doctrine that because God is all-powerful, all-knowing, and completely sovereign, He "from all eternity did by the most wise and holy

Chapter 6
History in the Bible

counsel of His own will, freely and unchangeably ordain whatsoever comes to pass."

We're told in Ephesians 3:11 *"according to the **eternal purpose** which He accomplished in Christ Jesus our Lord."* [Emphasis added]. His *"eternal purpose"* was to save men through Christ. Ephesians 1:4-5 tells us, *"Just as He [God] **chose us in Him** [Christ Jesus] before the foundation of the world, that we would be holy and without blame before him in love, **having predestined us to adoption as sons** by Jesus Christ to Himself, according to the good pleasure of His will."* [Emphasis added]

The Belgic Confession of 1561 (Article XVI) *affirmed that God delivers and preserves from perdition all whom he, in his eternal and unchangeable council, of mere goodness hath elected in Christ Jesus our Lord, without respect to their works.*

Some sixteenth century Christians believed that God picked those who would be saved before the world was created. However that is not how the verses above read; it is not that there are certain people that are predestined (picked) to salvation, but that **salvation is predestined for those who choose God**. Believers are therefore assured that they are among the predestined. God decreed the rules regarding salvation through Christ Jesus in advance. All who believe are saved – that is the statement of fact.

So what about the question of whether God's gift of saving grace depends on some action--or even decision--by man to accept that gift? Since salvation is "in Christ" then the only requirement of the believer is to accept Jesus Christ in order to be included in that predestined salvation. Nothing more, God's gift is solely by grace. This is put very plainly for us Romans 10:9: *"that if you confess with your mouth the Lord Jesus and believe in your heart that God has raised Him from the dead, you will be saved."* That is all we are asked to do and the rest is by grace. Do that and then you'll definitely be among the predestined and in the Lamb's book of life.

Another interesting verse regarding the Lamb's Book of Life again in Revelation 13:8 *"All who dwell on the earth will worship him, whose names have not been written in the Book of Life of* **the Lamb slain from the foundation of the world**.*"* [Emphasis added] The Lamb slain **from** the foundation of the world? So how can that be, Jesus died about 2,000 years ago and the creation was some 4,000 years before that?

John 3:16, *"For God so loved the world that He gave His only begotten Son, that whoever believes in Him should not perish but have everlasting life."* God's plan of redemption through Jesus was not his plan B; it wasn't some hastily devised scheme to bring man back into right standing with him after the fall in the Garden of Eden. No, it was always God's plan of love from the very outset. God *"gave"* His Son from the creation of the world. God lives outside of created time; therefore the death of Jesus was a literal event to God before Adam had disobeyed Him. The cleansing power of the blood of Jesus is available to every person that has ever lived even though the physical act of His death hadn't yet occurred. John 14:6, *"Jesus said to him, "I*

Chapter 6
History in the Bible

am the way, the truth, and the life. No one comes to the Father, except through me."" The **only** way to right standing with God is through Jesus. That applied to all mankind right from the creation of the world. If it had not, then mighty men of the Old Testament who had spent a lifetime living for God could not have obtained eternal life. That would have been a rather cruel trick by a loving God. No, God's salvation plan covers them too. Men like Abraham, Moses, David and Daniel all knew that they would be raised to life in the last days. And the only way that could be possible was through Jesus. God's plan of redemption started from the creation of the world. Because of his view of time he knew at the outset the names and details of every person who accepted Jesus as their Lord and Saviour. That is when He wrote the Lambs Book of Life. So we're not picked in advance, it's our acceptance of Jesus that God observed from time long before we were even born.

The people of the Old Testament didn't fully comprehend God's salvation plan but they chose to follow Him anyway. And through that they obtained redemption through Jesus Christ and hence eternal life. For us in our time we are without excuse, we have God's full restoration plan completely revealed to us as plain as day. Accept Jesus as your Lord and Saviour and you will be saved. It's a simple matter of choice. God's salvation plan outlines exactly what happens to all those who believe. All we have to do to be included in that predestined plan is to choose Jesus.

So getting back to the books; there is another reason why God keeps such detailed records and the reason is love. When we are recorded in the book of life all our sins (transgressions) are gone – because of the redemptive work of Jesus on the cross. Psalm 103:12 *"As far as the east is from the west, so far has He removed our transgressions from us."* Not much chance of them coming up again then is there?

The blotting out of our sins is only the first part of the deal. Malachi 3:16 *"Then those who feared the Lord spoke to one another, and the Lord listened and heard them; so a book of remembrance was written before Him for those who fear the Lord and who meditate on His name."* So God keeps a book of remembrance of all the good we do once we become a Christian "in Christ"? He keeps an account of all our tears and every hair on our head. The sum of these certainly indicates God is intensely interested in us. In His eyes everything His adopted sons in Christ do is so important that He immediately jots it down. It's amazing to comprehend that the Creator of the universe is absolutely besotted by every single one of those whom He has adopted.

Why all this writing about believers? The Apostle Paul tells us in 2 Corinthians 5:10 *"For we must all appear before the judgment seat of Christ, that each one may receive the things done in the body, according to what he has done, whether good or bad."* The expression "the judgment seat of Christ" has tended to cause a misconception which arises from the English word "judgement" that God perhaps will mete out some sort of

Chapter 6
History in the Bible

believer's retribution for sins in their life. Absolutely not – this is a place where rewards will be given or lost depending on how one has used his or her life for the Lord.

It is significant that the closing chapter of Revelation contains these words: (Revelation 22:12) *"And behold, I am coming quickly, and My reward is with Me, to give to every one according to his work."*

Salvation is a complete gift without anything further required. However, in addition, as this Revelation verse tells us, there are rewards given for faithfulness in the Christian life and loss of rewards for unfaithfulness. These rewards should be one of the great motivators of our Christian walk. But wait, does this infer "merit" instead of "grace," and don't we serve the Lord out of love and for God's glory? Of course, in true response to the gift of salvation our only option is to serve the Lord out of love and for God's glory, however the fact still remains that the Bible promises us rewards – quite clearly.

The purpose of the judgment seat of Christ is then to examine a Christian's total life. *"That each one may receive the things done in the body, according to what he has done, whether good or bad."* 2 Corinthians 5:10. The term *"receive the things"* refers to a summing up and evaluation of the total pattern of a believer's life. It's a time of reward, not punishment; there will be no record of any sin at this judgement seat. Yes I know it does say "good or bad". The original Greek word translated here as bad is "phaulos" which is defined as bad or worthless. Remember the verse is talking about us receiving what is due for the things done. Since there is no commendation for those in Christ Jesus I suggest that the worthless things will be mentioned in the context of what is achieved rather than what we did wrong. I liken it to an exam mark out of 100: some will achieve 100%, some 60%, and some 30%. Jesus himself talking about the fruit produced says in Matthew 13:8 *"But others fell on good ground and yielded a crop: some a hundredfold, some sixty, some thirty."*

What we must be clear on is that while born again believers won't ever be condemned for their sins, our present lives do affect what will happen at the Judgment Seat of Christ. Here's how: Sin and indifference in this life rob us of our present desire for serving the Lord. That in turn means a loss of rewards, because we will not have used our time to His glory. That is why Paul exhorts us in Ephesians 5:15-16, *"See then that you walk circumspectly, not as fools but as wise, redeeming the time, because the days are evil."* Sin and indifference cause us to pass up opportunities for service, which we would otherwise perform and be rewarded for.

The greatest consequence of unfaithfulness here on earth is that it disappoints Jesus. 1 John 2:28, *"And now, little children, abide in Him, that when He appears, we may have confidence and not be ashamed before Him at His coming."* That is a sobering thought--we could be ashamed as we stand before the Lord. At the same time, it should encourage us with the prospect of receiving his lavish rewards if we serve Him faithfully during our time here on earth.

Chapter 6
History in the Bible

Rev. A. B. Simpson explains this well in his writings on The Days of Heaven. [4]

It will not always be the day of toil and trial. One day, we shall hear our names announced before the universe, and the record read of things that we had long forgotten. How our hearts will thrill, and our heads will bow, as we shall hear our own names called, and then the Master shall recount the triumph and the services which we had ourselves forgotten! And, perhaps, from the ranks of the saved He shall call forward the souls that we have won for Christ and the souls that they in turn had won, and as we see the issue of things that have, perhaps, seemed but trifling at the time, we shall fall before the throne, and say, "*Not unto us, O Lord, not unto us, but unto your Name give glory!*"

Beloved, the pages are going up every day, for the record of our life. We are setting the type ourselves, by every moment's action. Hands unseen are stereotyping the plates, and soon the record will be registered, and read before the audience of the all the saints.

Oh, to hear those words Jesus recounted in his parable in Matthew 25:21 " *His lord said to him,* ***Well done, good and faithful servant;*** *you were faithful over a few things, I will make you ruler over many things. Enter into the joy of your lord.*" [Emphasis added].

Our good or pious works, no matter how many, will never bring about salvation for us. For salvation we simply submit to our Lord Jesus and He bestows His righteousness upon us. After that point our works do count, profoundly. So does that mean that all Christians should rush around filling their remaining years with as many good deeds as possible to maximize rewards? No; not at all. Jesus isn't looking for pious do-gooders. Once we are saved we're all filled with the Holy Spirit of God and He directs us. Every person has individual talents and abilities and the Holy Spirit will help focus our strengths to achieve exactly the right thing at precisely the right time to achieve the perfect outcome. This will bring about quality works which are a sweet smelling aroma to God and that's what brings out His writing pen.

God's prolific bookkeeping is yet further proof that He is intensely interested in us. He's passionately interested in every detail about every individual. Why else would the Bible record seemingly endless names of family lines and ancestral trees?

There is also another reason for all the names. The Bible is set in reality. The people in the Bible are all real people they all have genuine lives and families. The records are of actual events and circumstances that literally happened to the people named. The family trees demonstrate the reality of the nation of Israel. It brings the fullness of the people mentioned to life. It gives details of their length of life, who their brothers, parents and grandparents were.

What's interesting is that all the different books of the Bible mesh in with the life spans of the various named individuals and generally the Bible is laid out in chronological order. It's so

Chapter 6
History in the Bible

detailed that it's physically possible to trace history back to the date of creation. Considering that all the books were written over a 1600 year period this is nothing short of miraculous. The bottom line is that it's not a made up jumble of fictitious characters, it is real history.

So why do critics claim otherwise? Critics dismiss the Bible as history saying it's just "religious" writings. Personally I'm not absolutely clear on what they mean by religious writings or text so I checked out Wikipedia. Here's what they define religious texts as: *"the texts which various religious traditions consider to be sacred, or central to their religious tradition. Religious texts may be used to evoke a deeper connection with the divine, convey spiritual truths, promote mystical experience, foster communal identity, and to guide individual and communal spiritual practice."* The problem is this does not describe the Bible. Yes you could probably allocate the writings of the Apostle Paul into this loose definition but certainly not the majority of the Old Testament.

Generally the Bible reads as a factual news account of real events, places, people, and dialogue. Historians and archaeologists have repeatedly confirmed its authenticity. It is essentially an historical account of the people of God throughout hundreds of years. If you open almost any page in the Bible you will find a name of a place and/or a person. Much of this can be, and has been, verified from archaeology. Though archaeology cannot prove that the Bible is the inspired word of God, it has the ability to prove whether or not some events and locations described therein are true or false. So far, however, there isn't a single archaeological discovery that disproves the Bible in any way. This is an incredible fact – not a single archaeological find has disagreed with the Bible. Yes there are many things that have not yet been proven through archaeological discovery but that does not disprove the event. The Red Sea crossing is an example. Somewhere beneath the Red Sea are a myriad of chariot wheels waiting discovery. Man just hasn't looked in the right place yet.

Critics point to the Red Sea crossing and claim, solely based on human reasoning, that such an incident could not occur. And yes in straight human terms water does not naturally stand as a wall, Exodus 14:29 *"But the children of Israel had walked on dry land in the midst of the sea, and the waters were a wall to them on their right hand and on their left."* To those critics I say; this is not a book about human terms; the premise of the book is "God" – a God that is so amazing, so mighty, so incredibly powerful and so, so much greater than man. Of course a God of this power could easily make the water stand as a wall. Of course this great God could cause a global flood and provide for all the kinds of animals in a massive ark for nearly a year. Of course this great God could evoke all the plagues on Egypt. Of course this mighty God could have created the heavens and the earth and all the creatures in it in just six days. The Bible is all about God, all powerful, all knowing omnipresent, omnipotent. Man still suffers under the illusion that he is "like" God believing the lie the serpent told Eve in the Garden of Eden. Man in his natural state envisions a god,

Chapter 6
History in the Bible

perhaps slightly more powerful than him but not much, perhaps in the league of a more powerful big brother. Isaiah 55:8 "*My thoughts are nothing like your thoughts,*" *says the LORD. "And my ways are far beyond anything you could imagine."* (NLT) The God of the Bible is mighty; of course He caused miraculous events to occur through the course of history.

A kindergarten teacher was walking around observing her classroom of children while they were drawing pictures. As she got to one girl who was working diligently, she asked what the drawing was. The girl replied, "I'm drawing God." The teacher paused and said, "But no one knows what God looks like." Without looking up from her drawing, the girl replied, "They will in a minute."

The Bible has become a significant source book for secular archaeology, helping to identify such ancient figures as Sargon (Isaiah 20:1); Sennacherib (Isaiah 37:37); Horam of Gazer (Joshua 10:33); Hazar (Joshua 15:27); and the nation of the Hittites (Genesis 15:20). The Biblical record, unlike other "scriptures," is historically set, opening itself up for testing and verification. [5]

Two of the greatest 20th-century archaeologists, William F. Albright and Nelson Glueck, both lauded the Bible (even though they were non-Christian and secular in their training and personal beliefs) as being the single most accurate source document from history. Over and over again, the Bible has been found to be accurate in its places, dates and records of events. No other "religious" document comes even close.

The 19th-century critics used to deny the historicity of the Hittites, the Horites, the Edomites and various other peoples, nations, and cities mentioned in the Bible. Those critics have long been silenced by the archaeologist's spade, and few critics dare to question the geographical and ethnological reliability of the Bible.

The names of over 40 different Kings of various countries mentioned in the Bible have all been found in contemporary documents and inscriptions outside of the Old Testament, and they have all been found consistent with the times and places associated with them in the Bible. Nothing exists in ancient literature that has been, even remotely, as well-confirmed in accuracy as has the Bible.

History in the Bible can be relied on in equal standing with God's message of salvation. The whole of the Bible is the inspired word of God. Paul tells Timothy that **every** scripture is divinely inspired. **Every** means each verse in all the chapters. It's unimaginable to conceive God informing us of something incredible about say, the work of Jesus in one chapter then on the next page telling you a complete fabrication regarding an historical event in the next. Every verse is true!

But what exactly is history? Merriam-Webster defines the word; "as past events that relate to a particular subject, place, nation, etc." [6.] Basically just a day to day record of what has

Chapter 6
History in the Bible

previously occurred. There are significant events in history and then there are the in-between – just stuff that happens every day but immediately it's happened it's in the past.

Every one of us has a history whether we admit it or not. For some it's colourful and exciting while for others, outright boring. Nevertheless it is still history. Some have lived all their lives in complete obscurity then through one single event, occasionally not even of their own making, are thrust into the lime-light, their name and action forever etched in time. Some through a heroic feat, some through a ghastly error, while others have spent their lives at the forefront of public affairs, their every action recorded and admired or ridiculed.

At the very moment of most momentous historic events the participants are simply going about their daily routine or task, when something breaks that routine and they deal with it, quickly, efficiently and sometimes heroically and move on. Consider a hero on a battlefield, standing firm but cut off from his platoon, machine gun firmly in his grasp dispensing terror against wave after wave of enemy soldiers emerging against him, seemingly from everywhere. On the verge of exhaustion he glimpses in the distance a vehicle bristling with communication equipment. Feigning death to distract his immediate opponents, he tosses his machine gun, secures his rocket propelled grenade launcher and slithers forward on his stomach metre by metre to achieve an unrestricted view of the command vehicle. Plainly it is a target and with a clear shot certain without hesitation he fires. A massive explosion ensued and the mobile command centre is no more. Strangely the enemy guns so close all around fall silent immediately in unison and he senses his opponents hastily retreating into the background. Too exhausted to give chase he lies still, as in death.

After what seems an eternity he recognises familiar excited voices calling his name. Back at camp his commander explains to him that the command vehicle he'd destroyed contained the enemy's commander in chief. He has apparently driven with his Generals to observe what he believed was the knockout punch of his invasion, However following his demise his remaining Generals have quickly surrendered unconditionally. "Your heroic last ditch action has completely turned the war and gained us a comprehensive and unexpected victory. You will be forever a national hero," his commander proclaimed.

Now, in my little fictitious word picture it's easy to see why the unnamed solider became a hero. The truth is though that in the moment of battle his primary focus was only survival. That is until something in his years of training as a professional soldier prompted him to consider the importance of the bigger picture - removing that command vehicle. Not once during the entire situation did it enter his head - if only he could take out that vehicle then he would be a national hero finally receiving the true respect a fighter with his experience should command! Never, he was simply going about his job doing what he had been trained to do. That is how it is with history, it's rarely created by knowingly achieving the heroic at the time but

Chapter 6
History in the Bible

rather when we look back, after the fact, we realise that what was achieved was truly a milestone forever imprinted in time.

Viewing history in this way begs the question, what are we doing with our time? What are the likely outcomes of the predominant occupiers of our hour to hours? History revolves around others, other people, other things, what is useful and helpful for the greater good. Rarely do you find a figure recorded for good in history that had totally selfish ambitions. Believe me history certainly records plenty of selfish participants but how many are remembered for good?

What occupies your time? Me, Myself and I are all good people but in whose eyes? Everything today is centred on self, how I can do better, achieve more to be seen as right and good in the eyes of others. I challenge you to scroll through your last few Facebook postings. Be honest now, what was the primary motive for each post? How many of them are the real you, how many are Look At Me? I doubt that at the judgement seat of Christ there will be many recitings' of Facebook postings. Some maybe, but just think about your postings in that context – how many are truly Christ honouring? That's not to say Christians can't have some fun with their lives and of course God intended that. The question is what is the centre of our life? Facebook is often a good place to start when answering that question.

Not only does the Bible record history accurately it has also significantly influenced history, transforming many lives, leaving a mark forever on the lives of millions. The cultural influence of the Bible has significantly impacted the English language, specifically with the King James Version which had a special place in history because it was the common English version. Its popularity spanned many centuries, from when it was first printed in 1611 to well into the 20th Century. This impact is much greater than most English scholars would care to admit.

The following are 36 common English phrases all find their origins in Scripture. [7] There are literally hundreds of other less common ones.

- **Bite the Dust** Psalms 72:9, *"They that dwell in the wilderness shall bow before him; and his enemies shall lick the dust."* (KJV)

- **The Blind Leading the Blind,** Matthew 15:14, *"Let them alone: they be blind leaders of the blind. And if the blind lead the blind, both shall fall into the ditch."* (KJV).

- **By the Skin of Your Teeth**, Job 19:20. *"My bone clings to my skin and to my flesh, and I have escaped by the skin of my teeth."*

- **Broken Heart**, Psalms 34:18, *"The Lord is nigh unto them that are of a broken heart; and saveth such as be of a contrite spirit"* (KJV).

- **Can a Leopard Change his spots?** Jeremiah 13:23, *"Can the Ethiopian change his skin, or the leopard his spots?*

then may ye also do good, that are accustomed to do evil." (KJV)

- **Cast the First Stone.** John 8:7, "*So when they continued asking him, he lifted up himself, and said unto them, He that is without sin among you, let him first cast a stone at her*" (KJV).

- **Drop in a Bucket.** Isaiah 40:15 "*Behold, the nations are as a drop of a bucket, and are counted as the small dust of the balance: behold, he takes up the isles as fine dust*" (ESV).

- **Eat, Drink, and Be Merry.** Ecclesiastes 8:15, "*because a man hath no better thing under the sun, than to eat, and to drink, and to be merry: for that shall abide with him of his labour the days of his life, which God giveth him under the sun.*" (KJV)

- **Eye for Eye, Tooth for Tooth.** Matthew 5:38, "*Ye have heard that it hath been said, An eye for an eye, and a tooth for a tooth.*" (KJV)

- **Fall from Grace.** Galatians 5:4, "*Christ is become of no effect unto you, whosoever of you are justified by the law; ye are fallen from grace.*" (KJV)

- **Fly in the Ointment.** Ecclesiastes 10:1, ""*Dead flies cause the ointment of the apothecary to send forth a stinking savour: so doth a little folly him that is in reputation for wisdom and honour.*"" (KJV)

- **Forbidden Fruit**, Genesis 3:3 (when Adam and Eve were commanded not to eat from the tree of the Knowledge of Good and Evil.) *"But of the fruit of the tree which is in the midst of the garden, God hath said, Ye shall not eat of it, neither shall ye touch it, lest ye die."* (KJV)

- **Go the extra mile**. Matthew 5:41 *"And whosoever shall compel thee to go a mile, go with him twain"* (KJV).

- **Good Samaritan**, Luke 10:30-37, the Parable of the Good Samaritan.

- **He who lives by the sword dies by the sword**. Matthew 26:52, *"Then said Jesus unto him, Put up again thy sword into his place: for all they that take the sword shall perish with the sword."* (KJV)

- **How the Mighty have Fallen**. 1 Samuel 1:19, *"The beauty of Israel is slain upon thy high places: how are the mighty fallen!"* (KJV)

- **Let there be Light**. Genesis 1:3 *"And God said, "Let there be light," and there was light."* (KJV)

- **Money is the Root of All Evil**. This is almost always misquoted as the verse refers to the love of money not money itself. Here is the ESV translation of 1 Timothy 6:10 *"For the love of money is a root of all kinds of evils. It is through this craving that some have wandered away from the faith and pierced themselves with many pangs."* (ESV)

Chapter 6
History in the Bible

- **Nothing but skin and bones**, Job 19:20, "*I have been reduced to skin and bones*" [NLT]
- **The Powers that Be**, Romans 13:11 "*Let every soul be subject unto the higher powers. For there is no power but of God: the powers that be are ordained of God.*" (KJV)
- **Pride comes before a fall**, Proverbs 16:18, "*Pride goeth before destruction, and an haughty spirit before a fall.*" (KJV)
- **Put words in one's mouth**, 2 Samuel 14:3, "*And come to the king, and speak on this manner unto him. So Joab put the words in her mouth.*" (KJV)
- **Rise and shine**, Isaiah 60:1, "*Arise, shine, for your light has come, and the glory of the LORD shines over you.*" (KJV)
- **The Root of the Matter,** Job 19:28, "*But ye should say, Why persecute we him, seeing the Root of the matter is found in me?*" (KJV)
- **Scapegoat.** (the Old Testament Law) Leviticus 16:10 "*But the goat, on which the lot fell to be the scapegoat, shall be presented alive before the LORD, to make an atonement with him, and to let him go for a scapegoat into the wilderness.*" (KJV)
- **See eye to eye**, Isaiah 52:8, "*Thy watchmen shall lift up the voice; with the voice together shall they sing: for*

they shall see eye to eye, when the LORD shall bring again Zion." (KJV)

- **Sign of the times**, Matthew 16:3, "*And in the morning, It will be foul weather today: for the sky is red and lowering. O ye hypocrites, ye can discern the face of the sky; but can ye not discern the signs of the times?*" (KJV)

- **Straight and Narrow,** Matthew 7:14, "*Because strait is the gate, and narrow is the way, which leadeth unto life, and few there be that find it.*" (KJV)

- **Twinkling of an Eye**, 1 Corinthians 15:52, "*in a moment, in the twinkling of an eye, at the last trumpet; for the trumpet will sound, and the dead will be raised imperishable, and we will be changed.*" (KJV)

- **There's nothing new under the sun**. Ecclesiastes 1:9 "*The thing that hath been, it is that which shall be; and that which is done is that which shall be done: and there is no new thing under the sun.*" (KJV)

- **Wash your hands of the matter**. Matthew 27:24, "*When Pilate saw that he could prevail nothing, but that rather a tumult was made, he took water, and washed his hands before the multitude, saying, I am innocent of the blood of this just person: see ye to it.*" (KJV)

- **Weighed in the balance**, Job 31:6 "*Let me be weighed in an even balance that God may know mine integrity.*" (KJV)

Chapter 6
History in the Bible

- **What God has joined together let no man put asunder**, Matthew 19:6 *"Wherefore they are no more twain, but one flesh. What therefore God hath joined together, let not man put asunder."* (KJV)
- **Wit's End**, Psalm 107:27, *"They reel to and fro, and stagger like a drunken man, and are at their wits' end."* (KJV)
- **Wolves in Sheep's Clothing**, Matthew 7:15, *"Beware of false prophets, which come to you in sheep's clothing, but inwardly they are ravening wolves."* (KJV)
- **The Writing's on the Wall**, Daniel 5:5 *"In the same hour came forth fingers of a man's hand, and wrote over against the candlestick upon the plaster of the wall of the king's palace: and the king saw the part of the hand that wrote."*. (KJV)

Not only is the Bible a history book it's clear from the above list that in the English speaking world at least the Bible has become strongly entwined in our own history. Few would claim to have not heard of the expressions in the above list and most likely have used them in their day to day conversations, regardless of their religious beliefs.

The Bible – True, Relevant or a Fairy Tale?

"God is the Potter, Not Harry!"

Chapter 7
Writing of the Bible

Genesis, the first book in the Bible, was written by Moses after the exodus of the children of Israel from Egypt which historians calculate took place around 1445 B.C– about 2,550 years after the creation. Today is just over 2,000 years since Jesus lived on this earth. If someone began to write a detailed book about his life in our day how could we believe it was authentic? I for one may have some doubts, given the very long elapsed time since the event. However is it really that absurd? Could someone write an authentic account of the life and death of Jesus Christ thousands of years after the fact?

To consider that question you must first evaluate how it could be done. Could the author interview any eyewitnesses – no! What historic information is available to the writer – well copious volumes, as it happens? There are literally thousands of historic records and old manuscripts available and any prudent scribe would be well advised to begin by making a detailed study of them. Perhaps then it really could be possible in our day to put together a precisely detailed and accurate account of the life and death of Jesus given the quality of

Chapter 7
Writing of the Bible

material available. Naturally the work could not claim to be an original but provided adequate research was carried out it certainly would be authentic even though the subject matter was 2,000 years ago. Why? Because of the abundant amount of information available to the author.

So, back to Moses and his writing of the creation account, 2,550 years after the fact. Indeed he not only wrote about creation, his book Genesis, provides a complete and detailed genealogy of several family lines with bountiful details on the lives of many of the pillars of history and the patriarchs of the nation of Israel. Even the life of Abraham occurred some 430 years before Moses. Given the detail can this book be relied upon as accurate when it was penned so long after the events?

Firstly let's spell out one thing. Genesis is included in the Bible. This means it is part of scripture **"given by inspiration of God"**. 2 Timothy 3:16 *"All scripture is given by inspiration of God, and is profitable for doctrine, for reproof, for correction, for instruction in righteousness."*

Jesus himself validates Moses and also the creation account in Mark's gospel. Mark 10:2-9 *"The Pharisees came and asked Him, "Is it lawful for a man to divorce his wife?" testing Him. And He answered and said to them, "What did Moses command you?" They said, "Moses permitted a man to write a certificate of divorce, and to dismiss her." And Jesus answered and said to them, "Because of the hardness of your heart he wrote you this precept. But **from the beginning of the creation, God made them male and female**. For this reason a man shall leave his* *father and mother and be joined to his wife, and the two shall become one flesh; so then they are no longer two, but one flesh. Therefore what God has joined together, let not man separate."* [Emphasis added].

While the underlying subject matter in that discourse was regarding divorce my point is that Jesus completely authenticated what Moses had written when quoting him in his reply to the Pharisees. Not only did he validate Moses regarding the law, Jesus went further by tying his answer to a direct quote of Moses from Genesis 1:27 *"God created man in His own image; in the image of God He created him;* **male and female He created them**.*"* [Emphasis added]. Jesus is divine, the Son of God, and here He is quoting from the book of Genesis. Under no circumstance could Jesus have ever done that if there was any shadow of doubt regarding the authenticity of what Moses had written.

Jesus confirms what Moses wrote was definitely part of scripture and thereby inspired by God and, by extension, absolutely true and can be relied upon. Again how can this be, when he wrote it so long after the fact? Let's consider that in a little more depth.

Moses was very close to God. Exodus 33:11 *"So the Lord spoke to Moses face to face, as a man speaks to his friend."* [part verse]. Here is the Creator of the universe speaking directly with Moses, face to face. What did they talk about? The same chapter continues and provides a remarkable insight of Moses questioning God and seeking to learn and understand

Chapter 7
Writing of the Bible

more of His greatness together with God's answers to Moses. Exodus 33:12-23 *"Then Moses said to the Lord, "See, You say to me, 'Bring up this people.' But You have not let me know whom You will send with me. Yet You have said, 'I know you by name, and you have also found grace in My sight.' Now therefore, I pray, if I have found grace in Your sight, show me now Your way, that I may know You and that I may find grace in Your sight. And consider that this nation is Your people."*

And He said, "My Presence will go with you, and I will give you rest."

Then he said to Him, "If Your Presence does not go with us, do not bring us up from here. For how then will it be known that Your people and I have found grace in Your sight, except You go with us? So we shall be separate, Your people and I, from all the people who are upon the face of the earth."

So the Lord said to Moses, "I will also do this thing that you have spoken; for you have found grace in My sight, and I know you by name."

And he said, "Please, show me Your glory."

Then He said, "I will make all My goodness pass before you, and I will proclaim the name of the Lord before you. I will be gracious to whom I will be gracious, and I will have compassion on whom I will have compassion." But He said, "You cannot see My face; for no man shall see Me, and live." And the Lord said, "Here is a place by Me, and you shall stand on the rock. So it shall be, while My glory passes by, that I will put you in the cleft of the rock, and will cover you with My hand while I pass by. Then I will take away My hand, and you shall see My back; but My face shall not be seen."

Wow, clearly a very close relationship existed between God and Moses. He plainly tells Moses *"you have found favour in my sight, and I know you by name."* Perhaps because they were so closed that God just dictated the creation account and all the details of Genesis to Moses? That definitely could be a possibility as Moses did spend a lot of time in God's presence.

Further on we read in Exodus 34:28 *"So he was there with the Lord forty days and forty nights; he neither ate bread nor drank water. And He wrote on the tablets the words of the covenant, the Ten Commandments."* This makes it clear how Moses received the Ten Commandments and in fact the "He" reference in the above verse is not Moses but God as clarified in Exodus 31:18 *"And when He had made an end of speaking with him on Mount Sinai, He gave Moses two tablets of the Testimony, tablets of stone, written with the finger of God."*

In an earlier chapter we looked at the books that God keeps *"from the creation of the world"*. God would have had plenty of written information he could have perhaps shared with Moses to allow him to make a detailed account of the first 2,550 years of the history of man. Alternatively, God could have simply dictated all the detail to Moses during those 40 days on the mountain. All those are genuine possibilities but we are not told. Nothing in the writings of Moses give us any indication of how he came by the detail to write the book of Genesis.

Chapter 7
Writing of the Bible

One incredible thing about God is that yes, He is extraordinarily great – much greater than man – and can do anything He wishes just by speaking a word. When dealing with mankind however He very rarely acts unilaterally. The vast majority of great feats throughout the Bible occurred when mighty men rose up by the power of the Spirit of God. God deliberately chooses to use very ordinary human beings to carry out His work throughout the earth. He still does so even today. Jesus has left the spreading and impacting of the gospel of His Kingdom into the hands of those who have chosen to follow him. He has given His Holy Spirit to us to provide the power and ability to achieve exactly what He desires. God has placed a lot of responsibility into the hands of His adopted sons and daughters.

In keeping with this form it would seem more likely that while God inspired Moses to write the book of Genesis He did not dictate it to him. Rather Moses penned it from the accumulation of historic information that was available to him. Let's then explore a little what information could have been available to Moses and how accurate that might have been.

Firstly, how soon after the creation did the written word begin?

This earliest form of writing is known as pictographs (symbols which represented objects) and served to aid in remembering simple numeric commerce such as how many sheep were needed for sacrifices in the temples. [1] However around 3200 BC a more elaborate writing system developed, in the Sumerian city of Uruk, which became known as phonograms – symbols which represented sounds – and those sounds were the spoken language of the people. With phonograms precise meaning could be clearly conveyed and these quickly set the base for a true writing system that recorded the spoken word and contained signs for vowels and syllables. Clay tokens from this era, containing this form of writing, were discovered during the excavations of Uruk in Mesopotamia in 1850 to 1854.

Historians therefore generally agree that writing of the spoken word began approximately 3200 BC. Ok so that's about 800 years after the creation! A lot closer to the event than Moses but still many hundreds of years after it happened. Prior to the written word it is assumed that history and ancestry statistics were passed down by word of mouth. So for 800 years everything was solely by word of mouth. Where is the accuracy in that? The key lies in eyewitness account as the genealogy for the first 1700 years of history was dramatically different from today.

From Adam until Noah the common lifespan of man was well over 900 years. 900 years is a massive life span so how can that be? Surely someone got that wrong as man just doesn't live that long, especially when compared to today's average of about 80 to 90 years. However, Genesis clearly records the ages of all the pre-flood fathers when their sons were born, together with the number of days following that, then accurately ties it all together by providing the total years each one lived. The

Chapter 7
Writing of the Bible

record is very detailed, which leaves little room to explain a simple numerical miscalculation. The chronological order in which the linage is presented is flawless and from the Biblical record it's simple to calculate the number of years from Adam to Noah. In fact that same theme continues right through the entire book of Genesis to the time of Jacob and also Joseph in the land of Egypt. Really, these first fathers actually lived for nearly a thousand years?

Creation.com has a very informative article called "**Living for 900 years**" by Carl Wieland which explains this subject very ably. [2]

In the book of Genesis, the Bible routinely records human lifespans which seem outrageously different from our experience today. Adam lived to 930 years. Noah even longer, to 950 years These long lifespans are not haphazardly distributed; they are systematically greater before the Flood of Noah, and decline sharply afterwards.

These great ages are not presented in the Bible as if they are in any way extraordinary for their times, let alone miraculous.

Many people are quick to scoff at such ages, claiming they are 'biologically impossible'. Today, even if they avoid all fatal diseases, humans will generally die of old age before they reach much past 100. Even the very exceptional cases don't make it past 120 years

However, a look at the evidence related to aging suggests that the apparent upper limit on today's average lifespans is not something that is 'biologically inevitable' as such for humans or other multi-celled creatures.

Disease, diet, 'wear and tear' and other environmental factors undoubtedly play a part in how long we live. However, it now appears that underlying all these are factors somehow written into our genetic code, which determine what our 'upper limit' is. This is not really surprising; most of us know of families in which nearly everyone lives to a ripe old age—and the opposite, of course.

And although an average 'upper limit' seems to be 'programmed' into each species, breeding experiments have shown that this limit can be altered, even dramatically. Experiments with fruit-flies and worms have shown that extra longevity can be bred into and out of these populations. So you can have two populations of the same fly, with one group living many times longer than the other, on average. Even a genetic 'switch' involved in longevity has been identified in one species of worm.

Why do we wear out?

Why do multi-celled creatures (like people) all eventually wear out and die? It is not enough to simply say that there are physical laws which dictate that all fixed structures will eventually wear out. This is true, but biological machinery has

Chapter 7
Writing of the Bible

built-in 'intelligence' (programmed into the DNA) which gives it the ability to repair itself.

Why don't these cells keep on dividing, repairing and renewing the organ forever? That's why single-celled creatures like bacteria don't die of old age—they just divide into two new copies, each of which divides into two more, and so on. [Actually, there is now abundant evidence that single-celled creatures can in fact suffer senescence—i.e., aging and death, though being able to split off an identical 'fresh copy' suggests it is not completely comparable. Conversely, the Royal Society blog on 27 March 2014 wrote of the multi-celled creatures known as hydra: "There is some evidence to suggest that hydra possess biological immortality – failing an accident or carelessness – they can reproduce by budding and don't exhibit obvious senescence (aging to death).] Beings like us have organs (e.g., liver, kidneys etc.) which are made up of lots of individual cells. Why don't these cells keep on dividing, repairing and renewing the organ forever? If this were to happen, with worn-out cells replaced by newly manufactured ones, then none of your 'parts' would wear out. This of course means that you would never wear out. You might be killed by a falling tree or die of some infection, but you would never die of old age.

Of course, this isn't so. Our individual organs do wear out. The cells within them can multiply for a while, but not forever. After a certain number of times, they simply stop dividing. It is known that ordinary human cells will only divide some 80–90 times, then no more.

It appears that there is, on the tips of each of our chromosomes, a structure called a telomere. Think of it as a counting device, with a number of beads on the end. Every time the cell divides it is as if a bead is snipped off, shortening the telomere. Once all of the beads have gone cell division can no longer take place. From then on, as each cell 'runs down', it is not replaced by any new ones. So even if you avoid any sort of fatal accident or disease you will eventually succumb to failure of one or more organs.

The machinery by which cells divide is controlled by the instructions written on the DNA, the genetic code. So it looks as if some pre-programmed genetic limit, while not all there is to aging, could well be a big part of the story. **In short, there is no known biological reason why lifespans of 900 years or more would be impossible if that genetic limit were set at a different point.**

There is reason to think that there could indeed be great variation in this genetic 'upper limit'. We have already seen that simply reshuffling gene frequencies through breeding selection in fruit-flies can drastically increase their lifespan.

Genetic loss after the Flood; A cause for dropping lifespans?

There is a well-known and simple phenomenon called 'genetic drift', through which varying forms (alleles) of genes

Chapter 7
Writing of the Bible

(stretches of DNA coding for various characteristics) can become lost in small populations.

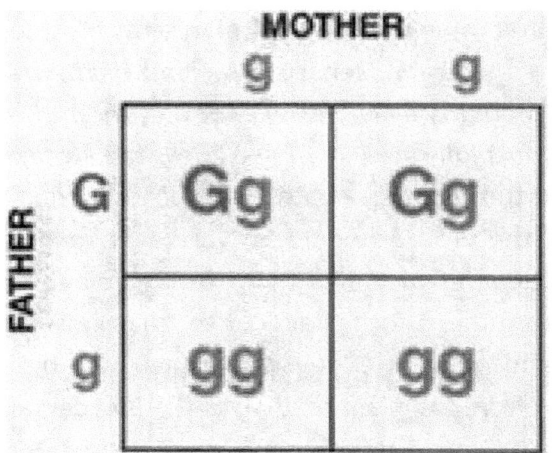

Genes come in pairs; you inherit one from your mother and one from your father. In the example shown above diagrammatically, the 'G' form of the gene is present in father and not in mother. Each of their children only has a 50–50 chance of inheriting the 'G' version of that particular gene, as shown. Therefore the possibility that none of the offspring will inherit this gene is not at all a remote one. (If they only have three children, the chance is 1 in 8). In a situation in which the entire human race was reduced down to Noah, his three sons and their wives, it is entirely feasible that some forms of the genes present in Noah were not passed on. Since it now appears that much of aging is under genetic control, loss of some of the genes for longevity may be the reason for the drop post-Flood. Perhaps subsequent population bottlenecks (at Babel) contributed further to this genetic elimination.

When God created man it wasn't his plan, at that time, for man to die. God told Adam in Genesis 2:17 *"but of the tree of the knowledge of good and evil you shall not eat, for in the day that you eat of it you shall surely die."* We know the story; man disobeyed God and through that death was placed on mankind. God created man; therefore it would be very easy for Him to reprogram a genetic limit of man's DNA to alter his lifespan. Initially it seems from the record that God set that limit to just under one thousand years. He doesn't tell us why but the chronicles are clear from the plain reading of the Biblical text.

Following the flood we're told in Genesis 6:3 *"And the Lord said, "My Spirit shall not strive with man forever, for he is indeed flesh; yet his days shall be one hundred and twenty years."* God intervened again with man's DNA and adjusted it to a maximum of 120 years. Later we're told in Psalm 90:10 *"The days of our lives are seventy years; and if by reason of strength they are eighty years."* At some point God adjusted things down to 70 – 80 years, and unquestionably this is where we're at today.

All right, so let's accept then that the pre-flood fathers did live that long. What impact would that have on passing down information? The following chronological graph gives a very interesting insight into the overlap of the various ancestors and just how many generations would be alive in the same time period.

Chapter 7
Writing of the Bible

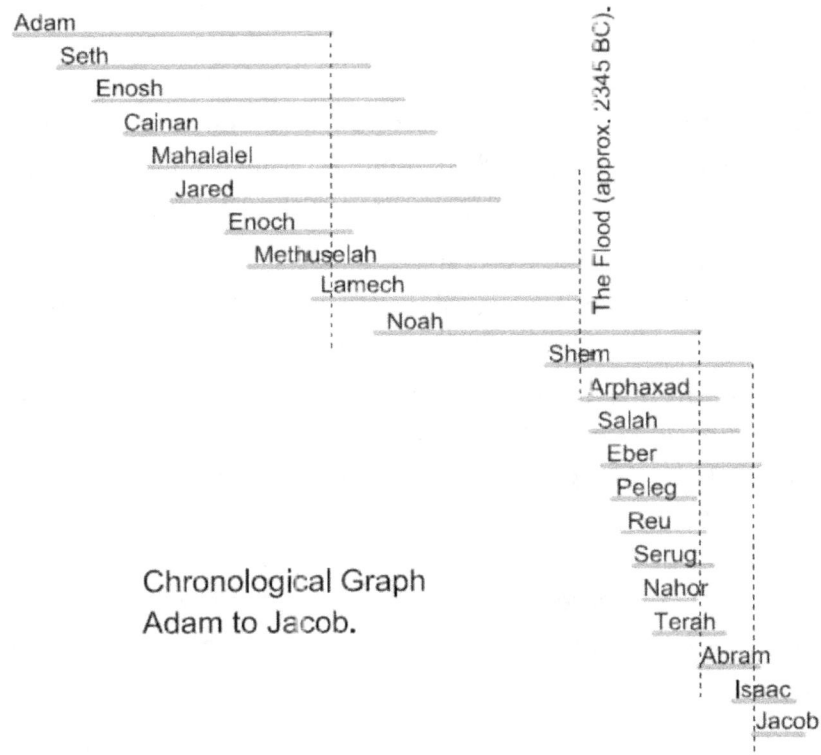

Chronological Graph
Adam to Jacob.

Amazingly, this graph shows us that Noah's father was a young man when Adam died. Theoretically it would have been completely feasible for Lamech to sit down with Adam and hear a first-hand account of the creation. Lamech in turn could have passed that directly onto Noah.

The Bible tells us that during this pre-flood era the whole earth had the same language. That continued after the flood but changed during the lifetime of Peleg, six generations after Noah. Genesis 10:25 *"To Eber were born two sons: the name of one was Peleg, for in his days the earth was divided; and his brother's name was Joktan."* The division of the language took place in a city called Babel which is the origin of the English phase we have today when we refer to someone as "babbling on" about something which we neither understand nor perhaps care about. Babel was the forerunner of the city of Babylon.

God created numerous different languages at that time and imposed them on man. Genesis 11:5-7 *"But the Lord came down to see the city and the tower which the sons of men had built. And the Lord said, "Indeed the people are one and they all have one language, and this is what they begin to do; now nothing that they propose to do will be withheld from them. Come, let Us go down and there confuse their language, that they may not understand one another's speech."* Genesis 11:9 *"Therefore its name is called Babel, because there the Lord confused the language of all the earth; and from there the Lord scattered them abroad over the face of all the earth."*

Prior to the flood understanding each other was no problem; everyone spoke the same language as Adam.

So, let's get back to the written word. We know from archaeological records that true writing was around in about 3200 BC. [1] In accordance with the Biblical chorological graph above Enoch, the 7th from Adam, was alive during the lifetime of Adam. Enoch only lived for 365 years and the Bible doesn't record his death only saying in Genesis 5:24 *"Enoch walked with God, and he was not found, for God took him."* The interesting thing about Enoch is that he lived from 3378 BC to

Chapter 7
Writing of the Bible

3013 BC. Writing came about during his lifetime. We also know that Enoch embraced this new technology as books attributed to him were quoted in the Bible by Jude. Jude 1:14 *"Now Enoch, the seventh from Adam, prophesied about these men also, saying, "Behold, the Lord comes with ten thousands of His saints,"* This prophecy can be found in the book of Enoch which is readily available to us today.

So clearly Enoch wrote down his prophecies and other writings and these were handed down and obviously Noah had a copy of them with him in the ark or they would have been lost. We know then that Enoch did write and we have his written account still today. But what else did he write? The Bible doesn't say, but it's highly conceivable that he became a prolific sponsor of this new technology.

Adam was 622 years old when Enoch was born and he lived on until Enoch was 308. There was a window of about 300 years when Enoch could have easily have sat down with Adam, clay tablet in hand and said "now tell me exactly the detail of creation"? Being the first man created would have given Adam a lot of kudos with his descendants, all of which were his direct blood relatives. I am assuming, but I would envisage that when Adam died there would have been a massive commemoration for him as probably he was the first person to die of old age. Others had died prior to that, such as Adam's son Able, but he was murdered.

The interest in Adam would have been massive and writing it down would have been logical. If Enoch didn't do it himself then I'm certain others at that time would have. The writings would have been highly accurate because it was an eyewitness account.

All right, so during Adam's lifetime details of the creation account and his bloodline were most likely written down to be made available for future generations. How did that information get passed along?

Noah was born after Enoch had been taken from the earth. However Noah's father Lamech was alive when both Adam and Enoch were, and very possibly he personally knew them both. Lamech could easily have obtained a copy of Enoch's writings which he could have passed onto Noah. God gave Noah one hundred years to prepare for the coming global flood. During that time he had to build the ark and prepare for the inbound animals. God made it very clear to Noah the reason for the flood and that it would only be him and his sons (and wives) that would survive – it would be catastrophic. While preparing for the flood, no doubt Noah would have gathered all the things that were important to him and placed them securely in the ark. An ark built to house a few thousand animals for over a year would certainly have room for a few manuscripts.

Enoch's son Methuselah died in the year of the flood (or perhaps even in the flood) and Noah himself was 600 years old when the flood came. Again a large window was available there for Noah to sit down with Methuselah and gather information. The art of writing clearly survived the flood as we have no record of it being reinvented, so it's reasonable to assume that

Chapter 7
Writing of the Bible

either Noah or his sons could also write. Noah not only recorded all that God told him before the flood but also during and after. It's again logical to assume Noah would have made sure he retained a complete record of all his ancestors' right back to Adam to uphold his place in history.

By making a few logical assumptions it's reasonably believable to understand how the record of creation could have been made and how this was preserved through the global flood. What about after the flood, how did this get passed on down to Moses? Again take a look at the chronological graph above. While long life quickly dropped back after the flood Noah and his son Shem still lived a very long time. Abraham's father was alive when Noah died and Abraham (Abram) was an old man when Shem died. Shem would have been famous on the earth because he'd lived through the great global flood.

Shem certainly would have had a direct understanding of God from his experience in watching his own father talk with God and receive his detailed instructions on building the ark. He would have experienced God shutting them in the ark and seen the literal fulfilment of everything God had spoken about of destroying everything that had the breath of life through a flood over the whole earth. It's very plausible that anyone with an understanding of God's ways would be very interested to sit down and chat with Shem. Somewhere Abram learned about God. The Bible doesn't mention anything about Abram's father Terah knowing God so somewhere somehow Abram as a young man learned to really trust and understand God. Abram was from the bloodline of Shem and it's very plausible they could have met, possibly more than once and likewise Shem could have instructed Abram in the ways of God. That is an educated guess on my part but given the circumstances, you be the judge.

If indeed the two men had met, which does seem highly plausible, it is also quite conceivable that Shem could have given Abram copies of manuscripts covering the creation, his genealogy and the flood. Abram would of course know his own ancestors and made those recordings too. Think about the detail and accuracy of such manuscripts coming to Abram at this point. All the information in them would have been from direct eyewitnesses, no second-hand accounts or years of oral history passed down. What an incredible base from which to write the book of Genesis.

That account of the written word passed on through no more than three hands over 2000 years from Adam to Abram is nothing short of miraculous. Records from Abram to Moses would certainly have been maintained and kept within the children of Israel. I believe it is without any doubt that Moses would have had several highly accurate eyewitness accounts to use to combine into the book of Genesis. All the information in Genesis can be fully relied upon, it is the inspired word of God and every part of it is absolute truth.

As for the other 4 books of Moses; Exodus, Leviticus, Numbers and Deuteronomy – Moses was an eyewitness of that entire period. He wrote everything that God told him to but he

Chapter 7
Writing of the Bible

also penned detailed records of everything that occurred during the forty plus years he led the Children of Israel.

There are 41 authors accredited to writing the various 66 books in the Bible and the following is a list of the book, their authors and when they were written. [3] We say about 40 authors because it's uncertain who wrote the book of Hebrews as unlike the other epistles the writer doesn't identify himself. If it is Paul, as some claim, then the number is 40.

Book	Author	Date Written
Job	Job?	1900 - 1700 BC?
Genesis	Moses	1445 B.C.
Exodus	Moses	1445 - 1405 B.C.
Leviticus	Moses	1405 B.C.
Numbers	Moses	1444 - 1405 B.C.
Deuteronomy	Moses	1405 B.C.
Joshua	Joshua	1404-1390 B.C.
Judges	Samuel	1374-1129 B.C.
Ruth	Samuel	1150? B.C.
First Samuel	Samuel	1043-1011 B.C.
Second Samuel	Ezra?	1011-1004 B.C.
First Kings	Jeremiah?	971-852 B.C.
Second Kings	Jeremiah?	852-587 B.C.
First Chronicles	Ezra?	450 - 425 B.C.
Second Chronicles	Ezra?	450 - 425 B.C.
Ezra	Ezra	538-520 B.C.
Nehemiah	Nehemiah	445 - 425 B.C.

Esther	Mordecai?	465 B.C.
Psalms	David	1000? B.C.
	Sons of Korah wrote Psalms 42, 44-49, 84-85, 87; Asaph wrote Psalms 50, 73-83; Heman wrote Psalm 88; Ethan wrote Psalm 89; Hezekiah wrote Psalms 120-123, 128-130, 132, 134-136; Solomon wrote Psalms 72, 127.	
Proverbs	Solomon wrote 1-29 Agur wrote 30 Lemuel wrote 31	950 - 700 B.C.
Ecclesiastes	Solomon	935 B.C.
Song of Solomon	Solomon	965 B.C.
Isaiah	Isaiah	740 - 680 B.C.
Jeremiah	Jeremiah	627 - 585 B.C.
Lamentations	Jeremiah	586 B.C.
Ezekiel	Ezekiel	593-560 B.C.
Daniel	Daniel	605-536 B.C.
Hosea	Hosea	710 B.C.
Joel	Joel	835 B.C.
Amos	Amos	755 B.C.
Obadiah	Obadiah	840 or 586 B.C.
Jonah	Jonah	760 B.C.
Micah	Micah	700 B.C.
Nahum	Nahum	663 - 612 B.C.
Habakkuk	Habakkuk	607 B.C.
Zephaniah	Zephaniah	625 B.C.

Chapter 7
Writing of the Bible

Haggai	Haggai	520 B.C.
Zechariah	Zechariah	520 - 518 B.C.
Malachi	Malachi	450 - 600 B.C.
Matthew	Matthew	60's
Mark	John Mark	late 50's to early 60's
Luke	Luke	60
John	John	late 80's to early 90's
Acts	Luke	61
Romans	Paul	55
1 Corinthians	Paul	54
2 Corinthians	Paul	55
Galatians	Paul	49
Ephesians	Paul	60
Philippians	Paul	61
Colossians	Paul	60
1 Thessalonians	Paul	50 - 51
2 Thessalonians	Paul	50 - 51
1 Timothy	Paul	62
2 Timothy	Paul	63
Titus	Paul	62
Philemon	Paul	60
Hebrews	(Paul, Apollos, Barnabas??)	60's
James	James, half-brother of Jesus	40's or 50's

1 Peter	Peter	63
2 Peter	Peter	63 - 64
1 John	John	late 80's to early 90's
2 John	John	late 80's to early 90's
3 John	John	late 80's to early 90's
Jude	Jude, half-brother of Jesus	60's or 70's
Revelation	John	late 80's to early 90's

Finally a picture of the past:

Brother Phillip was the apprentice of Father John; both were mature monks of the recently established Order of Minims. Their monastery was set in the serene countryside of rural Catholic France and the year was 1482. Father John was a master of calligraphy and his order was tasked with replicating the Biblical cannon for various dioceses of their region.

Brother Phillip was now ten years as an understudy. His work ethic was unquestionably studious and steadfast however his finished manuscripts clearly lacked finesse. Any of his reproductions that did not meet Father John's exacting standards were immediately discarded to the fire, irrespective of the fact that they had been slaved over for several months.

Chapter 7
Writing of the Bible

Brother Phillip stood back proudly admiring the completion of his fifth attempt of an unblemished replica. Father John sat back-facing behind him, completely engrossed in the development of yet another work of art. Leaning forward proudly to admire the brilliant calligraphy of his own letters, the broad sleeve of Brother Phillip's black wool tunic accidentally brushed the top of his resting quill, causing the inkpot to spin across the table dispensing as it went copious globules of bright red ink all over his prized creation. Unfortunately what immediately sprang from Brother Phillip's lips was neither hymn nor praise.

Father John, completely absorbed in his work, nonchalantly and absentmindedly replied to what he thought Brother Phillip had uttered, "Well done Brother Phillip, finally you've achieved success". Sadly we can't record precisely what ensued, but it's sufficient to say that ten years of Brother Phillip's pent up frustration spewed to the surface and now unfortunately Father John also faces replicating several of his most recent successes.

"How to have a better marriage every Thursday at 6.30pm"

Chapter 8
Conflicts within the Bible

Maybe this is going to be a very short chapter as I must state right at the outset that "there are no conflicts within the Bible." "All right, if you say so; but why then do we hear so many people shouting the opposite?" I've had several people tell me, "Oh you can't trust the Bible, it conflicts itself on almost every page". My first question in reply, "Perhaps you could show me one or two of them?" At which point the mumbled reply is: "Well they hadn't actually read the Bible themselves, but that's what they had heard." Why then all this discrediting of the Bible in this way, where do these apparent conflicts arise from?

Often the problem of apparent conflict arises when a Bible verse is taken out of context. By context I mean the setting of or intended audience for whom it was written. When looking at the Bible as a whole and understanding its teachings there are simply no contradiction which is remarkable for a book of the Bible's age, size and scope.

On face value there may appear to be a small number of apparent discrepancies but these are more curiosity than

Chapter 8
Conflicts within the Bible

calamity. They do not touch on any major event or article of faith. Here is an example of a so-called apparent contradiction.

When Jesus was crucified Pilate ordered that a sign be posted on the cross above where Jesus hung. Three of the Gospels record what was written on that sign:

- Matthew 27:37, "*This is Jesus, the king of the Jews.*"
- Mark 15:26, "*The king of the Jews.*"
- John 19:19, "*Jesus of Nazareth, the king of the Jews.*"

In each of these the wording is slightly different, hence the apparent contradiction. The remarkable thing, though, is that all three very different writers describe the same event in such detail -- Jesus was crucified. On this they all agree. They even record that a sign was posted on the cross, and the base meaning of the sign is the same in all three accounts – the King of the Jews!

What about the exact wording? In the original Greek of the Gospels, they didn't use a quotation symbol as we do today to indicate a direct quote. The Gospel writers were making an indirect quote, which would account for the subtle differences in the passages. Were they originating this in English the words "The king of the Jews" would be in brackets as defining the actual quote, thereby clarifying that the related comments were by the writer. Whatever explanation is given I'm sure you'll agree the consequences of such a conflict are minimal.

A further apparent contradiction arises regarding the length of time Jesus was in the tomb prior to His resurrection. Prior to His crucifixion Jesus said in Matthew 12:40, *"For as Jonah was three days and three nights in the belly of the great fish, so will the Son of Man be three days and three nights in the heart of the earth."* Mark records another statement that Jesus made, Mark 10:33-34) *"Behold, we are going up to Jerusalem, and the Son of Man will be betrayed to the chief priests and to the scribes; and they will condemn Him to death and deliver Him to the Gentiles; and they will mock Him, and scourge Him, and spit on Him, and kill Him. And the third day He will rise again."*

Tradition has it that Jesus was killed on Friday (Good Friday) and the resurrection was discovered on Sunday. Try as you might, it is impossible to fit three days and three nights between a Friday afternoon burial and an early Sunday morning resurrection.

The Gospels are clear that Jesus died and His body was hurriedly placed in the tomb late in the afternoon, just before sundown when a Sabbath began. Mark 15:42-46 *"Now when evening had come, because it was the Preparation Day, that is,* **the day before the Sabbath,** *Joseph of Arimathea, a prominent council member, who was himself waiting for the kingdom of God, coming and taking courage, went in to Pilate and asked for the body of Jesus. Pilate marveled that He was already dead; and summoning the centurion, he asked him if He had been dead for some time. So when he found out from the centurion, he granted the body to Joseph. Then he bought fine linen, took*

Chapter 8
Conflicts within the Bible

Him down, and wrapped Him in the linen. And he laid Him in a tomb which had been hewn out of the rock, and rolled a stone against the door of the tomb." [Emphasis added].

This verse unmistakably defines the burial day as the "Day before the Sabbath." Since the Sabbath is Saturday naturally the before day is Friday? Clearly something doesn't add up. Either Jesus misspoke about the length of time He would be in the tomb, or the "Good Friday–Easter Sunday" timing is not Biblical or accurate. Obviously both cannot be true, so which one is right?

The answer is surprisingly simple and relates to the setting and culture at the time of the event.

We first must understand that God doesn't begin and end days at midnight as we do in Western culture today. Genesis 1:5 *"God called the light "day", and the darkness He called "night". So the evening and the morning were the first day.."* God counts a day as beginning with the evening (the night portion) and ending at the next evening" He further defines this for us in Leviticus 23:32 *"It shall be to you a sabbath of solemn rest, and you shall afflict your souls; on the ninth day of the month at evening, **from evening to evening**, you shall celebrate your sabbath."* [Emphasis added] This is why Joseph of Arimathea and Nicodemus hurriedly placed His body in Joseph's nearby tomb just before sundown as a Sabbath was beginning at nightfall when all work would have to cease.

The question is, which Sabbath?

Most people assume John is speaking of the regular weekly Sabbath day, observed from Friday sunset to Saturday sunset. From John's unambiguous statement, most people assume Jesus died and was buried on a Friday—thus the traditional belief that Jesus was crucified and died on "Good Friday."

We read in John 19:31, *"The Jews therefore, because it was the preparation, that the bodies should not remain upon the cross on the Sabbath day, (for that Sabbath day was an **high day**,) besought Pilate that their legs might be broken, and that they might be taken away."* (KJV) [emphasis added]. So what was this *"High Day"* that immediately followed the hurried entombment of our Lord and Saviour?

The Gospels tell us that on the evening before Jesus was condemned and crucified, He kept the Passover with His disciples Luke 22:14-15 *"When the hour had come, He sat down, and the twelve apostles with Him. Then He said to them, "With fervent desire I have desired to eat this Passover with you before I suffer."*

Leviticus 23 lists God's festivals. He tells us in Leviticus 23:5-7. *"On the fourteenth day of the first month at twilight is the Lord's Passover. And on the fifteenth day of the same month is the Feast of Unleavened Bread to the Lord; seven days you must eat unleavened bread. On the first day you shall have a **holy convocation**; you shall do no customary work on it."* [emphasis added]. A *"holy convocation"* and a *"High Day"* have the same meaning.

Chapter 8
Conflicts within the Bible

So Jesus kept the Passover with his disciples and in the evening (the very start of the day) of the 14th day of the first month. Remember the Passover day began at sundown and ended the following day at dusk. Jesus kept the Passover with His disciples, and then was arrested later that night. After daybreak the next day He was questioned before Pontius Pilate, crucified, then hurriedly entombed just before the next sunset when the "High Day," the first day of the Feast of Unleavened Bread, began. Incredibly Jesus was actually crucified on the Passover day in a literal fulfilment of the symbolic Passover lamb.

It is possible to calculate historic Jewish dates back in time as the months were related to a new moon. According to the US Naval Observatory, Nisan 14 in the year AD 31 fell on Wednesday, April 25. The Passover meal was eaten just after sundown on Wednesday at the very start of Nisan 14. (Remarkably this date fits exactly with Daniel's prophecy of the 7 weeks and 62 weeks - 69 weeks - but that's a whole further subject for another time.)

Jesus was arrested later that Nisan 14 night and was crucified and entombed on that same day. He was placed in the tomb late Wednesday (that day ended at sundown) and remained there Thursday, Friday and Saturday nights (3 full nights) and of course three days Thursday (the High Day), Friday and Saturday (regular Sabbath day) (3 full days). The Good Friday–Easter Sunday tradition simply isn't true or Biblical.

Can we find further proof of this in the Gospels? Yes, certainly!

Mark 16:1: *"Now when the Sabbath was past, Mary Magdalene, Mary the mother of James, and Salome bought spices, that they might come and anoint Him."* They bought (purchased) the spices after the Sabbath.

During those times, if the body was placed in a tomb rather than being buried directly in the ground, loved ones would commonly place aromatic spices in the tomb alongside the body to reduce the smell as the remains decayed.

Since Jesus' body was placed in the tomb just before the special Thursday Sabbath began, the women had no time to buy those spices before that Sabbath. On any Sabbath day all shops are firmly shut so their first opportunity to purchase the spices was the Friday. Thus, Mark says, they bought the spices after the Sabbath — "when the High Day Sabbath was past."

We are told in Luke 23:55-56, *"And the women who had come with Him from Galilee followed after, and they observed the tomb and how His body was laid. Then they returned and prepared spices and fragrant oils. And they rested on the Sabbath according to the commandment."*

Mark 16 clearly states that the women bought the spices after the Sabbath —"when the Sabbath was past." Luke tells us that the women prepared the spices and ointments, after which "they rested on the Sabbath according to the commandment."

Chapter 8
Conflicts within the Bible

Mark tells us they bought the spices after the Sabbath, but Luke says they prepared the spices before resting on the Sabbath. Is this a clear contradiction between these two Gospel accounts— unless of course two Sabbaths were involved!

All quite simple really, when understood in context. Mark is talking about the *"High Day"* Sabbath, which began after Passover day on the Wednesday evening at sundown and ended Thursday evening at sundown, and then on the Friday the women went out and bought the spices to anoint Jesus' body. Luke then tells us that the women prepared the spices on the Friday then they rested on the Sabbath (the normal weekly Sabbath day, observed Friday sunset to Saturday sunset).

By comparing details in both accounts, it's obvious that two different Sabbaths are mentioned along with a workday in between.

The original Greek in which the Gospels were written also plainly tells us that two Sabbath days were involved in these accounts. In Matthew 28:1 *"Now after the Sabbath, as the first day of the week began to dawn, Mary Magdalene and the other Mary came to see the tomb."* In the original Greek the word here for Sabbath is sabbatōn which is plural and therefore should more correctly be translated "Sabbaths".

Hence, our Lord Jesus Christ was crucified and entombed on a Wednesday evening, just before an annual Sabbath began. So when was He resurrected?

We read in John 20:1-2, *"Now the first day of the week Mary Magdalene went to the tomb early, while it was still dark, and saw that the stone had been taken away from the tomb. Then she ran and came to Simon Peter, and to the other disciple, whom Jesus loved, and said to them, "They have taken away the Lord out of the tomb, and we do not know where they have laid Him."* Three points from this; it was Sunday, it was still dark and the tomb was empty.

I've heard the argument that since Jesus was resurrected at sunrise on Sunday morning then that would count for a day in the tomb! But that has the appearance of cheating which is impossible for someone as Holy as Jesus and besides John tells us it was still dark – the day hadn't started yet. So when did his resurrection take place then? It is all there, if we just read the words of Jesus himself, without the blinders of years of "traditional" learning.

Matthew 12:40 *"For as Jonah was three days and three nights in the belly of the great fish, so will the Son of Man be three days and three nights in the heart of the earth."*

There was no trickery or sleight of hand; Jesus was entombed — placed *"in the heart of the earth"* — just before sundown on a Wednesday. If we count forward from that, one day and one night brings us to Thursday at sundown. A second day and night brings us to Friday at sundown. A third day and night brings us to Saturday at sundown. After the Saturday sundown it was Sunday the first day of the week.

Chapter 8
Conflicts within the Bible

According to the words of Jesus, in Matthew 12:40; He is to be resurrected "three days and three nights" after He was entombed. When Mary arrived "while it was still dark" on Sunday morning the tomb was already empty. Jesus rose from the dead at some point soon after sundown on Saturday which was already the first day of the week and hence our Sunday.

It is interesting to note that none of the Gospels mention the soldiers that were sent to guard the tomb being anywhere around when the disciples began arriving early that Sunday morning. It seems they had long since realised the tomb was empty and went off to report the matter to their superiors. This further demonstrates that Jesus rose sometime after sunset Saturday night.

I love these types of demonstration in scripture when, despite years of traditional teaching to the contrary, the clear and obvious answer is all there in plain sight in the word. Reading the Bible in context together with understanding the culture and history of a recorded event will greatly enhance our understanding of what is meant. Discrepancies, apparent or otherwise, simply disintegrate.

When considering possible discrepancies in the Bible it's necessary to appreciate that the vast majority of what we read today may not be precisely what the authors actually wrote. They scribed in their native tongue and only a small percentage of the world's population today speak those languages. The Bible (the whole or in part) has been translated into about 2,426 different languages, covering 95% of the world's population. While the vast majority of the translators have done a fantastic job its nigh-on impossible to convey the exact meaning of every verse from one language to another and for this reason "apparent" discrepancies can result.

And what language did the original writers use? Moses, the writer of the first five books, penned in Hebrew, his native language. During the thousand plus years of its composition, almost the entire Old Testament was written in Hebrew. The exceptions are a few chapters in the prophecies of Ezra and Daniel and one verse in Jeremiah which were written in a language called Aramaic. This language became very popular in the ancient world and for a time became dominant, in the way that English is today. Aramaic was the common language spoken in Israel in Jesus' time, and it was possibly the language He spoke day by day although clearly He communicated with and fully understood the Jewish scribes and teachers of the law who only used Hebrew.

Some Aramaic words are even used by the Gospel writers in the New Testament. The New Testament is written in Greek, as this was the language of scholarship during the years of its composition from 50 to 100 AD. Greek became so prevalent that eventually many Jews could no longer read Hebrew. So, around 200 BC a translation of the Old Testament from Hebrew into Greek was completed. Gradually this Greek translation of the Old Testament, called the Septuagint, was widely accepted and was even used in many synagogues. It also became a

Chapter 8
Conflicts within the Bible

wonderful missionary tool for the early Christians, for now the Greeks could read all God's Word in their own tongue.

Nowadays of course English is the most widely spoken language and the focus of interpretation has been from Hebrew and Greek to English. Unfortunately this has resulted in a vast array of versions, not only for the English but of numerous other tongues as well. There are literally dozens of different translations of the Bible into English and for many this huge variety is confusing as they just don't know which Bible to choose or if there is essentially any difference between them. How did we get into this situation anyway?

At the heart of the problem are two views as to what a translation should be. On one side are those who feel a translation should stick just as closely as possible to every word of the original Hebrew and Greek. They want the translation to be a literal transfer, word for word, of the original words into English. They feel this will provide the greatest accuracy possible and, after all, this is the aim, isn't it?

Unfortunately, that approach encounters real-world problems. Some words simply don't have an exact equivalent in English. The word order and the entire sentence structure just don't match from one language to another. So these word-for-word translations tend to be wooden and unnatural. They can be very useful for close study, but they often fail in terms of comprehension and readability. Opposing a literal translation are those who feel a translation should transfer the message, that is, the exact thought and emotion of the original text. To do this, it should use as many words as are necessary to reproduce the idea precisely in English, so that the reader understands it. In the end, they say, a thought-for-thought translation is actually more accurate as well as more understandable.

Translations also differ as to the targeted reading level of the reader which may vary from a third grade to a twelfth grade reading level. The lower reading level translations have shorter sentences, draw from a smaller English word pool, and avoid all uncommon words. Some employ a vocabulary limited to 1000 different words.

The King James Version (KJV) was the first English translation and dates from 1611. Today however the KJV contains seemingly archaic language and the real message of its verses are often very difficult to decipher. In more recent versions such as the New International Version (NIV) the thoughts within the passages come through with distinctly more clarity.

The King James Version is loved for the majesty of its language and for the way God has used it in ministering to millions down through the centuries. Some Christians feel that no other translation can possibly replace it. I was brought up in a church that insisted that the seventeenth century language used in the King James Bible was the only way to speak to God as "we must always be reverent when speaking to Him". Even all prayer had to utilise words such as thee, thy and thou etc. Such a concept is utterly ridiculous when you think about it.

Chapter 8
Conflicts within the Bible

Why would our loving God be more accepting of us just because we used 17th century English? If they really wanted to be pious I guess they should have all used Hebrew as that was probably the language that Jesus spoke to His Father with, during His time on this earth. I have no idea what native language God himself uses and of course it's unquestionably of no relevance. God not only is completely fluent in every language on earth today (remember He created all the different languages at the tower of Babel incident) but He also completely comprehends all the tongues of men and angels. It's only to man that language is a problem; God understands everything regardless of the dialect we use and we're told He even knows all our thoughts and intentions of our heart. Hebrews 4:12 *"For the word of God is living and powerful, and sharper than any two-edged sword, piercing even to the division of soul and spirit, and of joints and marrow, and is a discerner of the thoughts and intents of the heart."*

So, which English version is best? That's difficult to answer directly but the following are some of the better known ones.

- The New International Version is widely distributed and utilized translation worldwide. It is a thought-for-thought translation, but employs a moderately traditional tone that makes it appropriate for both public worship and personal reading.
- The New King James Version is also very widely read and it is an accurate translation following closely to the text of the KJV except in plain English.

- A recent translation that is gaining widespread acceptance and uses contemporary terminology is the New Living Translation. It is both accurate and very readable.
- Another widely used translation is the New American Standard Bible, which is a more literal rendition.
- The New Revised Standard Version is a contemporary thought-for-thought translation.
- Many Roman Catholic readers prefer the New Jerusalem Bible.

Remember that, regardless of the translation, the word of God has abundant power to transform your life. Though the cadence and the terminology may differ, the voice of God can speak to you through each one. The question is: how will you respond to God's voice as He speaks to you from the pages of this life-changing book?

One version necessary to mention at this point is "The Message Bible" by Eugene Peterson. [1]

The Message is not actually a translated rendition of the Bible at all but is a paraphrase - a rephrased, simplified, and shorter version of written word – and there is a massive difference. Yes it is definitely easy to read but it contains segments watered down from the original in order to widen its appeal. This book uses street language in attempts to be "hip" and in tune with the language of our culture. It is written with a

Chapter 8
Conflicts within the Bible

very free rendering of the Greek. The text has chapter numbers, but no verses. The verse numbers are probably omitted to make the text look more like normal English literature. When receiving instructing on how to learn about God and the way to eternal life, there is zero room for misdirection.

Because of its interpretive and idiosyncratic nature, The Message should never be used for doctrinal study or church teaching. If read for enlightenment or entertainment, the reader should follow the advice of Saint Augustine, as quoted in the original preface to the KJV, "Variety of translations is profitable for finding out the sense of the Scriptures." Acts17:11 applauds the Bereans for evaluating Paul's teaching with the Old Testament Scriptures. In the same manner, The Message needs to be evaluated against more consistent and traditional translations, especially when its renderings evoke a response such as, "I didn't know the Bible said that!" or, "Now I understand what it means."

So while the phrase "The Message" is the author's rendition of "The Gospel," not everything in The Message should be treated as gospel. I cringe whenever I hear a Pastor teach from this book as a part of his sermon.

There are some clear examples in scripture where the literal meaning of a verse is difficult to portray in the English language. One such example is in John 21 where Jesus asked Peter three times if he loved him. It has been dubiously suggested by some that this was because Jesus had previously healed Peter's mother-in-law when she was at the point of death! (Luke 4:38). Sorry no Biblical theology points there and the real meaning is certainly much deeper and far more significant.

It's impossible to interpret the subtleties in this John 21 dialogue between Jesus and Peter without digging deeper and taking a look at the Greek origin. With the advent of the Internet, tools are readily available to all Christians with internet access. There are a number of sites but one I have personally found very useful is www.biblica.com. This site provides multiple avenues to explore any verse in the Bible including comparing it directly to the original Greek or even Hebrew.

Let's take a look at exactly how this conversation plays out. First the plain English version in John 21:15-19 *"After breakfast Jesus asked Simon Peter, "Simon son of John, do you love me more than these?"*

"Yes, Lord," Peter replied, "you know I love you."

"Then feed my lambs," Jesus told him.

Jesus repeated the question: "Simon son of John, do you love me?"

"Yes, Lord," Peter said, "you know I love you."

"Then take care of my sheep," Jesus said.

A third time he asked him, "Simon son of John, do you love me?"

Peter was hurt that Jesus asked the question a third time. He said, "Lord, you know everything. You know that I love you."

Chapter 8
Conflicts within the Bible

Jesus said, "Then feed my sheep.

"I tell you the truth, when you were young, you were able to do as you liked; you dressed yourself and went wherever you wanted to go. But when you are old, you will stretch out your hands, and others will dress you and take you where you don't want to go." Jesus said this to let him know by what kind of death he would glorify God. Then Jesus told him, "Follow me."" (NLT)

What lies at the heart of this discourse between Jesus and Peter is the word love. The Greek language distinguishes at least four different ways by which the term love is used and it has a distinct word for each: agápe, éros, philía, and storgē. It's difficult to separate the true meanings of these words when used outside of their respective contexts; nonetheless, their general senses are as follows:

- Agápe (ἀγάπη agape) means "love: esp. charity; the love of God for man and of man for God." Agape is used to express the unconditional love of God for His children.

- Éros (ἔρως érōs) means "love, mostly of the sexual passion."

- Philía (φιλία philō) means "affectionate regard, friendship," usually "between equals." It is a dispassionate virtuous love, expressed variously as loyalty to friends (specifically, "brotherly love"), family, and community, and requires virtue, equality, and familiarity.

- Storgē (στοργή storgē) means "love, affection" and "especially of parents and children" It's the common or natural empathy, like that felt by parents for offspring. It is also known to express mere acceptance or putting up with situations, as in "loving" the tyrant. This is also used when referencing the love for one's country or a favourite sports team.

Then there's the English word "know." This too has different meanings in the Greek.

- Oidas (οἶδα oida) means "properly, to see with physical eyes, as it naturally bridges to the metaphorical sense: perceiving ("mentally seeing"). This is akin to the expressions: "I see what you mean"; "I see what you are saying."

- Ginóskō (γινώσκω ginoskeis) means "properly, to know, especially through personal experience" (first-hand acquaintance).

Herein ends our short Greek lesson. [2] Now, getting back to our John 21 verse;

Unapparent in the English there is interplay going on here between two Greek words for love, Agape and Philo. Jesus asks of Peter's love with one word, but Peter responds with another. There is also a subtle shift in the use of another verb meaning "to know." Peter moves from oidas to ginoskeis. Both can be translated "you know" but again the question is why the shift and how should this be interpreted?

Chapter 8
Conflicts within the Bible

Let's reproduce the dialogue with the Greek distinctions stitched in:

Jesus: "Simon, son of John, do you love (agápe) me more than these?"

Peter: "Yes, Lord, You know (oidas) that I love (philō) you."

Jesus: "Simon, son of John, do you love (agápe) me?"

Peter: "Yes, Lord, You know (oidas) that I love (philō) you."

Jesus: "Simon, son of John, do you love (phileis) me?"

Peter: "Lord, you know (oidas) everything; you know (ginoskeis) that I love (phileis) you."

The use of different words for love is highly significant. Jesus is asking Peter for agape love. Agape love being the highest and most spiritual love. Jesus is calling Peter to love him above all things and all people, including himself. But Peter, finally being honest says to Jesus in effect, Lord you know that I love you (only) with brotherly love (philō). Jesus in return entrusts the role of Chief Shepherd to Peter anyway. But again He asks for agape love and Peter answers the same. A third time Jesus asks, but this time He comes to Peter's level and says, in effect, "OK Peter then do you love me with brotherly love (phileis me)?"

This makes Peter sad who now becomes more emphatic and says Lord, you know (oidas) everything; you know (ginoskeis) that I (only) love with brotherly love (philō). Note here that Peter's exasperation includes a shift in the verb "know." He shifts from the verb of know from oidas (meaning more literally "you have seen") to the verb ginoskeis (meaning a deeper sort or perception that includes understanding by personal experience). Peter surrendered to Jesus at that point, he acknowledged to Jesus that "Lord you know everything there is to know about me." Following that submission the Lord could use him.

So perhaps the final sentence translated with these distinctions in mind would read: "Lord! You have seen everything; and you understand that I'm only capable of loving you with brotherly love." The Lord then goes on to tell Peter that one day he will die a martyr's death. Almost as if to say, "Peter I **do** understand that you only love me now with brotherly love. But there will come a day when you will finally be willing to die for me and you will give over your physical life. Then you will truly be able to say that you love me with Agape love."

Truly understanding God's word throughout the Bible is not simply a case of reading and learning. It's about in-depth understanding. For the Christian we have an incredible advantage through God's wonderful gift of His Holy Spirit. John 14:26 *"But the Helper, the Holy Spirit, whom the Father will send in My name, He will teach you all things, and bring to your remembrance all things that I said to you."* We are without excuse when it comes to understanding; this verse tells us that the Holy Spirit will teach you **all** things – nothing is left out! Always ask the Holy Spirit to reveal His word as you read and I

Chapter 8
Conflicts within the Bible

guarantee He will give you fresh understanding every single time.

"Give God what's right not what's left"

Chapter 9
History of the Bible

Understanding the how we came to get our Bible is important. Some youngsters may believe that milk only comes from a supermarket. As they grow, they usually discover that farming and cows are also involved. Perhaps many Christians just view the Bible as another bookstore book and have very little appreciation or understanding of how our present English translations of the Bible came to us.

The Old Testament was and in fact still is the Bible of the Jewish faith, Judaism. Before and during the time of Jesus it was considered the only scripture. Jesus frequently quoted from it throughout His ministry time on earth, as in Luke 24:44 *"Then He said to them, "These are the words which I spoke to you while I was still with you, that all things must be fulfilled which were written in the Law of Moses and the Prophets and the Psalms concerning Me."* Notice Jesus here refers to three parts; the Law of Moses, the Prophets and the Psalms. This three part distinction is important as it not only clarifies exactly what He was referring to, it also defines how it was fashioned. Let's take a closer look at these three sectors.

Chapter 9
History of the Bible

The Law of Moses

The opening books of the Old Testament date back some 3,450 years and have been held as the word of God from the outset. And God told Moses to write them. Exodus 34:27 *"Then the Lord said to Moses, "Write these words, for according to the tenor of these words I have made a covenant with you and with Israel."* Deuteronomy 31:24-26 *"So it was, when Moses had completed writing the words of this law in a book, when they were finished, that Moses commanded the Levites, who bore the ark of the covenant of the Lord, saying: "Take this Book of the Law, and put it beside the ark of the covenant of the Lord your God, that it may be there as a witness against you;"*

These books of Moses are considered the authoritative text of the Jewish Bible (the Tanakh) and collectively are known as the Torah. The Torah refers to the "Five Books of Moses" or the Pentateuch, meaning "five scroll-cases" and consists of Genesis, Exodus, Leviticus, Numbers, and Deuteronomy.

The Prophets

Nevi'im [1] meaning "Prophets" is the second main division of the Tanakh (Jewish Bible). It contains two sub-groups, the Former Prophets and the Latter Prophets.

The Former Prophets include the books of Joshua, Judges, Samuel (1 & 2) and Kings (1 & 2). The Latter Prophets are further divided into two groups, the "major" prophets, Isaiah, Jeremiah and Ezekiel, and the Twelve Minor Prophets, collected into a single book including Hosea, Joel, Amos, Obadiah, Jonah,

Micah, Nahum, Habakkuk, Zephaniah, Haggai, Zechariah and Malachi. The minor prophet collection is divided into twelve individual books in the Christian Old Testament, one for each of the prophets.

The Psalms (the Writings)

Ketuvim [2] meaning "the writings" is the third and final section of the Tanakh. The Ketuvim are believed, in Judaism, to have been written under the Holy Spirit but with one level less authority than that of prophecy. It contains:

- Three poetic books: Psalms, Proverbs and Job.
- Five Scrolls: Song of Songs, Ruth, Lamentations, Ecclesiastes and Esther.
- Other books: Daniel, Ezra, Nehemiah and Chronicles.

In Masoretic manuscripts, Psalms, Proverbs and Job are presented in a two-column form emphasizing the parallel stichs (lines of poetry) in the verses, which are a function of their poetry. Collectively, these three books are known as Sifrei Emet (an acronym of their titles in Hebrew) which is also the Hebrew for "truth".

These three books are also the only ones in the Tanakh with a special system of cantillation notes that are designed to emphasize parallel stichs within verses. However, the beginning and end of the book of Job are in the normal prose system.

Chapter 9
History of the Bible

The Tanakh was written in Hebrew except for some small portions (Ezra 4:8–6:18 and 7:12–26, Jeremiah 10:11, Daniel 2:4–7:28) which were written in Aramaic.

The Septuagint

The Septuagint [3] is a translation of the Hebrew Tanakh together with some related texts into Greek which began in Alexandria in the late 3rd century BC and was completed by 132 BC. As the work of translation progressed, the canon of the Greek Bible expanded. The Torah always maintained its pre-eminence as the basis of the Greek canon but the Nevi'im had various hagiographical works added to it. (Hagiographical works admire or represent someone as much better than they really are). These additional books are Tobit, Judith, Wisdom of Solomon, Wisdom of Jesus son of Sirach, Baruch, the Letter of Jeremiah, additions to Daniel (The Prayer of Azarias, the Song of the Three Children, Susanna and Bel and the Dragon), additions to Esther, 1 Maccabees, 2 Maccabees, 3 Maccabees, 4 Maccabees, 1 Esdras, Odes, including the Prayer of Manasseh, the Psalms of Solomon, and Psalm 151.

The Septuagint formed the basis for the Old Latin, Slavonic, Syriac, Old Armenian, Old Georgian and Coptic versions of the Christian Old Testament. The Roman Catholic and Eastern Orthodox Churches use most of the books of the Septuagint, while Protestant churches usually do not. After the Protestant Reformation many Protestant Bibles began to follow the Jewish canon and exclude the additional texts, which came to be called Biblical Apocrypha. The Apocrypha are included under a separate heading in the English language King James Version of the Bible.

The Septuagint version was discarded in favour of Theodotion's version in the 2nd to 3rd centuries AD. In Greek-speaking areas, this happened near the end of the 2nd century, and in Latin-speaking areas it occurred in the middle of the 3rd century. History does not record the reason for this but Theodotion's Greek translation of the Hebrew more closely resembles the Tanakh.

The Christian Bible

The books which make up the Christian Old Testament [4] differ between the Catholic, Orthodox, and Protestant churches, with the Protestant movement accepting only those books contained in the Hebrew Bible, while Catholics and Orthodox have wider canons. A few groups consider particular translations to be divinely inspired, notably the Greek Septuagint and the Aramaic Peshitta. Most Protestants Bibles do not contain the Apocrypha as they don't accept these additional books as the inspired word of God.

The Old Testament has always been central to the life of the Christian church. Jesus himself often quoted scripture from Moses, the Psalms and the Prophets. In Acts 17:11 it tells us; *"These were more fair-minded than those in Thessalonica, in that they received the word with all readiness, and searched the Scriptures daily to find out whether these things were so."* These early Berean Christians regarded the "holy writings" of

Chapter 9
History of the Bible

the Israelites as necessary and instructive for the Christian. Paul tells Timothy in 2 Timothy 3:15 "*And that from childhood you have known the Holy Scriptures, which are able to make you wise for salvation through faith which is in Christ Jesus.*" The only Holy Scriptures at that time was the Old Testament.

The New Testament

The Christian New Testament [5] is a set of books that Christian denominations regard as divinely inspired and thus constitutes scripture. It forms the second and final portion of the Christian Bible and Jesus Christ is its central figure. Although the Early Church primarily used the Septuagint for the Greek speakers or the Targums among Aramaic speakers, the apostles did not leave a defined set of new scriptures; instead the canon of the New Testament developed over time.

The term "New Testament" came into use in the second century following a controversy among Christians over whether or not the Hebrew Bible should be included with the Christian writings as sacred scripture. The New Testament presupposes the inspiration of the Old Testament and is also considered to be an infallible source of doctrine, historical and factual detail. It's a collection of 27 books of 4 different genres, The Gospels, the Acts of the Apostles, Epistles and an Apocalypse.

During the 2nd and 3rd centuries the early Christian Church retained various inspired writings which, through a divinely directed process, would become the New Testament. Somewhat different lists of accepted works continued to develop in antiquity until the 4th century when a series of synods produced a list of texts equal in standing to the 39 book canon of the Old Testament. Most notably, the Synod of Hippo in 393 AD finalised the 27-book canon of the New Testament, and in 400 AD Jerome produced a definitive Latin edition of the Bible (the Vulgate), which at the insistence of the Pope, was in strict accord with the earlier Synods. This process affirmatively set the New Testament canon which is still in use today.

Textual history

By the 2nd century AD Jewish groups had called the Bible books the "scriptures" and referred to them as "holy." Christians quickly accepted the term and named the Old and New Testaments of the Christian Bible "The Holy Bible" or "the Holy Scriptures." The Bible was divided into chapters in the 13th century by Stephen Langton and into verses in the 16th century by French printer Robert Estienne and today all scripture is usually cited by book, chapter, and verse.

The oldest extant copy of a complete Christian Bible (Old and New Testament) in Greek is an early 4th-century parchment book preserved in the Vatican Library, and known as the Codex Vaticanus. The oldest known copy of a complete Latin (Vulgate) Bible is the Codex Amiatinus, dating from the 8th century.

English Bible History [6]

The fascinating story of how we got our English language version of the Bible in its present form begins with the

Chapter 9
History of the Bible

"Morning Star of the Reformation", by John Wycliffe who in 1380 AD produced the first hand-written English language Bible manuscripts.

John Wycliffe, an Oxford professor, scholar, and theologian was well-known throughout Europe for his opposition to the teaching of the organized Church, which he believed to be contrary to the Bible. With the help of his followers, called the Lollards, and his assistant Purvey, and many other faithful scribes, Wycliffe produced dozens of hand written copies of the English language manuscript of the scriptures. They were translated from the Latin Vulgate, which was the only source text available to Wycliffe. The Pope was so infuriated by his translation of the Bible into English that 44 years after Wycliffe had died, the Pope ordered his bones to be dug-up, crushed, and scattered in the river!

John Hus

One of Wycliffe's followers, John Hus, actively promoted Wycliffe's ideas: that people should be permitted to read the Bible in their own language, and they should oppose the tyranny of the Roman church who threatened anyone possessing a non-Latin Bible with execution – serious stuff! Hus was burned at the stake in 1415, with Wycliffe's manuscript Bibles used as kindling for the fire. The last words of John Hus were that, "in 100 years, God will raise up a man whose calls for reform cannot be suppressed." Almost exactly 100 years later, in 1517, Martin Luther nailed his famous 95 Theses of Contention (a list of 95 issues of heretical theology and crimes of the Roman Catholic Church) into the church door at Wittenberg. The prophecy of Hus had come true! Martin Luther went on to be the first person to translate and publish the Bible in the commonly-spoken dialect of the German people; a translation more appealing than previous German Biblical translations. Foxe's Book of Martyrs records that in that same year, 1517, seven people were burned at the stake by the Roman Catholic Church for the crime of teaching their children to say the Lord's Prayer in English rather than Latin.

Johann Gutenberg

Johann Gutenberg invented the printing press in the 1450s, and the first book to ever be printed was a Latin language Bible, printed in Mainz, Germany. Gutenberg's Bibles were surprisingly beautiful, as each leaf Gutenberg printed was later colourfully hand-illuminated. Ironically, though he had created what many believe to be the most important invention in history, Gutenberg was a victim of unscrupulous business associates who took control of his business and left him in poverty. Nevertheless, the invention of the movable-type printing press meant that Bibles and books could finally be effectively produced in large quantities in a short period of time. This was essential to the success of the Reformation.

Thomas Linacre

In the 1490s an Oxford professor, and the personal physician to Kings Henry the 7th and 8th, Thomas Linacre decided to learn Greek. After reading the Gospels in Greek, and comparing it to the Latin Vulgate, he wrote in his diary, "Either this (the original Greek) is not the Gospel or we are not Christians." The Latin had become so corrupt that it no longer even preserved the message of the Gospel, yet the Catholic Church still threatened to kill anyone who read the scripture in any language other than Latin even though Latin was not an original language of the scriptures.

John Colet

In 1496, John Colet, another Oxford professor and the son of the Mayor of London, started reading the New Testament in Greek and translating it into English for his students at Oxford, and later for the public at Saint Paul's Cathedral in London. The people were so hungry to hear the Word of God in a language they could understand, that within six months there were 20,000 people packed in the church and at least that many outside trying to get in! Fortunately for Colet, he was a powerful man with friends in high places, so miraculously he managed to avoid execution.

Desiderius Erasmus

In considering the experiences of Linacre and Colet, the great scholar Erasmus was so moved to correct the corrupt Latin Vulgate that in 1516, with the help of printer John Froben, he published a Greek-Latin Parallel New Testament. The Latin part was not the corrupt Vulgate, but his own fresh rendering of the text from the more accurate and reliable Greek, which he had managed to collate from a half-dozen partial old Greek New Testament manuscripts he had acquired. This milestone was the first non-Latin Vulgate text of the scripture to be produced in a millennium and the first ever to come off a printing press. The 1516 Greek-Latin New Testament of Erasmus further focused attention on just how corrupt and inaccurate the Latin Vulgate had become. He understood how important it was to go back and use the original Greek New Testament and original Hebrew Old Testament languages to maintain accuracy when translating them into the languages of the common people, whether English, German, or any other tongue. No sympathy for this "illegal activity" was to be found from Rome however.

William Tyndale

William Tyndale was the Captain of the Army of Reformers, and was their spiritual leader. Tyndale holds the distinction of being the first man to ever print the New Testament in the English language. Tyndale was a true scholar and a genius, so fluent in eight languages that it was said one would think any one of them to be his native tongue. He is frequently referred to as the "Architect of the English Language", (even more so than William Shakespeare) as so many of the phrases Tyndale coined are still in our language today.

Martin Luther had a small head-start on Tyndale, as Luther declared his intolerance for the Roman Church's corruption on 31st October in 1517, by nailing his 95 Theses of Contention to the Wittenberg Church door. Luther, who would be exiled in

Chapter 9
History of the Bible

the months following the Diet of Worms Council in 1521 that was designed to martyr him, would translate the New Testament into German for the first time from the 1516 Greek-Latin New Testament of Erasmus, and publish it in September of 1522. Luther also published a German Pentateuch in 1523 and another edition of the German New Testament in 1529. In the 1530s he would go on to publish the entire Bible in German.

William Tyndale was keen to use the same 1516 Erasmus text as a source to translate and print the New Testament in English for the first time in history. Tyndale showed up on Luther's doorstep in Germany in 1525, and by year's end had translated the New Testament into English. Tyndale had been forced to flee England, because of the wide-spread rumour that his English New Testament project was underway, causing inquisitors and bounty hunters to be constantly on Tyndale's trail to arrest him and prevent his project. God foiled their plans, and in 1525-26 the Tyndale New Testament became the first printed edition of the scripture in the English language. Subsequent printings of the Tyndale New Testament in the 1530s were often elaborately illustrated.

The Bishop of the day confiscated and burnt as many printed copies he could lay his hands on, but they did trickle through to the general public and one actually ended up in the bedroom of King Henry VIII. The more the King and Bishop resisted its distribution, the more fascinated the public at large became. The church declared it contained thousands of errors as they torched hundreds of New Testaments confiscated by the clergy, although in fact they burned them because they could find no errors at all. One risked death by burning at the stake if caught in mere possession of Tyndale's forbidden books.

Having God's Word available to the public in English, the language of the common man, spelt disaster to the Catholic Church. No longer could they control access to the scriptures. If people were able to read the Bible in their own tongue the church's income and power would crumble. How could they possibly continue to get away with selling indulgences (the forgiveness of sins) or selling the release of loved ones from church-manufactured "Purgatory?" People would begin to challenge the church's authority if the church were exposed as frauds and thieves. The contradictions between what God's Word said, and what the priests taught, would open the public's eyes and the truth would set them free from the grip of fear that the institutional church held. Salvation through faith, not works or donations, would be understood. The need for priests would vanish through the priesthood of all believers. The veneration of church-canonized Saints and Mary the mother of Jesus would be called into question. The availability of the scriptures in English was the biggest threat imaginable to the wicked church. Neither side would give up without a fight.

Today, there are only two known copies left of Tyndale's 1525-26 First Edition. Tyndale's flight was an inspiration to freedom-loving Englishmen who drew courage from the 11

Chapter 9
History of the Bible

years that he was hunted. Books and Bibles flowed into England in bales of cotton and sacks of flour. Ironically, Tyndale's biggest customer was the King's men, who would buy up every copy available to burn them and undeterred Tyndale used their money to print even more! In the end, Tyndale was caught: betrayed by an Englishman whom he had befriended. Tyndale was incarcerated for 500 days before he was strangled and burned at the stake in 1536. Tyndale's last words were, "Oh Lord, open the King of England's eyes". This prayer would be answered just three years later in 1539, when King Henry VIII finally allowed, and even funded, the printing of an English Bible known as the "Great Bible". However in the meantime the battle continued.

Myles Coverdale

Myles Coverdale and John "Thomas Matthew" Rogers had remained loyal disciples the last six years of Tyndale's life, and they carried the English Bible project forward and even accelerated it. Coverdale finished translating the Old Testament, and in 1535 he printed the first complete Bible in the English language, making use of Luther's German text and the Latin as sources. Thus, the first complete English Bible was printed on October 4, 1535, and is known as the Coverdale Bible.

John Rogers

John Rogers went on to print the second complete English Bible in 1537 which was the first English Bible translated from the original Biblical languages of Hebrew and Greek. He printed it under the pseudonym "Thomas Matthew", (an assumed name that had actually been used by Tyndale at one time) as a considerable part of this Bible was the translation by Tyndale. It was a composite, made up of Tyndale's Pentateuch and New Testament (1534-35 edition) and Coverdale's Bible and some of Rogers' own translation of the text. It remains known commonly as the Matthew-Tyndale Bible. It went through a nearly identical second-edition printing in 1549.

Thomas Cranmer

In 1539, Thomas Cranmer, the Archbishop of Canterbury, hired Myles Coverdale at the bequest of King Henry VIII to publish the "Great Bible". It became the first English Bible authorized for public use, as it was distributed to every church, chained to the pulpit, and a reader was even provided so that the illiterate could hear the Word of God in plain English. It would seem that William Tyndale's last wish had been granted, just three years after his martyrdom. Cranmer's Bible, published by Coverdale, was known as the Great Bible due to its great size: a large pulpit folio measuring over 14 inches tall. Seven editions of this version were printed between April of 1539 and December of 1541.

King Henry VIII

It was not that King Henry VIII had a change of conscience regarding publishing the Bible in English. His motives were more sinister. The Lord sometimes uses the evil intentions of

Chapter 9
History of the Bible

men to bring about His glory. King Henry VIII had in fact, requested that the Pope permit him to divorce his wife and marry his mistress. The Pope refused. King Henry responded by marrying his mistress anyway and thumbing his nose at the Pope by renouncing Roman Catholicism, taking England out from under Rome's religious control, and declaring himself, the reigning head of State, to also be the new head of the Church. This new branch of the Christian Church, neither Roman Catholic nor truly Protestant, became known as the Anglican Church or the Church of England. King Henry acted essentially as its Pope. His first act was to further defy the wishes of Rome by funding the printing of the scriptures in English – the first legal English Bible.

Queen Mary

The ebb and flow of freedom continued through the 1540's and into the 1550's. Following the reign of King Henry VIII, King Edward VI took the throne, and after his death, the reign of Queen "Bloody" Mary was the next obstacle to the printing of the Bible in English. She was obsessed in her quest to return England to the Roman Church. In 1555, John "Thomas Matthew" Rogers and Thomas Cranmer were both burned at the stake. Mary went on to burn reformers at the stake by the hundreds simply for the "crime" of being a Protestant. This era was known as the Marian Exile, and the refugees fled from England with little hope of ever seeing their home or friends again.

John Foxe

In the 1550's, the Church at Geneva, Switzerland, was very sympathetic to the reformer refugees and was one of only a few safe havens for a desperate people. Many of them met in Geneva, led by Myles Coverdale and John Foxe (publisher of the famous Foxe's Book of Martyrs, which is to this day the only exhaustive reference work on the persecution and martyrdom of Early Christians and Protestants from the first century up to the mid-16th century), as well as Thomas Sampson and William Whittingham. There, with the protection of the great theologian John Calvin and John Knox, the great Reformer of the Scottish Church, the Church of Geneva determined to produce a Bible that would educate their families while they continued in exile.

John Calvin

In 1557 John Calvin completed his English translation of New Testament, followed by the Old Testament and, in 1560, his first complete Bible was published. It became known as the Geneva Bible. Unfortunately due to a passage in Genesis describing the clothing that God fashioned for Adam and Eve upon expulsion from the Garden of Eden as "Breeches" (an antiquated form of "Britches" — nowadays translated as clothes), some people referred to the Geneva Bible as the Breeches Bible.

Chapter 9
History of the Bible

John Knox

The Geneva Bible was the first Bible to add numbered verses to the chapters, so that referencing specific passages became vastly easier. Every chapter was also accompanied by extensive marginal notes and references so thorough and complete that the Geneva Bible is also considered the first English "Study Bible". William Shakespeare quotes from the Geneva translation of the Bible hundreds of times in his plays. The Geneva Bible became the Bible of choice for over 100 years of English speaking Christians. Between 1560 and 1644 at least 144 editions of this Bible were published. Examination of the 1611 King James Bible clearly shows that its translators were influenced much more by the Geneva Bible than by any other source. The Geneva Bible itself retains over 90% of William Tyndale's original English translation. It truly was the "Bible of the Protestant Reformation."

With the end of Queen Mary's bloody reign, the reformers could safely return to England. The Anglican Church, now under Queen Elizabeth I, reluctantly tolerated the printing and distribution of Geneva version Bibles in England. The marginal notes, which were vehemently against the institutional Church of the day, did not rest well with its rulers. Another version, with a less inflammatory tone was desired, and the copies of the Great Bible were getting to be decades old. In 1568 a revision of the Great Bible known as the Bishop's Bible was introduced. Despite 19 editions being printed between 1568 and 1606, this Bible, referred to as the "rough draft of the King

James Version", never gained much popularity among the common people.

By the 1580s the Roman Catholic Church saw that it had lost the battle to suppress the will of God that all the scripture would be available in the English language. In 1582 the Church of Rome surrendered their fight for "Latin only" and decided that if the Bible was to be available in English they would at least have an official Roman Catholic English translation. And so, using the corrupt and inaccurate Latin Vulgate as the only source text, they went on to publish an English Bible with all the distortions and corruptions that Erasmus had revealed and warned of 75 years earlier. Because it was translated at the Roman Catholic College in the city of Rheims, it was known as the Rheims New Testament. The Douay Old Testament was translated by the Church of Rome in 1609 at the College in the city of Douay. The combined product is commonly referred to as the "Douay/Rheims" Version. In 1589 Dr. William Fulke of Cambridge published the "Fulke's Refutation" in which he printed in parallel columns the Bishop's Version alongside the Rheims Version, attempting to show the error and distortion of the Roman Church's corrupt compromise of an English version of the Bible.

King James I

With the death of Queen Elizabeth I, Prince James VI of Scotland became King James I of England. The Protestant clergymen approached the new King in 1604 and announced their desire for a new translation to replace the Bishop's Bible

Chapter 9
History of the Bible

first printed in 1568. They knew that the Geneva Version had won the hearts of the people because of its excellent scholarship, accuracy, and exhaustive commentary. However, they were against the controversial marginal notes (proclaiming the Pope an Anti-Christ, etc.). The leaders of the church desired a Bible for the people, with scriptural references only for word clarification or cross-references.

This "translation to end all translations" (for a while at least) was the result of the combined effort of about fifty scholars. They took into consideration: The Tyndale New Testament, The Coverdale Bible, The Matthews Bible, The Great Bible, The Geneva Bible, and even the Rheims New Testament. The great revision of the Bishop's Bible had begun. From 1605 to 1606 the scholars engaged in private research. From 1607 to 1609 the work was assembled. In 1610 the work went to press, and in 1611 the first of the huge 16 inch (40cm) tall pulpit folios known today as "The 1611 King James Bible" came off the printing press. A typographical discrepancy in Ruth 3:15 rendered a pronoun "He" instead of "She" in that verse in some printings. This caused some of the 1611 First Editions to be known by collectors as "He" Bibles, and others as "She" Bibles. Starting just one year after the huge 1611 pulpit-size King James Bibles were printed and chained to every church pulpit in England printing began on the earliest normal-size printings of the King James Bible. These were produced so individuals could have their own personal copy of the Bible.

John Bunyan

The Anglican Church's King James Bible took decades to overcome the more popular Protestant Church's Geneva Bible. One of the greatest ironies of history is that many Protestant Christian churches today embrace the King James Bible exclusively as the "only" legitimate English language translation yet it is not even a Protestant translation! It was printed to compete with the Protestant Geneva Bible, by authorities who throughout most of history were hostile to Protestants and killed them. While many Protestants are quick to assign the full blame of persecution to the Roman Catholic Church, it should be noted that even after England broke from Roman Catholicism in the 1500's the Church of England (The Anglican Church) continued to persecute Protestants throughout the 1600s. One famous example of this is John Bunyan who, while in prison for the crime of preaching the Gospel, wrote one of Christian history's greatest books, Pilgrim's Progress. Throughout the 1600's as the Puritans and the Pilgrims fled the religious persecution of England to cross the Atlantic and start a new free nation in America, they took with them their precious Geneva Bible and rejected the King's Bible. America was founded upon the Geneva Bible, not the King James Bible.

Protestants today are largely unaware of their own history and unaware of the Geneva Bible which is textually 95% the same as the King James Version, but 50 years older, and not influenced by the Roman Catholic Rheims New Testament that the King James translators admittedly took into consideration.

Chapter 9
History of the Bible

Nevertheless, the King James Bible turned out to be an excellent and accurate translation, and it became the most printed book in the history of the world, the only book ever to have over one billion copies in print. In fact, for over 250 years until the appearance of the English Revised Version of 1881-1885, the King James Version reigned without much of a rival. One little-known fact is that for the past 200 years all King James Bibles published in America actually use the 1769 Baskerville spelling and wording revision of 1611 King James Version. The original "1611" preface is decevingly included by the publishers and no mention of the fact that it is really the 1769 version is to be found, because that may have hurt sales.

John Eliot

Although the first Bible printed in America was written in the native Algonquin Indian Language by John Eliot in 1663, the first English language Bible to be printed in America, by Robert Aitken in 1782, was a King James Version. Robert Aitken's 1782 Bible was also the only Bible ever authorized by the United States Congress. He was commended by President George Washington for providing Americans with Bibles during the embargo of imported English goods due to the Revolutionary War. In 1808 Robert's daughter, Jane Aitken, would become the first woman to ever print a Bible and to do so in America. In 1791 Isaac Collins vastly improved upon the quality and size of the typesetting of American Bibles and produced the first "Family Bible" printed in America also a King James Version.

Similarly in 1791 Isaiah Thomas published the first Illustrated Bible printed in America – the King James Version.

Noah Webster

While Noah Webster, just a few years after producing his famous Dictionary of the English Language, would produce his own modern translation of the English Bible in 1833 the public remained too loyal to the King James Version for Webster's version to have much impact. It was not really until the 1880s that England's own planned replacement for their King James Bible the English Revised Version (E.R.V.), would become the first English language Bible to gain popular acceptance as a post King James Version modern-English Bible. The widespread popularity of this modern-English translation brought with it another curious characteristic: the absence of the 14 Apocryphal books.

Up until the 1880s every Protestant Bible (not just Catholic Bibles) had 80 books, not 66! The inter-testamental books written many years before Christ called "The Apocrypha," were part of virtually every printing of the Tyndale-Matthews Bible, the Great Bible, the Bishop's Bible, the Protestant Geneva Bible, and the King James Bible until their removal in the 1880s! The original 1611 King James contained the Apocrypha and King James threatened anyone who dared to print the Bible without the Apocrypha with heavy fines and a year in jail. Only for the last 135 years has the Protestant Church rejected these books, and removed them from their Bibles. This has left most modern-day Christians believing the popular myth that there is

Chapter 9
History of the Bible

something "Roman Catholic" about the Apocrypha. There is, however, no truth in that myth, and no widely-accepted reason for the removal of the Apocrypha in the 1880s has ever been officially issued by a mainline Protestant denomination.

The Americans responded to England's E.R.V. Bible by publishing the nearly-identical American Standard Version (A.S.V.) in 1901. It was also widely-accepted and embraced by churches throughout America for many decades as the leading modern-English version of the Bible. In the 1971 it was again revised and called New American Standard Version Bible. This New American Standard Bible is considered by nearly all evangelical Christian scholars and translators today to be the most accurate, word-for-word translation of the original Greek and Hebrew scriptures into the modern English language that has ever been produced. It remains the most popular version among theologians, professors, scholars, and seminary students today. Some, however, have taken issue with it because it is so direct and literal a translation (focused on accuracy), that it does not flow as easily in conversational English.

For this reason, in 1973, the New International Version (N.I.V.) was produced, which was offered as a "dynamic equivalent" translation into modern English. The N.I.V. was designed not for "word-for-word" accuracy but rather, for "phrase-for-phrase" accuracy, and ease of reading even at a Junior High-School reading level. It was meant to appeal to a broader (and in some instances less-educated) cross-section of the general public. Critics of the N.I.V. often jokingly refer to it as the "Nearly Inspired Version", but that has not stopped it from becoming the best-selling modern-English translation of the Bible ever published.

In 1982 Thomas Nelson Publishers produced what they called the "New King James Version". Their original intent was to keep the basic wording of the King James to appeal to King James Version loyalists, while only changing the most obscure words and the Elizabethan "thee, thy, thou" pronouns. This was an interesting marketing ploy. However, upon discovering that this was not enough of a change for them to be able to legally copyright the result they had to make more significant revisions, which defeated their purpose in the first place. It however is an accurate translation and is taken seriously by scholars with good public acceptance.

In 2002 a major attempt was made to bridge the gap between the simple readability of the N.I.V., and the extremely precise accuracy of the N.A.S.B. This translation is called the English Standard Version (E.S.V.) and is rapidly gaining popularity for its readability and accuracy. The 21st Century will certainly continue to bring new translations of God's Word in the modern English language.

As Christians we must be very careful to make intelligent and informed decisions about what translations of the Bible we choose to read. On the liberal extreme, we have people who would give us heretical new translations that attempt to change God's Word to make it politically correct. One example

Chapter 9
History of the Bible

of this, which has made headlines recently, is the Today's New International Version (T.N.I.V.) which seeks to remove all gender-specific references in the Bible whenever possible! Not all new translations are good and some are very bad.

But equally dangerous is the other extreme of blindly rejecting ANY English translation that was produced in the four centuries that have come after the 1611 King James. We must remember that the main purpose of the Protestant Reformation was to get the Bible out of the chains of being trapped in an ancient language that few could understand and into the modern, spoken, conversational language of the present day. William Tyndale fought and died for the right to print the Bible in the common, spoken, modern English tongue of his day. As he boldly told one official who criticized his efforts, "If God spares my life, I will see to it that the boy who drives the ploughshare knows more of the scripture than you, Sir!"

When we fully comprehend the path the Bible has taken to get into our hands it seems extremely callous the way many Christians respect it today. Many men lost their lives, others lived in ridicule, some banned from their posts and others forced in exile to bring this God inspired book to us. Yet nowadays, while most Christians feel it's still essential to own a Bible, many leave them discarded, unread, considering its contents to be irrelevant. Where is the fire gone whereby I'll go to any lengths to secure my personal copy and then cherish the fact I can read it in my native tongue? It is still God's word today! Nothing has changed about that.

Imagine you heard of a special limited edition year book on your favourite sports team, or national hero and it was only available for a short period in a distant town. All your life you sought ownership such a book and here is the opportunity. After driving for hundreds of miles, standing in line for hours and paying a princely sum, what would you do with it upon arriving back home. Throw it in a drawer and discard it? I doubt that, I expect you'd be reading every word, making sure you have understood each fact and feat. You would likely display it in a prominent position and proudly go through it with every friend that came by.

While I expect not many of us would admit to being that person I guess we all know someone precisely that fanatical. If we would do that for some man-made entertainment why should we not do it for the living word of God? Someone once said familiarity breeds contempt. How many times have you read your Bible this week or this past year? Jesus tells us in Luke 8:18 *"Therefore take heed how you hear. For whoever has, to him more will be given; and whoever does not have, even what he seems to have will be taken from him."* How well are you hearing?

Chapter 10
Knowledge

*"God wants spiritual fruit
not religious nuts"*

Chapter 10
Knowledge

A well-known Pastor was once invited to a debate at the annual conference of the atheist association. "What's the debate about?" the Pastor asked. "That there is no God, of course," the convenor replied. "Our leader will speak first for 20 minutes and then you are allotted 10 minutes to reply," he continued. "Oh 10 minutes is more than enough," the Pastor responded, "I'll doubt I even need that long."

The day arrived and the Pastor entered the packed venue overflowing with confirmed atheists certain they were about to witness their legendary orator utterly humiliate this unsuspecting God-promoter and his grossly out-dated beliefs. The atheist leader stood up and raged on for a full 30 minutes powerfully expressing his philosophies on the non-existence of God from every viewpoint. As he finished he turned to the sole God believer in the room inviting him to come forward and attempt to refute his compelling argument in his allotted 10 minutes.

The Bible – True, Relevant or a Fairy Tale?

As the Pastor approached he called to the atheist leader asking him if he would mind staying on stage with him for a moment as he needed his help. The leader quickly agreed as, naturally, the Pastor's only option was to concede defeat. "He would be gracious in his acceptance," the leader mused.

The Pastor walked over to a whiteboard and drew a large circle on it. He then asked the atheist, "Imagine this circle represents all the knowledge in the universe, absolutely everything it's possible to know. How much of this knowledge would you honestly say you knew?" The atheist considered for a short time and said, "Well, I do have two PhD's and I have studied for many years so modestly I would say about this much." Following which he drew a line across the top of the circle and shaded it in.

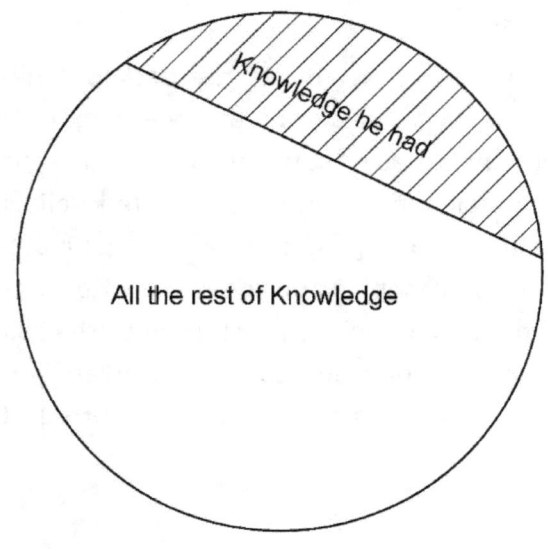

The Pastor, pointing to the atheist shaded area, said, "So you confirm that of all the knowledge in the whole universe this is what you know – about 7% say, of everything?" "Yea that's about

Chapter 10
Knowledge

right," replied the atheist, not certain of where the Pastor was heading. "And" continued the Pastor, "all the rest of this vast area is stuff you don't know?" Again the atheist confirmed his bemused agreement.

"So here's my question to you," continued the Pastor, pointing to the board, "within all this huge expanse of stuff that you just confirmed that you know nothing about couldn't it just be possible that somewhere within all that, God really does exist?

The Pastor left the gobsmacked atheist staring at the obvious truth portrayed on the whiteboard, and returned to his seat as the audience clapped in half-hearted polite acknowledgment of a speedy rebuttal of their long-held conviction.

Man is simply not capable of knowing everything, as that little story demonstrates. Many people understand a lot about specific specialist subjects and some people know a little about a lot of things, but no man knows everything. The extreme depth of God's incredible creation is mind boggling. The more we learn it seems the more there is to know. Unfortunately man is very possessive of his knowledge and is often ashamed to admit it when he doesn't know something. At least our atheist had admitted there was plenty he didn't know. It's what we don't know that's usually dangerous to us. We've all heard people's excuses; "I didn't know that would happen" or "You should have told me."

Knowledge is to be accumulated and never disseminated. We're told in Proverbs 23:23 *"Buy the truth, and do not sell it, Also wisdom and instruction and understanding."* And God is the only one that knows absolutely everything. 1 John 3:20, *"For if our heart condemns us, God is greater than our heart, **and knows all things**."* [Emphasis added].

Ok, so what exactly is knowledge? Here's a dictionary definition: [1]

- Facts, information, and skills acquired through experience or education; the theoretical or practical understanding of a subject. *"A thirst for knowledge"*

- Awareness or familiarity gained by experience of a fact or situation. *"The programme had been developed without his knowledge"*

More importantly is what knowledge is not. It's not about ideas, theories or philosophies, it's is about real facts, information, skills and awareness – things that are real.

Ok, you say, that's all good but where are we going with this; how's this related to the Bible?

In the Garden of Eden there were two trees that God makes special mention of; Genesis 2:9 *"And out of the ground the Lord God made every tree grow that is pleasant to the sight and good for food. **The tree of life** was also in the midst of the garden, and **the tree of the knowledge of good and evil**."* [Emphasis added].

Chapter 10
Knowledge

Then God put man in this wonderful Garden He'd planted and instructed him in Genesis 2:15-17, *"Then the Lord God took the man and put him in the garden of Eden to tend and keep it. And the Lord God commanded the man, saying, "Of every tree of the garden you may freely eat; but **of the tree of the knowledge of good and evil**; for in the day that you eat of it, you will surely die.""* [Emphasis added].

So here's the question, "why didn't God want man eating from the tree of good and evil?" Surely God would want man to have an understanding of good and evil? What's so bad about knowledge?

Notice He didn't warn man not to eat from the tree of life? Why, simple reality is, it wasn't God's plan for man to die – ever. God's original plan was that man should live in close relationship with Him for eternity and that there would be no death. This tree of life is mentioned a few times through the Bible and it appears again in Revelation 22:2 *"In the middle of its street, and on either side of the river, was the tree of life, which bore twelve fruits, each tree yielding its fruit every month. The leaves of the tree were for the healing of the nations."* So this tree is eternal and has a purpose in God's future plans.

Again, why block Man from the knowledge of good and evil? The answer is in understanding the meaning of knowledge. Look again at the dictionary explanation – *skills acquired through experience or education, and familiarity gained by experience.* Newly created man had absolutely no experience in the knowledge of good and evil and no decent parent (or Creator in this instance) will allow their kids play with something dangerous.

Observe something else too; it's all about the "knowledge" of good and evil. It wasn't about good and evil itself it was the knowledge of it gained by experience or familiarity. So God said "No." Undeterred man took it anyway! Why?

Let's look again to what occurred at the fall in the Garden of Eden.

Firstly Satan created doubt in the woman's mind via the serpent Genesis 3:1 *"Now the serpent was more cunning than any beast of the field which the Lord God had made. And he said to the woman,* **"Has God indeed said***, 'You shall not eat of every tree of the garden'?""* [Emphasis added]. The women should have just said "Yes, He did" to the serpent right there and walked away. But because the seed of doubt was sown she felt the need to clarify things and replies. Genesis 3:2-3 *"The woman said to the serpent, "And the woman said to the serpent, "We may eat the fruit of the trees of the garden; but of the fruit of the tree which is in the midst of the garden,* **God has said***, You shall not eat it, nor shall you touch it, lest you die.' "* [Emphasis added]. She knew well enough exactly what God had said and also what the consequences of eating it were. Interesting though the doubt seed was already working because the women adds that God had told them *"nor shall you touch it"*. Acutually, God didn't say that, God only told them not to eat it as we already saw in Genesis 2:15-17 quoted

Chapter 10
Knowledge

above. Doubt brings confusion and this very short conversation between the woman and the Serpent shows just how subtle doubt is and how quickly it begins to work.

Once the Devil knew the doubt was working he goes in for the big lie. Genesis 3:4-5 *"Then the serpent said to the woman, "You will not surely die. For God knows that in the day you eat of it your eyes will be opened, and you will be like God, knowing good and evil."* For us in hindsight it's abundantly clear what was going on here but for the woman right in the thick of it, not so clear unfortunately. First the big lie *"You will not surely die"* – completely untrue and directly opposite of what God had very clearly said. However to get the women to believe his lie the Devil again uses doubt. He continues immediately *"For God knows"* suggesting God was somehow deliberately keeping the truth from Adam and Eve – doubt again.

The first part of what the Devil says next is true enough but then he continues with another massive lie *"the day you eat it, your eyes will be opened, and you will be like God, knowing good and evil.".* Yes, some of that was accurate. Genesis 3:6-7 *"So when the woman saw that the tree was good for food, that it was pleasant to the eyes, and a tree desirable to make one wise, she took of its fruit and ate. She also gave to her husband with her, and he ate.* **Then the eyes of both of them were opened***, and they knew that they were naked; and they sewed fig leaves together and made themselves coverings."* Yes their eyes were opened but what on earth made them think that being naked was evil and needed correcting immediately?

None of the other creatures God created wore clothes and no fellow humans were there to leer at them. Surprisingly though this is what they saw as their most pressing problem and it had to be dealt with immediately, using their newly obtained knowledge! Don't fret, I'm not about to advocate nudity, the point is they had no idea how to apply this knowledge, no experience. Apart from why clothes as the first adjustment, why fig leaves? Again no experience as I suspect fig leaves may have been a little raspy and definitely not that practical. Not only would they tear easily, what about when they dried and became brittle? Yes they had knowledge but absolutely no experience, a fact I expect they quickly realised when they later compared their fig leaf garments to the nice leathers that God made for them? Genesis 3:21 *"Also for Adam and his wife the Lord God made tunics of skin, and clothed them."*

Wait a bit, I hear you say. The tree was called the **knowledge** of good and evil, so surely if they ate the fruit they would gain all the knowledge too? Look again at the meaning of knowledge it also includes facts and information. For sure Adam and Eve received all the facts and information about good and evil but the knowledge of how to configure those facts is only gained by experience. Most of us have seen the do-gooder, fresh out of four years of university, crammed with knowledge on every subject but hopeless when it comes to practical applications of that learning. The situation is identical for these first two humans. Lots of knowledge but they were clueless on how to use it.

Chapter 10
Knowledge

The often forgotten part of Satan's lie in Genesis 3:5 is where he says *"you will be like God"*. Mankind bought that lie hook, line and sinker and very firmly clings to it even today. The crowning point of the so called theory of evolution is that man is at the absolute apex of all evolved development. Nothing anywhere is greater than man. Man thinks he is just like God. Let's ignore for a moment the vast magnitude of how wrong that statement truly is and consider the implication of such thinking.

Here is Man (mankind) having acquired, through direct disobedience, a knowledge of good and evil with no skills or understanding on how to use it, but then at the same time believing he is akin to God. Consider it in the same terms as finding a six year old who has just picked up a loaded AK47 automatic assault rifle and now believes he's a grown-up and totally knows how and when to use it.

For some 6,000 years now man has believed that he sets the standards for what is good and what is evil and everything in between. I expect you've heard the term, "if it feels good, do it?" That pretty much sums up man's moral code of good and evil in today's world.

Have you ever seriously considered why God gave the children of Israel the Ten Commandments? Most people, Christians or not, can quote some or all of them. God wrote these for Moses on two tablets of stone about 2,550 years after the fall in the Garden of Eden. Here's the list.

1. I am the Lord thy God, which have brought thee out of the land of Egypt, out of the house of bondage. Thou shalt have no other gods before me.
2. Thou shalt not make unto thee any graven image.
3. Thou shalt not take the name of the Lord thy God in vain.
4. Remember the Sabbath day, to keep it holy.
5. Honour thy father and thy mother.
6. Thou shalt not kill (murder).
7. Thou shalt not commit adultery.
8. Thou shalt not steal.
9. Thou shalt not bear false witness against thy neighbour.
10. Thou shalt not covet (neighbour's house, neighbour's wife, neighbour's servants, animals, or anything else).

Nothing particularly complicated in that list, is there? Man had struggled for 2,550 years with his own idea of a moral benchmark for good and evil. The book of Genesis is littered with the result. Murder, deceit, rape, idolatry, envy and slavery, just to name a few. When God called out the Children of Israel to be His chosen people; He in effect told them, "Look I know you've been having a bit of bother maintaining your own moral yardstick. Here are ten simple rules to get you started. See how you go with these."

Chapter 10
Knowledge

The amazing thing is that since the day God gave Moses these ten simple commands not one single person has been able to live his entire life and not fail at least one of them. Except of course for our Lord Jesus Christ, He never failed at anything. Matthew 5:17 *"Do not think that I came to destroy the Law or the Prophets. I did not come to destroy but to fulfill."* Of course Jesus is God, as Son of God naturally he didn't have any problem complying with all of God's law. Man on the other hand – hopeless.

Man recognises that God's law is good and if you take a look at most nations on earth today their laws are all based around these ten commands. At least the ones they believe they live by. I may be wrong but I don't think there is a single nation on earth today that doesn't have a law against murder. Little bit of plagiarising going on perhaps?

In addition, most individuals have adopted the concept of the Ten Commandments for their own personal moral code. Some are very proud of the fact they are able to keep most of them. They proudly tell you they have never murdered or certainly don't steal but these same ones become strangely silent regarding taking the Lord's name in vane or committing adultery. James tells James 2:10 *"For whoever shall keep the whole law, and yet stumble in one point, he is guilty of all."*

So why is it that man has so much trouble keeping these ten seemingly simple rules? It all comes down to the first one. "I am the Lord thy God, thou shalt have no other gods before me." Man in his perceived knowledge of good and evil says "you're not the only God; I'm like you and I decide who and what I serve." Romans 1:25 *"who exchanged the truth of God for the lie, and worshiped and served the creature rather than the Creator, who is blessed forever. Amen."* The "who" in that verse is clarified in verse 18 of that same chapter in Romans *"men who suppress the truth in unrighteousness."* The writer of Romans is talking about mankind in this verse. But what is the lie that they exchanged for the truth? It's the one that the Devil told Eve in the Garden of Eden that *"you will be like God"*. The result of accepting that lie is that he *"worshiped and served the creature rather than the Creator"*. Man worships himself instead of God. What is meant by worship, you ask? The dictionary explains it as "the feeling or expression of reverence and adoration for a deity." In other words man believes and acts as if he is a deity *"you will be like God."*

Humanism has been around for centuries but in the last 100 years it has seriously taken root in society throughout the world. The term was coined by theologian Friedrich Niethammer [2] at the beginning of the 19th century. In modern times humanist movements are typically aligned with secularism and, today humanism refers to a non-theistic life stance centred on the human agency and looking to science rather than revelation from a supernatural source to understand the world.

So let's see if we have this straight. Through disobedience Man obtained the "knowledge of good and evil" believing that then he will be "like God". Now after thousands years of

Chapter 10
Knowledge

experimenting with how to use it Man chooses to look to science to understand his world instead of looking to God for answers? So perhaps he now has so much practical understanding of good that he actually believes he really is a god?

The theory of evolution popularised through Charles Darwin provides the foundation to make this absurd concept a reality in their minds. If man can prove through "science" that the earth somehow just happened and that life appeared out of nothing, evolving through an extremely long evolutionary process, then clearly there is no reason or place for God. Mankind indeed is at the very apex and he is the master of all he surveys and truly is god of his universe. Unfortunately this thinking has become main-stream in Western culture today. Man lives fully convinced he is "like God".

Nowadays with man self-assured that he is god, has no reason to accept God's criterion of good and evil as he possesses his own "knowledge" of it. The Ten Commandments are discarded by this way of thinking and Man displays his creative talents. Let's take something straight forward like "Thou shalt not murder". I doubt you would find many people today that would disagree with that commandment, but is that really true. Remember man is in charge (in his eyes) of our moral measure and perhaps he needs the term murder to be more clearly defined. Some claim that destroying a human embryo is okay – provided it's not more than a curtain number of weeks advanced, or so long as the baby's head hasn't left the mother's birth canal, or heaven forbid if some generic defect is detected while in the womb! No, they believe, that's not murder because man as god has determined that an unborn embryo is not a real person despite the fact it has its own heartbeat, capable of feeling pain and has independent movement within the mother's womb. Cunning Man renamed this to abortion, a term meaning to abandon, bring a halt to or terminate, so of course it's not murder – so they claim!

Next he looks at death at life's end. Man has decided that if someone is suffering and is terminally ill then they should have the right to choose when and how they die. Often such a person may need assistance to end their life but provided certain conditions are met then assisted death is permitted. Such assistance of course is not murder if it's nicely termed euthanasia.

Both these redefinitions of murder have come about because a strong vocal minority cried out to those in authority to be allowed to have this right. Since God's word was no longer the standard to base the law on, how then must it be established? Man has reasoned using his "knowledge of good and evil" that if it seems acceptable to the people affected by such things then the majority rule should apply and the definition of murder is reinvented.

So let's take this reasoning to the next level. There is no God and man is the sole determiner of good and evil.

Chapter 10
Knowledge

- A baby is born and it has a previously undetected severe defect and is going to cost a fortune to keep it alive.

- A child develops a chronic learning disorder and will never be a positive in society and experience suggests that a life of crime and years of expensive incarceration are a certainty.

- A previously healthy adult comes down with a crippling disease and while it's not terminal in the near term it will result in years of expensive intensive care.

- Finally there is the old lady, no relatives and although generally healthy, is suffering from moderate dementia and requires round the clock care.

Currently society has a heart and all these distressing examples are catered for completely. But what if "Man" (as in society) decided that the billions of dollars all of these cases collectively require were better spent on other things such as enhanced education for bright and gifted children or technology development? Wouldn't that better enriched society as a whole? The vast majority of people on this earth today would be categorically horrified at the thought of killing off these dependant citizens for the sake of a few dollars and quite rightly so. But I put it to you, go back 100 years and from what we know of a God fearing people of that time, how many of them do you honestly believe would consent to our current laws on abortion or euthanasia? If man continues to determine good and evil by his standard why couldn't laws terminating such dependants, in the interests of economics, become reality within the next 100 years? Will that happen? I have no answer. Could that happen? Absolutely. Remember Man has the knowledge of good and evil and thinks he is just like God. In his eyes whatever he wants will happen.

Fortunately regardless of what mankind believes God is still very much in overall control. He not only gave us the Ten Commandments He also gave us a perfect example of moral living through our Lord Jesus Christ. In addition the New and Old Testaments are full of information on how to live in right standing with God. The only way to be delivered from this lie of the Devil's, that we are like God, is to surrender our lives completely to Jesus Christ. Once we've done that the curse of the fall in the Garden of Eden is removed from our lives and we revert to a right relationship with God living by His standard in accordance with His word by the power of the Holy Spirit.

Humanism within society is easy to recognise as generally it evokes the standard that mankind is the apex of all things living – there is nothing greater. What about in the Church, has humanism had an influence there? Oh, of course not, I hear you respond. God is still front and centre in the Church!

On a visual level that would seem to be the case. I doubt there are many Christian churches throughout the world that maintain Man is somehow equal with God. The devil is much more subtle than that. He comes in by stealth and uses his old trick of doubt, "did God really say?" With so many different versions of the English translation of the Bible today it's

Chapter 10
Knowledge

relatively easy, especially when a verse is taken out of context, to find a scripture that would support almost any particular bias or leaning.

I have no intention of getting into the whole homosexuality debate as much has been said on that by others. The only point I will make is that God makes it extremely clear what will happen to those who continue to practice it. 1 Corinthians 6:9-10 *"Do you not know that the unrighteous will not inherit the kingdom of God? Do not be deceived. Neither fornicators, nor idolaters, nor adulterers, nor homosexuals, nor sodomites, nor thieves, nor covetous, nor drunkards, nor revilers, nor extortioners will inherit the kingdom of God."* This verse is very clear that not a single person who is one of those things will a part of His eternal plans. So is there any hope if someone is a homosexual? Fortunately there is, the passage continues, 1 Corinthians 6:11 "***And such were some of you.*** *But you were washed, but you were sanctified, but you were justified in the name of the Lord Jesus and by the Spirit of our God."* [emphasis added]. There is hope in Jesus Christ for all regardless of your past life.

What is interesting in God's eyes is that the sexually immoral etc. are in the same league as the drunkards, swindlers and the greedy. Unless we repent, turn away and are cleansed from ***all*** sin our fate is sealed. Now society has announced it is completely acceptable to be a homosexual and even marriage has been redefined to accommodate them. Man has a free choice and God is not intervening, just yet, to punish such laws or acts particularly. Man is free to do as he chooses and God will respect that choice. However that will never change what God thinks about it. He is very clear on the fate of those who continue in those things.

Society tells us clearly that we must not discriminate against those who have a different sexual preference to the majority, and rightly so. God wants every person included in His salvation plan regardless of what they have done or what lifestyle choices they had made, 2 Peter 3:9 *"The Lord is not slack concerning His promise, as some count slackness, but is longsuffering toward us,* **not willing that any should perish** *but that all should come to repentance."* [Emphasis added]. Everyone that comes to repentance will be saved regardless of what they have done. There is no basis for any discrimination relating to any person. What God hates is the sinful act as we saw in the 1 Corinthians 6:9 verse above. God discriminates between the person and the sin and holds out His love to every person regardless of their sin until the time of death or judgement arrives. We're all sinners saved by grace so none of us have any rights to be choosy about whomever God extends His love towards, but God never expects us to accept the sin of any other person. Murder, greed, drunkenness, adultery and homosexuality, just to name a few, are all sin and sin is what God hates and every person that has been cleansed by the blood of Jesus will by nature now hate those things too.

Man will of course tell us that, "no you can't place adultery or homosexuality in the same list as murder". They're not "sin"

Chapter 10
Knowledge

as some people are just born different, that's how nature made them, they have no choice in the matter. Perhaps that may be so, but that does not mean they have to practice their tendency. Someone may have a strong preference for alcohol and seemingly perhaps because of their genes have no control over how much they drink once they start. However that person cannot be termed a drunkard unless he actually drinks alcohol – that he literally lives out the difference he was born with. Just because we may be born with some particular tendency does not mean we have to follow that tendency and, if we do follow that tendency, that does not mean it is ok.

Humanism is so prevalent that it shouts from every side the lie of doubt on so many issues. Of course they shout, the Church must accept the right of a same sex couple to be married by it, if that's what the couple require. Of course the church must accept openly gay pastors to lead their flock! It is one thing for society to demand these things but it's a whole other level when the Church starts to accept these things.

God's word in the Bible is very clear as we've already discussed. However there have been numerous cases of church elders deliberating for hours questioning what God really meant. "Did God say"? Doubt arises when human reasoning is applied to God's word. When you read the verses in 1 Corinthians 9 quoted above (and there are numerous others) they leave no doubt. Why would a Church father who likely has a theological degree even debate such issues? Would they seriously advocate allowing a practicing drunkard or active swindler to lead a church? I doubt there would be little debate on that. Sadly there are a number of churches that have allowed the devil's seed of doubt to colour their interpretation of a Bible verse and have inducted practicing gay pastors or willingly performed marriages for same sex couples. Naturally "Society" embraces such things as wonderful, and points to love and tolerance. God's view certainly has not changed in the slightest, His word still stands firm.

The reason why this has happened is simple – some are not listening to God's Holy Spirit. When Jesus returned to heaven He sent the Holy Spirit and part of the work of the Holy Spirit is to give us understanding. John 14:26 *"But the Helper, the Holy Spirit, whom the Father will send in My name, He will teach you all things, and bring to your remembrance all things that I said to you."* Every believer has the Holy Spirit dwelling inside of them 2 Corinthians 1:22 *"and he has identified us as his own by placing the Holy Spirit in our hearts as the first installment that guarantees everything he has promised us."* (NLT) This is God's own Spirit residing in every single believer. Why? *"To teach you all things."* No Church father acting under the teaching of the Holy Spirit could ever embrace a personal bias on any scripture.

Clearly these churches who have embraced society's wishes or demands that are contrary to God's word have abandoned the Holy Spirit. Perhaps the lie of the devil – you will be like God – lives on in some in the church still.

Wake up my fellow believers in our Lord Jesus Christ. There is only one fount of all knowledge and that is God. He imparts

Chapter 10
Knowledge

His knowledge to us through His word in the Bible and gives us a detailed understanding of it through His gift of the Holy Spirit who dwells in each of us. Using Man's knowledge of good and evil is the literal handling of stolen goods. It's based on a lie and will always end in death. Man will never be like God that way but, amazingly, we will through God's way. In fact, even better that that He has made us His children and joint heirs with Jesus Christ. Romans 8:16-17 *"The Spirit Himself bears witness with our spirit that we are children of God, and if children, then heirs—heirs of God and joint heirs with Christ, if indeed we suffer with Him, that we may also be glorified together."* Not only do we get to share His knowledge but we also share His glory.

Glory to Jesus!

*"Be an organ donor
give your heart to Jesus"*

Chapter 11
What is the Real Story?

I haven't personally counted them but apparently there are 770,430 words in the NKJV Bible. With so many words what's really the underlying statement the Bible makes? Many people shy away from reading the Bible because of what they think is in it – intolerance, bigotry, rules and narrow mindedness. They perceive God to be ever ready to harshly punish our least mistake in order to teach us how to obey Him. Having read the Bible from cover to cover many times I can personally assure you that none of that has the slightest basis in truth. The Bible reveals the gospel – the good news of a tender loving God and of salvation through our Lord Jesus Christ. It truly is all good news.

Throughout this book we have focused a lot of attention on the book of Genesis, in particular the first few chapters. Why is that important? Why is it necessary for a Christian to believe the creation account? So what if it's taken millions of years to get us to today? Science confirms that man evolved doesn't it? Why would a loving God destroy all mankind in a global flood? Man couldn't possibly live for nearly 1,000 years, especially

Chapter 11
What is the Real Story?

given the lack of any modern day health care systems. Wow, steady on with all the questions! Perhaps there is a simple answer.

Firstly the Bible account is unambiguous. In just six days God created the heavens and the earth and all that is in it. God created Man and placed him in the Garden of Eden. Man rebelled against God through disobedience and received God's curse. The term for day in Genesis 1 means 24 hours – one day just as it is today.

Man's account says everything evolved. A big bang from nothing caused the universe to form over billions of years. Life began on earth spontaneously. All life evolved through an evolutionary process and man developed into his present form some 60,000 years ago.

These are two very startlingly different accounts. Clearly someone got it wrong or perhaps straight out lied. Both cannot be true.

I've heard various theoretical enlightenments trying to reconcile the two accounts. Perhaps the days were actually a thousand years long. Perhaps the creation account is metaphoric recorded as it was passed down by word of mouth by early generations. Lots of man-made explanations but none are very persuasive.

Paul told Timothy that **every** scripture is God breathed, 2 Timothy 3:16 *"All Scripture is breathed out by God and profitable for teaching, for reproof, for correction, and for* *training in righteousness,"* (ESV) Every scripture includes the book of Genesis. No doubt left there, the book of Genesis – all of it – is the word of God.

Some theologians tell us to simply dismiss the debate about creation as it's not relative anymore. It was a long time ago and we live in the day of salvation through the blood of Jesus. Here's why that's so wrong.

Let's assume for a moment that perhaps God did create man but that He did it over a very long time period and that animals and man have been around a very long time. If that were the case then many generations of animals and man would have passed by the end of the "six day" creation period. Death would have been everywhere with animals eating their fill and man reaching old age. There would have been many more than two humans living. Just two humans living in isolation in a utopian garden would be totally implausible.

Extend this scenario further to the fall in the Garden of Eden. Who were the couple that lived in this garden that had never been affected by death? If we assume man had already been around thousands of years the Garden of Eden situation becomes ridiculous as why would Man refrain from eating the fruit of just one tree through fear of death when death was already widespread? It becomes completely irrelevant and quite unbelievable.

Remove the "fall" in the Garden of Eden and how do we explain the relationship between God and Man? Did God

Chapter 11
What is the Real Story?

always intend Man to live with Him surrounded by death and suffering? Perhaps Man never actually fell out of favour with God and death was just His way of treating those that loved Him? Finally if there was no "fall" then there would be no need for Man to be redeemed through the blood of Jesus Christ as what is the relationship being restored to – more death? Remove Jesus from the equation and we have no hope of eternal life, why bother giving God the time of day?

Now my scenario may have many variables to the eyes of my critics but regardless of how you might play it, the bottom line is there could be no death before the Garden of Eden and that there were only two people living at that time Adam and Eve. Remove those factors and everything from that point on becomes ludicrous.

It is a very slippery slope when we start to reinvent God's word. What is written in Genesis – all of it – is completely and utterly true. But you say science has proved otherwise! No, mainstream science has surmised its narrative of observations through a fixed evolutionary bias. A bias that has it's starting point that God did not create. It's surprising to many to find there are thousands of renowned scientists who have allowed the possibility of God creating to be a factor in their observation and their narrative supports the Bible account of creation completely. Unfortunately their voices are quickly drowned out by the very vocal evolution scientists, as allowing God into the equation utterly discredits their entire hypothesis. Creation.com has a vast number of articles written by some of the greatest living scientists which fully support the creation account. Science truly does support and verify the six day creation account, including human life starting with just two people. Evolution absolutely does not.

Taking then everything written in the Bible as true and literal it becomes an amazing story of God's creation, the fall of humankind into sin and finally God's sacrifice of Jesus, paying the price for the sin of all people. Knowing the whole overarching Bible story helps us put each of the books and stories contained within it into context. It helps us understand how it all fits together and we get an amazing picture of God's love for people.

In the beginning God created the heavens and the earth. [1] In six days He created day and night (time), oceans and sky, land and plants, the sun, moon and stars, fish, birds and land animals. God created man, who is called Adam, in His image and likeness and gave him authority over everything on the earth. He bestowed extreme favour on man building him a helper and companion – woman, named Eve. He placed him in a special garden in Eden fashioned especially for him and God came and spoke with them regularly. Clearly God was delighted with Man and enjoyed spending time with His creation which He saw was very good. On the seventh day God rested.

One day the serpent tricked Eve into eating fruit from the tree of knowledge of good and evil. Desiring the same knowledge God had, she ate and shared the fruit with Adam. They instantly realised they had disobeyed God and tried to

Chapter 11
What is the Real Story?

hide from Him in the garden. Not wanting the man and woman to eat from the tree of life and therefore live forever in that state, God drove them out of the garden, sentencing Eve to pain during childbirth and Adam to work the ground for food. The special relationship Man had enjoyed with God had been destroyed through this one act of disobedience, no longer was Man able to delight in spending time with his Creator. Death and suffering was now entrenched in his life.

Adam and Eve then had two sons, Cain and Abel. Cain worked the ground and Abel was a keeper of sheep. Overcome with jealousy for his brother, Cain one day killed Abel in the field. Adam and Eve had another son, Seth, who also had children. As people populated the earth God saw that human hearts and thoughts were constantly filled with evil. God was sorry He had ever made humans. Only one man, Noah, pleased God.

God told Noah to build an Ark, because He was going to put an end to the sinful human race. Noah built the Ark as God commanded and filled it with a male and female of every kind of animal. God flooded the entire earth, and destroyed every living thing.

When the flood subsided God promised Noah that he would never again curse the ground because of humankind or destroy every living thing. He placed a rainbow in the clouds as a reminder to the human race of His promise.

The population grew, but the sinful desires of humans led them to build a tower to the heavens at Babel, attempting to establish their own glory, not that of God. God destroyed the tower and scattered the people and their languages over the earth.

Sometime after this God chose one man, Abraham, from whom would come an entire nation that would worship Him. He promised this nation a special land where they would live. It was to be from this nation that a saviour would come who would be a blessing to the people of the world.

Abraham was called at the age of 75 to go to the land of Canaan. Abraham and his wife Sarah had a son, Isaac, who in turn had two sons, Esau and Jacob. Jacob (also called Israel) had twelve sons whose families formed the twelve tribes of Israel. Jacob's favourite son, Joseph, was sold into slavery in Egypt by his jealous brothers.

After proving himself a faithful servant Joseph was put in charge over all of Egypt, second only to Pharaoh himself. He advised Pharaoh to store food in preparation for a coming famine. When the famine began Joseph's brothers came to Egypt to buy food. Joseph forgave his brothers and invited them to live with him in Egypt. Joseph realised his slavery, imprisonment and promotion were part of God's plan to settle his family in Egypt.

The Israelites grew in number and were in exile in Egypt for about 430 years. Fearing the growing power of the Israelites, a

Chapter 11
What is the Real Story?

new King of Egypt, who knew nothing of Joseph, decided to use the Israelites as slaves. God heard the cries of His people and chose one man, Moses, an unlikely candidate, to lead His beloved people to freedom and into the Promised Land.

After receiving God's instructions Moses asked Pharaoh to let the Israelites go, but Pharaoh denied the request. God then sent ten plagues into the land of Egypt to force Pharaoh to let the Israelites go, but after each plague Pharaoh remained stubborn. The final plague killed all firstborn children, except those of the Israelites who were instructed to put the blood of a lamb on their doors. Every door entrance that was protected by the blood was passed over by the destroying angel and the Israelite firstborn were saved from certain death.

After obtaining the Egyptian's silver, gold, jewellery and clothing (the Egyptians gave everything to them), the Israelites left Egypt, following God as a pillar of cloud during the day and a pillar of fire at night. By the time the Israelites came to the Red Sea Pharaoh had changed his mind and was pursuing them. God parted the Red Sea and the Israelites escaped. They came to Mount Sinai where God entered into a covenant with the people to be their God. Moses was given the Ten Commandments by God.

While at Mount Sinai God gave further instructions to Moses concerning sacrifices, offerings and worship, ceremonial cleanliness as well as feasts and holy days. God's desire was for His people to be holy. He required a response of submission and obedience from the people.

After a year had passed at Mount Sinai God led the Israelites to the edge of the Promised Land where they sent out spies. The spies reported that while the land was indeed flowing with milk and honey there were also significant adversaries present. The people complained against God, Moses and Aaron. God then sentenced the Israelites to years of wandering in the desert until that generation of unbelieving adults had died.

After 40 years in the desert Moses retold the story (of what had gone before) to the new generation of Israelites and reminded them of the commandments and requirements God had given them. Moses then went up Mount Nebo where God allowed him to see the Promised Land confirming to him that this was the land He had promised to give to Abraham. Moses died without entering the land.

God appointed Joshua to lead the Israelites into the Promised Land. When they entered the land God's 700 year old promise to Abraham was fulfilled. Jericho's walls collapsed before Joshua's army as they took possession of the land. The land was divided up among the twelve tribes. After the death of Joshua there was no formal leadership except for judges who were called from time to time by God, as the need arose. The judges had several functions: military leadership, spiritual leadership and as judge in case hearings and administering justice in Israel. However, during the 200 years Israel was governed by judges there was little law and order.

Chapter 11
What is the Real Story?

Samuel was the last judge; he brought peace and security to the nation of Israel. But the people rejected God as their ruler and began to want a king like the surrounding nations to provide military leadership and protect them from their enemy, the Philistines. God warned the people of the consequences of having such a king but granted the people their request. Saul became Israel's first king.

Saul did not follow God's commands and did not trust God. Because of this God rejected his kingship. One of Saul's amour-bearers, David, a man after God's heart, was chosen by God to be the next king. David was a great spiritual and political leader and wrote many of the Psalms. David unified Israel and won victories over all of Israel's traditional enemies: the Philistines, Edomites, Moabites, Ammonites and Syrians. He ruled over the entire Promised Land from the River of Egypt to the River Euphrates all the area that God had originally promised to Abraham. God was pleased with David and told him that he would never fail to have a descendant sit on his throne and that his kingdom would last forever.

After David his son Solomon became king of Israel. Solomon was a wise king who built the temple in Jerusalem and extended the wealth and boundaries of Israel to levels never before attained. To the Israelites it looked as though God's promises to Abraham were finally complete. But as Solomon grew old he gave way to pressure from his 1,000 foreign wives and concubines to build temples for their gods. Because of this God grew angry with Solomon and the peace and security Israel had experienced collapsed. When Solomon died Israel split into two countries: Israel in the North and Judah in the South.

Rehoboam, one of Solomon's sons, was appointed King over the entire nation, but lost Israel in a civil rebellion although he retained Judah. Israel was then led by Jeroboam.

Israel was by far the larger nation but was to exist for only 200 years. During this time God repeatedly sent prophets such as Hosea, Joel, Amos and Micah to warn the Israelites to turn back to Him, away from their unfaithfulness through idol worship and immorality. But all of Israel's 20 kings fell short in God's eyes and the nation was eventually destroyed by the Assyrians in 722 B.C.

Judah survived slightly longer than Israel: 350 years. During the first 50 years Judah was almost constantly at war with Israel. Of Judah's 19 kings and one queen, only eight did what was right in God's eyes. Many kings led Judah to worship other gods. God sent prophets such as Isaiah, Jeremiah, Habakkuk and Zephaniah to warn them to turn back to God. But continued unfaithfulness led to Judah coming under threat from Assyria. Unlike Israel, Judah with God's help fended off Assyria but later fell under Egyptian control until the Babylonians defeated the Egyptians at Carchemish in 605 B.C., thus becoming part of the Babylonian empire. In 597 B.C., Judah rebelled against Babylonian rule and was subsequently punished when King Nebuchadnezzar besieged Jerusalem. Judah's leading citizens were exiled to Babylon. After a second

Chapter 11
What is the Real Story?

rebellion in 586 B.C. the Babylonians burned Jerusalem and took more citizens into exile.

God's presence remained with the people of Judah who began calling themselves Jews. Ezekiel was sent by God to tell the Jews that God was still in control, even though Jerusalem was destroyed and they would be under Babylonian rule for a long time.

After Persia defeated Babylon in 539 B.C., King Cyrus of Persia sent the first wave of exiles back to Jerusalem in 538 B.C. They began rebuilding the temple which was completed, after many interruptions, in 516 B.C.

There was about 400 years between the last recorded events of the Old Testament and the coming of Jesus Christ in the New Testament. During this time Alexander the Great conquered the huge territory ranging from Greece in the West to Pakistan in the East, and in the process took control of the province of Judea, the home of the Jews.

After Alexander died in 323 B.C. the Greek empire split into two with Judea the buffer zone between them. The Jews suffered for this, first being ruled by the Ptolemies (from Egypt to the south) for 125 years, then the Seleucids (from Syria to the north) from 198 B.C. onwards.

One Seleucid king, Antiochus Epiphanies, invaded Judea and desecrated the Temple in 167 B.C. This was the last straw for the Jews who fought back and unexpectedly defeated the Seleucids and re-consecrated the Temple.

In 63 B.C. Roman general Pompey took control of Judea, assimilating it into the Roman Empire. Herod the Great was made King of Judea. It was under Herod's rule that Jesus Christ was born.

The Messiah God had promised through His prophet Isaiah was born to a Jewish couple named Mary and Joseph in the town of Bethlehem in about 3 B.C. Jesus was a direct descendant of David exactly as God had promised. Not much is chronicled about his childhood and early adult life.

At the age of about 30 He was baptized by John the Baptist and began His ministry by announcing that He was the fulfilment of the prophecy of the coming Messiah. He called twelve disciples to be His apostles and began teaching them about the Kingdom of God, and who will enter it. He travelled with His disciples throughout the land of Israel (particularly the Sea of Galilee) teaching people, healing the sick, challenging the religious establishment, demonstrating God's grace and mercy, and modelling an intimate relationship with God.

However, some Jewish religious leaders arrested Jesus for proclaiming He was the Son of God and for rejecting their ritualistic implementation of God's Law. Jesus was tried before Pilate and Herod and sentenced to death by crucifixion. He was crucified at Golgotha and His body taken to a nearby garden tomb.

Three days later He rose from the dead as He had promised. He appeared to the apostles and followers, and even ate with

Chapter 11
What is the Real Story?

them. He then ascended to heaven to be with God, His sacrifice a full atonement for the sins of all people, from Adam and Eve to the end of time. His death and resurrection established a new covenant of salvation by grace allowing a right relationship between God and Man to be fully restored.

Ten days after Jesus ascended to Heaven the Holy Spirit was given to the apostles exactly as Jesus had promised. The church began to grow rapidly and followers of Jesus became known as Christians. A Jewish Pharisee and Roman citizen named Saul was one of the leading persecutors of the early church.

One day as Saul approached Damascus, he encountered Jesus and was converted. His name changed to Paul. Paul was sent by God to preach the message of Jesus to the Gentiles (non-Jews), offering salvation and the forgiveness of sin through the death and resurrection of Jesus. The apostle Peter was tasked with preaching the message of Jesus to the Jewish people.

The church grew throughout Asia Minor, Greece, Macedonia and Cyprus as Paul and his companions travelled. Paul was eventually placed under house arrest. Although his fate is not mentioned in the Bible it is widely accepted that he was later executed by the Romans.

Before his death Paul wrote many letters to churches and individuals that make up much of the remainder of the New Testament. These letters describe how to live as a Christian by following the example of Christ.

The Bible concludes with a prophecy about the events that will lead to the return of Jesus in the book of Revelation. The entire Bible, from Abraham to Revelation covers a period of about 2,000 years.

Now that's a very simplified brief of the Bible and defines the principal facts and experiences. It generally leaves out the truth and teaching behind many of these events for the sake of simplicity. The underlying truth surrounding these happenings is somewhat less obvious at first glance.

In the beginning God created Man. He created him in His image and likeness with the desire to have a close relationship with him. Man failed in keeping God's one simple request and aligned himself with Satan who had attempted and failed to make himself like God. The relationship between God and Man was destroyed. Because of God's holiness it was not possible for Man to be redeemed back to God without the shedding of blood – death. This created an impossible paradox for Man; how could he relate to God and live? Romans 5:12, *"Therefore, just as through one man sin entered the world, and death through sin, and thus death spread to all men, because all sinned."*

God created a nation from the seed of Abraham and called them to be a holy nation before Him. Through Moses He demonstrated His awesome power through many mighty miracles so the people would understand and see his greatness. He gave them the law to live their lives by; a standard that would be acceptable to Him. He made allowances for their

Chapter 11
What is the Real Story?

fallen state to be cleansed from sinful acts through the sacrifice of animals. While this cleansed their personal wilful acts the blood of animals was never enough to cleanse man from the curse of the fall. This is clarified in the book of Hebrews 10:1-4 *"For the law, having a shadow of the good things to come, and not the very image of the things, can never with these same sacrifices, which they offer continually year by year, make those who approach perfect. For then would they not have ceased to be offered? For the worshipers, once purified, would have had no more consciousness of sins. But in those sacrifices there is a reminder of sins every year. For it is not possible that the blood of bulls and goats could take away sins."*

God allowed the Israelite nation to live under this law for hundreds of years. While there were many mighty men and women of God that lived during that period none of them obtained eternal life during their lifetime and they all eventually saw death – (the realisation of eternal life was of course released to them later through the blood of Jesus). Many Israelites, perhaps amounting into the millions, lived during the time of the law; however, not one single one of them was ever able to keep all of the law. Every person failed on at least some part of it. It wasn't that God set the bar incredibly high which made it difficult for man; no, it was because of man's ill-gotten desire to be like God, using their own knowledge of good and evil. Man lived on under the curse God pronounced on man at the Garden of Eden.

The only way man could be restored to complete and right standing with God was for someone who had never sinned to die for him. God in His incredible love for all mankind provided the answer. John 3:16, *"For God so loved the world that He gave His only begotten Son, that whoever believes in Him should not perish but have everlasting life."*

Jesus Christ, who is the bodily form of God, became a man and lived a perfect life right here on earth. He died and offered His very own blood to cleanse all those who came to believe in Him. Romans 8:1-4 *"There is therefore now no condemnation to those who are in Christ Jesus, who do not walk according to the flesh, but according to the Spirit. For the law of the Spirit of life in Christ Jesus has made me free from the law of sin and death. For what the law could not do in that it was weak through the flesh,* **God did by sending His own Son in the likeness of sinful flesh, on account of sin: He condemned sin in the flesh,** *that the righteous requirement of the law might be fulfilled in us who do not walk according to the flesh but according to the Spirit."* [Emphasis added]

What a wonderful loving God we have. First He unequivocally proved to man that regardless of what man did he wasn't the slightest bit capable of getting or keeping himself in right standing with God. Next He gave of himself, His own body in the form of man to cleanse our sin and make a way for all mankind to come back into a full relationship with him that would last for all eternity. How amazing!

Chapter 11
What is the Real Story?

So is this salvation provided by Jesus automatic? Absolutely not. God requires one thing only from us. Romans 10:9, *"that if you confess with your mouth the Lord Jesus and believe in your heart that God has raised Him from the dead, you will be saved."* All we're required to do is to believe in and submit to, Jesus Christ. No great acts or works to do to obtain salvation, just believe in our heart. The verse is very clear that by this simple action you will be saved. But saved from what? Romans 5:9 *"Much more then, having now been justified by His blood, we shall be saved from wrath through Him."*

Ok but what is God's wrath? Romans 2:5-9 *"But in accordance with your hardness and your impenitent heart you are treasuring up for yourself wrath in the day of wrath and revelation of the righteous judgment of God, who "will render to each one according to his deeds": eternal life to those who by patient continuance in doing good seek for glory, honor, and immortality;* **but to those who are self-seeking and do not obey the truth, but obey unrighteousness—indignation and wrath,** *tribulation and anguish* **on every soul of man who does evil,** *of the Jew first, and also of the Greek."* [Emphasis added]. This is how God's plans for the human race will end. Those who have accepted Jesus and persist with Jesus will go to eternal life and those that do not will be judged and subjected to the full wrath of God. Clearly that will not be pleasant. To avoid it is simple; accept Jesus Christ as your Lord and Saviour. Perhaps you have never actually done that and you're thinking right at this moment " don't like the sound of being punished by God especially when the alternative is not onerous." You're absolutely right. If that's you I would like you to stop for a moment a recite this little prayer, aloud so you will confess with your mouth.

"Dear Lord Jesus,

I admit that I am a sinner, in need of you and your forgiveness. I turn now from my sinful past and make you the Lord, the King, the Boss of my life. I believe in my heart and confess with my mouth that you are the Lord Jesus Christ and that you died on the cross in my stead for all my sins, you were buried and rose again to life. I thank you for the Father's gift of eternal life through faith and I believe in you alone. I surrender every part of my life to you Lord Jesus, forever and ever. Thank you for the gift of your Holy Spirit which I receive from you now."

God bless you if you've just genuinely prayed that prayer, you have received eternal life. You are guaranteed to be spared from God's judgement through Jesus. I recommend you find a church, if you don't already have one and read your Bible every day and talk to your Pastor about getting baptised. Praise the Lord!

When we come to Jesus in this way it's vital we literally surrender everything to Him. That is the meaning of making him Lord of your life. There is a modern trend in many church circles to teach that you need to invite Jesus into your life. On face value that seems absolutely correct as things certainly do go better with Jesus around. The problem is that inviting Jesus

Chapter 11
What is the Real Story?

into your life is not found anywhere in the Bible. Just the exhortation to "ask Jesus into your heart," if that's the whole message leaves out some very important aspects such as repentance and faith.

The Bible does mention the fact that, in some sense, Jesus resides in our hearts: Paul prayed in Ephesians 3:17 *"that Christ may dwell in your hearts through faith; that you, being rooted and grounded in love."* However this is written to believers who had already received salvation and it's not an evangelistic appeal. Paul is not telling the Ephesians to "ask Jesus into their hearts"; he is simply elevating their awareness that Jesus is present within them through the Holy Spirit.

The verse commonly quoted in this context is taken from Revelation 3:20, *"Behold, I stand at the door and knock. If anyone hears My voice and opens the door, I will come in to him and dine with him, and he with Me."* The passage does not deal with a person calling on the Lord for salvation and it doesn't mention the heart. In context, this verse is speaking to the church of Laodicea. This church had effectively excluded Jesus from their fellowship, and the Lord was seeking to restore that fellowship. The word is very clear about Jesus coming into collective situations Matthew 18:20 *"For where two or three are gathered together in My name, I am there in the midst of them."*

The gospel is the good news of Jesus' death and resurrection for the forgiveness of our sin it requires a proper response: to believe, receive and repent. We must change our minds about our sinful state and about who Christ is, believe that Jesus died and rose again, and receive the gift of eternal life by faith. None of the apostles ever told someone to "ask Jesus into your heart."

Simply asking Jesus to enter our lives without properly surrendering to His Lordship would be very limiting. Jesus is God and is currently with the Father. He resides in the heavenly realm outside of time and sees and does everything from that perspective. Inviting Jesus into your life is the same as asking Him to restrict His divine power to human standards within the confines of time. The proper and in fact only response we are required to give is total unconditional surrender to our Lord Jesus Christ. Doing that allows God the Father to open the floodgate of His favour which He bestows upon us. He sees us in the same reflection as His Son Jesus and we are made joint heirs with Christ.

When sharing the gospel we should be careful what we say and how we say it. Even the word "believe" can be misleading if it is presented as mere intellectual assent (agreeing that certain facts are true) instead of as trust (relying on those true facts). Salvation is not about believing a list of facts or even believing in God as we're told in James 2:19 *"You believe that there is one God. You do well. Even the demons believe—and tremble!"* Salvation is not about asking Jesus to come into your heart. Salvation is not even about asking God to forgive you, although that is a positive start. Salvation is about totally and

Chapter 11
What is the Real Story?

unconditionally trusting in Jesus as your Lord and Saviour, receiving the forgiveness He offers by grace through faith.

The other massive factor regarding salvation is that it's totally based on grace. Grace simply put, is unmerited favour – God giving us favour and good things that we do not deserve and could never possibly earn. Human nature teaches us there is no such thing as a free lunch – everything in life has a related cost somewhere. It's instinctive within us to work, or do something, to earn everything we have and to be weary of receiving something for nothing as there must be a catch. Because we live in a fallen world separated from God then this characteristic is favourable and helps us in our natural lives. In God's world it's a hindrance. Man inherently believes that he must do something to deserve eternal life from God. Perhaps if he does the right thing or enough good things during his lifetime then "hopefully" that will be enough for God to accept him into eternity. Rather risky way to live, me thinks! How would you ever know for sure?

The problem is that even the very best man can offer is actually putrid to God as we're wholly contaminated by the fallen world we reside in. It's explained clearly in the prophet Isaiah 64:6 *"But we are all like an unclean thing, and all our righteousnesses are like filthy rags; we all fade as a leaf, and our iniquities, like the wind, have taken us away."* I can't imagine God being very interested in dirty laundry (filthy rags), can you?

The only single thing we're asked to do, to receive salvation, is to surrender to the Lord Jesus Christ, nothing more nothing less. Do that and you have everything in God, don't do it and you have absolutely nothing. There goes that binary term again.

Every person alive, at least everyone I've ever met, loves getting free stuff. God delights in showering His children in Christ Jesus with gifts. He starts with eternal life Romans 6:23 *"For the wages of sin is death, but **the gift of God is eternal life in Christ Jesus our Lord.**"* [Emphasis added] Next comes the gift of the Holy Spirit, Acts 2:38 *"Then Peter said to them, "Repent, and let every one of you be baptized in the name of Jesus Christ for the remission of sins; and you shall receive **the gift of the Holy Spirit**."* [Emphasis added] Then there's the list of spiritual gifts that God gives which includes wisdom, knowledge, faith, healing, miracles, prophecy, discerning of spirits, speaking in tongues, and interpretation of tongues. See 1 Corinthians 12:8-10 for the full list.

Jesus goes even further when speaking in Matthew 7:11 *"If you then, being evil, know how to give good gifts to your children, how much more will your Father who is in heaven give good things to those who ask Him!"* Gifts that we ask Him for – truly His love knows no bounds! Do you start to get the picture of just how much God does love us? Nothing is too much for Him.

After reading that naturally the human mind says, "Anything? Ok I'll have that new wardrobe, that new house,

Chapter 11
What is the Real Story?

new car etc. etc." And then you might ask, "If this is true, why don't we see all Christians as the super-rich of this world?" Remember the starting point of God's gifting to us is total and unconditional surrender to our Lord Jesus Christ. Once we have done that our priorities change dramatically, things we've held as absolutely imperative suddenly fall way down the list. Jesus becomes our perspective not material things. That doesn't mean God may not provide those for his children but generally if he does it is because it will be used to further his work on this earth. With more gifting, becomes greater responsibility.

When discussing things that are precious to us here on earth I'm reminded of a story of the God-loving man who had been a gold trader all his life. He absolutely loved gold and declared that when he died he was taking at least one bar of fine gold with him to heaven to remind him of the enjoyment of his life's work. He lay on his death bed determinedly gripping a crumpled brown paper bag containing the most brilliant bar of fine gold from his life's collection.

He apparently arrived at heaven's pearly gates and was met by the Apostle Peter who quickly noticed the brown paper bag still clinging to his chest. "Wait a minute" Peter called, "you can't come in here with that." "Oh, please," begged the gold trader, "it's very precious to me and I really must have it with me as a reminder of my work." "Let me take a look," Peter answered, following which he walked over, opened the paper bag and looked inside. "Street paver" Peter exclaimed, "Why would you want to bring that in here, we've got millions already?

Revelation 21:21 *"The twelve gates were twelve pearls: each individual gate was of one pearl. And the street of the city was pure gold, like transparent glass."*

We touched on it above and many people ask; "What of all the millions of people that may have loved God but died long before Jesus lived, died and rose again? Does God exclude them from eternal life just because they were born too early?"

We're told in Revelation 13:8 *"All who dwell on the earth will worship him, whose names have not been written in the Book of **the Lamb slain from the foundation of the world**."* [Emphasis added]. The Lamb that was slain "from" the foundation (or creation) of the world! So how can that be, Jesus only died about 2,000 years ago and the creation was some 4,000 years before that?

John 3:16, *"For God so loved the world that He gave His only begotten Son, that whoever believes in Him should not perish but have everlasting life."* God's plan of redemption through Jesus was not His plan B; it wasn't some hastily devised scheme to bring man back into right standing with Him. No, it was always God's plan of love from the very outset. God "gave" His Son from the creation of the world. God lives outside of created time therefore the death of Jesus was a literal event to God before Adam had ever disobeyed Him. The cleansing power of the blood of Jesus is available to every person that has ever

Chapter 11
What is the Real Story?

lived even though the physical act of His death hadn't yet occurred. John 14:6, *"Jesus said to him, "I am the way, the truth, and the life. No one comes to the Father except through Me."* The only way to right standing with God is through Jesus. That applies to all mankind, right from the creation of the world. If it has not, then mighty men of the Old Testament who have spent a lifetime living for God could not have obtained eternal life. That would have been a rather cruel trick by a loving God. No, God's salvation plan covers them too. Men like Abraham, Moses, David and Daniel all knew that they will be raised to life in the last days. And the only way that could be possible was through Jesus. God's plan of redemption started from the creation of the world. Because of His view of time He knew at the outset the names and details of every person who accepted Jesus as their Lord and Saviour. That is when He wrote the Lambs' Book of Life.

The people of the Old Testament didn't fully comprehend God's salvation plan but they chose to follow Him anyway. Through that they obtained eternal life after Jesus died on the cross. For us, in our time, we are without excuse, we have God's full restoration plan completely revealed to us as plain as day. To be included in His restoration plan today we must accept Jesus Christ as our Lord and Savour before we die. Hebrews 9:27, *"And as it is appointed for men to die once, but after this the judgment."* Once we're dead it's too late, if we haven't accepted Jesus in our lifetime the only destination after death is to face God's judgement and wrath.

I'll make one final point. Don't you hate it when a pastor says that during his sermon? I've never heard a pastor yet who proclaims his final point but takes at least 20 minutes to cover it off! I promise you I'll explain this quickly. Why an Old testaments and a New Testament?

Firstly, what is a Testament? A testament, in this sense, is in effect a will; it sets out the will of the testator on how he wishes to have his property disposed of after his death.

So who died in the Old Testament? Adam did and the whole of the Old Testament deals with the aftermath and fallout from that. The Old Testament contains God's law given to man through Moses. The law was preparatory, temporary, and limited but did contain many promises of better to come. The Apostle Paul explains this well in Galatians 3:19-22 *"What purpose then does the law serve?* **It was added because of transgressions***, till the Seed should come to whom the promise was made; and it was appointed through angels by the hand of a mediator. Now a mediator does not mediate for one only, but God is one. Is the law then against the promises of God? Certainly not! For if there had been a law given which could have given life, truly righteousness would have been by the law. But the Scripture has confined all under sin, that the promise by faith in Jesus Christ might be given to those who believe."* [Emphasis added]

The New Testament is the will of Christ; its seal is the blood of Jesus. The testator of this will is Jesus, God's Son who fulfilled God's law from the Old Testament, to absolute

Chapter 11
What is the Real Story?

perfection. The inheritance is eternal life. The terms are faith and obedience. The period of probation is the Christian age which will end when Christ returns. The beneficiaries are all men who accept the terms and the executors of the will are the apostles. The New Testament is complete, eternal, and universal.

We continue with the Apostle Paul's words in Galatians 3:23-29 *"But before faith came, we were kept under guard by the law, kept for the faith which would afterward be revealed. Therefore the law was our tutor to bring us to Christ, that we might be justified by faith. But after faith has come, we are no longer under a tutor. For you are all sons of God through faith in Christ Jesus. For as many of you as were baptized into Christ have put on Christ. There is neither Jew nor Greek, there is neither slave nor free, there is neither male nor female; for you are all one in Christ Jesus. And if you are Christ's, then you are Abraham's seed, and heirs according to the promise."*

The two testaments are so closely related it can be said about them that the Old is the New concealed and the New is the Old revealed. [2]

Since the time of the cross, including in our age today, every one lives under the law of Christ rather than under the Law of Moses. Christ Jesus fulfilled the Old Covenant, the Law of Moses, nailed it to His cross and ended it there. Thus no portion of the Old Testament binds us today; even the 10 commandments have been replaced by better requirements. Jesus illustrates this during his Sermon on the Mount. Matthew

5:27-28 *"You have heard that it was said to those of old, 'You shall not commit adultery.' But I say to you that whoever looks at a woman to lust for her has already committed adultery with her in his heart. "* It's about the heart, not the law, and Jesus is the only way to obtain that kind of heart.

Chapter 12
Who is the God of the Bible?

"Honk your car horn, if you love Jesus
Text while driving, if you want to meet him"

Chapter 12
Who is the God of the Bible?

Many folks, rightly or wrongly, have built up a certain picture of God in their minds perhaps because of things they've heard or some impression gained through something they've experienced or read. It's surprising to learn that these "folks" are not just unbelievers; I've met many Christians whose impression of God was far from whom the Bible describes. Why? They have either never read their Bibles or if they have they simply have not believed what they read.

Man's continued belief that he is "like God" is the problem. It's not that perhaps some have such an elevated opinion of themselves that they believe they're a god. No, it's far more subtle; they bring God down to human terms. If we compare God to others we know, our natural fathers, friends or relatives, then that is enveloping God in human thinking. It immediately brings up trust, belief, confidence and abilities. The first key to this is belief.

We have previously mentioned how imperative it is to believe all that's written in the Bible. Remember the Bible starts with the phrase *"In the beginning God."* If we cannot accept He really does exists when we read the Bible we're never going to take seriously what it says about Him. Hebrews 11:6 *"But without faith it is impossible to please Him, for he who comes to God must believe that He is, and that He is a rewarder of those who diligently seek Him."* All that's needed is a simple step of faith. "Ok God I really do accept you exist."

In Mark we have the account of Jesus healing a young boy of an evil spirit Mark 9:22-24 *"And often he has thrown him both into the fire and into the water to destroy him. But **if you can do anything**, have compassion on us, and help us."* Jesus said to him, *"**If you can believe, all things are possible to him who believes.**" Immediately the father of the child cried out and said with tears, "**Lord I believe. Help my unbelief!**"* [Emphasis added] This is an interesting scripture because this man had come to Jesus to get his son healed but he only saw Jesus in human terms and actually questioned Jesus' ability by asking *"if you can do anything?"* A very low level of faith obviously but Jesus doesn't rebuke him He replies plainly in a surprised tone questioning the man's word and telling him the key is belief and finishes up with an infinite phase *"**all things** are possible to him who believes."* All things – no limits! The man quickly realised he was in the presence of an entity much greater than his human reasoning and instead of requesting Jesus again to heal his son the man asks Jesus to help him overcome his unbelief. Unbelief was the hindrance to this man, he had almost zero faith. Once his faith level was raised, by him understanding what was possible if only he believed, then Jesus was able to heal his son immediately.

Chapter 12
Who is the God of the Bible?

In the same way when we approach God believing in faith that He exists, that is the starting point for everything. Once we truly accept that God is almighty as opposed to something a bit above humans then that arouses immense curiosity. A God for example that can do exceeding abundantly above whatever I ask or think! Once you realise that's the true God of the Bible then our quest turns urgent and we begin to "earnestly seek him." The Hebrews 11 verse above tells us that God will reward us just for doing that – *"he is a rewarder of those who seek him."* If that is our starting point it paints an immediate positive picture of exactly who God is. Have faith and believe.

Trust is the next thing that stops us getting to know God fully. Again I've met Christians who do believe in Jesus as their Savour but are afraid to completely surrender their lives to Jesus. Their reasoning is that they're afraid God might do something awful to them, even as far as taking their life! Where they got such thinking from beats me but it's very real to them. Somehow they have this sadistic image of God who might gain pleasure from deliberate misfortune in their lives. This being the very same God who loved us so much that He gave His own Son to die in our stead to cleanse our sinful sate. 1 John 4:9 *"In this the love of God was manifested toward us, that God has sent His only begotten Son into the world, that we might live through Him."* The very same God, who bestows on us the free gift of eternal life, if we give our lives to Jesus and whom provides freely his Holy Spirit to dwell within us?

Fear is the demolisher of trust. Our natural selves tell us that because stuff has happened to us in the past that we must be very, very careful to maintain full control at all times. We're afraid if we lose control then that same thing will rear its ugly head again. 1 John 4:18 *"There is no fear in love; but perfect love casts out fear, because fear involves torment. But he who fears has not been made perfect in love."* God's love is perfect and continually shines upon us and never includes punishment. When we begin to comprehend just a little of exactly how much God really loves us then it becomes very easy to surrender completely and totally to Him.

The God of the Bible, our God and Father is truly remarkable. What are some of His attributes? Volumes could be written about each of these distinct characteristics of God but I'll give only a very brief description. [1]

Self-existent

God's self-existence means that He does not need us or the rest of creation for anything. While everything other than God depends on God for everything, God depends on no one for existence. He is absolute reality, with whom we have to reckon. Exodus 3:14 *"And God said to Moses, "I AM WHO I AM," and He said, "Thus you shall say to the children of Israel, 'I AM has sent me to you.'"*

Self-sufficient

"The Scriptures tells us that God does not need anything that we humans need to survive. He requires no water, air,

Chapter 12
Who is the God of the Bible?

food, sleep or money. He is self-sufficient in all capacities. Psalm 50:12-13 *"If I were hungry, I would not tell you; for the world is Mine, and all its fullness. Will I eat the flesh of bulls, or drink the blood of goats?"*

Eternal

God exists forever, meaning He has no beginning or end. He has always existed in the same way: fully and completely as God. Psalm 90:2 *"Before the mountains were brought forth, or ever You had formed the earth and the world, even from everlasting to everlasting, You are God."*

Infinite

God is not subject to any of the limitations of humanity or His creation. Psalm 147:5 *"Great is our Lord, and mighty in power. His understanding is infinite."*

Unchanging

Also called immutability, this means that God never changes in His being, who He is, or what He promises. Malachi 3:6 *"For I am the Lord, I do not change; therefore you are not consumed, O sons of Jacob."*

All-knowing - Omniscient

God knows all things. This includes the past, the present and the future. He knows what will happen and He knows what would or could happen. There was never a time when God did not know everything. Psalm 139:1-4 *"O Lord, You have searched me and known me. You know my sitting down and my rising up; You understand my thought afar off. You comprehend my path and my lying down, and are acquainted with all my ways. For there is not a word on my tongue, but behold, O Lord, You know it altogether."*

All-wise

God has all wisdom. He works everything out for the good of His people, and for the display and enjoyment of His glory. He never fails, never lacks any foresight, and never estimates. He knows all, and plans all, and He loves to display the glory and beauty of His wisdom by accomplishing the seemingly impossible. Romans 11:33, *"Oh, the depth of the riches both of the wisdom and knowledge of God! How unsearchable are His judgments and His ways past finding out!"*

All-powerful – Omnipotence

God has all power. He can exercise dominion over the entire universe, carry out the purposes of his wisdom, govern the hearts of men and even create things out of nothing. Psalm 65:6 *"Who established the mountains by His strength, being clothed with power;"*

Immaterial

God is not fundamentally composed of matter, for He is spirit, and He created all matter. This does not mean that God is absolutely nothing, ("immateriality" as a word can sometimes mean this) rather it means that God is nothing physical. John 4:23-24 *"But the hour is coming, and now is, when the true worshipers will worship the Father in spirit and truth; for the*

Chapter 12
Who is the God of the Bible?

Father is seeking such to worship Him. God is Spirit, and those who worship Him must worship in spirit and truth."

Everywhere-present – Omnipresence

God is everywhere. This does not mean that God's form is spread out so that parts of Him exist in every location. God is spirit; He has no physical form. He is present everywhere in that everything is immediately in His presence. At the same time He is present everywhere in the universe. No one can hide from Him and nothing escapes His notice. Psalm 139:7-10 *"Where can I go from Your Spirit? Or where can I flee from Your presence? If I ascend into heaven, You are there; if I make my bed in hell, behold, You are there. If I take the wings of the morning, and dwell in the uttermost parts of the sea, even there Your hand shall lead me, and Your right hand shall hold me."*

Impassable

God is not overwhelmed by any emotion, He is not incapacitated or weakened or stifled by any event or any amount of grief or love. Rather, God is totally self-controlled. While God does grieve, and does passionately love, He does so completely on purpose. Hebrews 2:18, *"For in that He Himself has suffered, being tempted, He is able to aid those who are tempted."*

Good

The goodness of God is one of the attributes of God as well as a description of His very essence. God, by nature, is inherently good. Psalm 34:8 *"Oh, taste and see that the Lord is good; blessed is the man who trusts in Him!"*

Just

God is deeply concerned with making wrongs right. He lets no sinner off the hook without a fitting punishment, or a fitting substitutionary atonement. Daniel 9:14 *"Therefore the Lord has kept the disaster in mind, and brought it upon us; for the Lord our God is righteous in all the works which He does, though we have not obeyed His voice."*

Merciful

God shows His mercy by not giving us the punishment we deserve. Mercy as used in the Bible frequently has a much wider sense which may be translated "loyal love". Psalm 86:15 *"But You, O Lord, are a God full of compassion, and gracious, longsuffering and abundant in mercy and truth."*

Gracious

God loves to give us what we don't deserve. He loves to pardon sin and lavish us with His goodness. He takes pleasure in giving gifts to people to display the glory of His resourcefulness, patience, and mercy. Hebrews 4:16 *"Let us therefore come boldly to the throne of grace, that we may obtain mercy and find grace to help in time of need."* Grace is unmerited favour.

Chapter 12
Who is the God of the Bible?

Love

God is concerned for His creatures, and especially His people. He is tender toward them, and does not take pleasure in their suffering or condemnation. He seeks the best for us, and He offered up His Son in love as a substitution for sin. 1 John 4:8 *"He who does not love does not know God, for God is love."*

Holy

To say that God is holy is to say that He is eternally separate and distinct from all impurity. The term holiness in Hebrew, qodesh, has the notion of separation, of uniqueness, of one-of-kindness as it were. Psalm 47:8 *"God reigns over the nations; God sits on His holy throne."*

Sovereign

The Sovereignty of God is the Biblical teaching that all things are under God's rule and control, and that nothing happens without His direction or permission. The sovereignty of God is not merely that God has the power and right to govern all things, but that He does so, always and without exception. Ephesians 1:11 *"In Him also we have obtained an inheritance, being predestined according to the purpose of Him who works all things according to the counsel of His will,"*

Jealous

The jealousy of God involves His protectiveness of His glory and for the faithfulness of His people. God's desire for glory drives His constant revelation of Himself in the lives of His people. He wants to be known, and recognized for who He is, so that He will receive the glory owed to Him. Exodus 34:14 *"for you shall worship no other god, for the Lord, whose name is Jealous, is a jealous God"*

Ok; so what about the Trinity? Critics are quick to point out that the actual word trinity is not used in the Bible and they're correct, nowhere does that word appear. God however clearly reveals Himself as a triune God: God the Father, God the Son, and Holy Spirit of God. Each person is called God, given worship as God, exists eternally, and is involved in doing things only God could do. God is one and cannot be divided. All are involved completely whenever one of the Three is active.

This concept to the human mind is very difficult to comprehend. God, however, gives us a big clue in the book of Genesis, on how to make sense of it. Genesis 1:26 *"Then God said, Let us make man **in Our image, according to Our likeness;** let them have dominion over the fish of the sea, over the birds of the air, and over the cattle, over all the earth and over every creeping thing that creeps on the earth."* [Emphasis added]. First of all who was God talking to? Let "us" make man! It wasn't the angels because we don't have the image and likeness of angels as they're described in the Bible. We know the Holy Spirit was there at creation as it says in Genesis 1:2 *"The earth was without form, and void; and darkness was on the face of the deep. **And the Spirit of God** was hovering over the face of the waters."* [Emphasis added] Jesus was also there

Chapter 12
Who is the God of the Bible?

as we're told in John 1:1-3 "*In the beginning was the Word, and the **Word was with God**, and the Word was God. **He was in the beginning with God.** All things were made through Him, and without Him nothing was made that was made.*" [Emphasis added]. So who was the Word, we're told in John 1:14 "*And the Word became flesh and dwelt among us, and we beheld His glory, the glory as of the **only begotten of the Father**, full of grace and truth.*" [Emphasis added]. The only Son of the Father is of course Jesus. So the Holy Spirit, Jesus and the Father were all present when God said "let us make man in our image and likeness." He was speaking to them.

God was talking about His very own image and His own likeness. God didn't say He was making man after His glory or power, no, He was very precise, His likeness and image – His triune being. Now that is an incredible thought, we're made just like God with a spirit, heart and body. This is confirmed in 1 Thessalonians 5:23 "*Now may the God of peace Himself sanctify you completely; and may **your whole spirit, soul, and body** be preserved blameless at the coming of our Lord Jesus Christ.*" [Emphasis added] Understanding who we are will clarify our understanding of our triune God. So what of our own triune state? We are a spirit being, we live in a body and we possess a soul.

Our Body

Our bodies are what we live in while we are here on earth. God formed Adam's body out of the dust of the earth Genesis 2:7 "*And the Lord God formed man of the dust of the ground,* and breathed into his nostrils the breath of life; and man became a living being." Man's body is not eternal as we're told in Psalm 104:29 *"You hide Your face, they are troubled; You take away their breath, they die and return to their dust."* These verses tell us that our body is only temporary and will have life for as long as God provides our breath. God provides the breath at the start and takes it away at the end. After that the body dies and returns to dust. It is provided to us as a temporary shell and the Apostle Peter refers to his body as a tent, 2 Peter 1:13-14 *"Yes, I think it is right, as long as I am in this tent, to stir you up by reminding you, knowing that shortly I must put off my tent, just as our Lord Jesus Christ showed me."*

Peter's description of our bodies being a tent begs the question of what's inside the tent. 1 Corinthians 3:16 *"Do you not know that you are the temple of God and that the Spirit of God dwells in you?"* Our bodies then are a temple and God's Spirit lives in there. This temple also contains our own spirit and our heart. Our body is simply a temporary container in which to hold these intangible items.

The body we currently have is not intended to last forever in our human state. However God has plans regarding believer's bodies, as the Apostle Paul writes in 1 Corinthians 15:42-49 *"So also is the resurrection of the dead. The body is sown in corruption, it is raised in incorruption. It is sown in dishonor, it is raised in glory. It is sown in weakness, it is raised in power. It is sown a natural body, it is raised a spiritual body. There is a natural body, and there is a spiritual body. And so it is*

Chapter 12
Who is the God of the Bible?

written, "The first man Adam became a living being." The last Adam became a life-giving spirit. However, the spiritual is not first, but the natural, and afterward the spiritual. The first man was of the earth, made of dust; the second Man is the Lord from heaven. As was the man of dust, so also are those who are made of dust; and as is the heavenly Man, so also are those who are heavenly. And as we have borne the image of the man of dust, we shall also bear the image of the heavenly Man."

At the time of the return of Jesus Christ we (believers) will all receive a new imperishable body, one that can never experience death, and is eternal. It will have all the characteristics of the heavenly man – that man is Jesus Christ. This is the culminating action of the redemptive work of Jesus in which we will become a physical new creation raised in power. This body will be perfect in every way and not capable of growing old, getting sick or being injured. In that body we'll live with God for ever. But these bodies are only for those who have surrendered their lives to Jesus before they died – those written in the Lamb's book of life. What of the unbelievers?

Sadly the Bible gives a very dark end for those not written in the Book of Life. The book of Revelation calls these ones "the dead". They will be brought before God and judged according to their works. It doesn't mention them getting any kind of body at this time, it seems it's just their souls and hearts which are eternal that stand before God at the great white throne and are judged. Revelation 20:11-15 *"Then I saw a great white throne and Him who sat on it, from whose face the earth and the heaven fled away. And there was found no place for them. And I saw the dead, small and great, standing before God, and books were opened. And another book was opened, which is the Book of Life. And the dead were judged according to their works, by the things which were written in the books. The sea gave up the dead who were in it, and Death and Hades delivered up the dead who were in them. And they were judged, each one according to his works. Then Death and Hades were cast into the lake of fire. This is the second death. And anyone not found written in the Book of Life was cast into the lake of fire."* What an absolutely ghastly way to end your days. The time to avoid that judgement is right now. This event is a real and literal event that will occur about 1,000 years after Jesus Christ returns to claim his saints.

All those written in the Lamb's book of life will already have been raised and received their heavenly bodies 1,000 years before this judgement so no believer will suffer this fate.

So let's recap about our bodies. The scriptures show it's a temporary tent which currently houses our soul and spirit. All born again Christians will however get a new heavenly body which is eternal and designed to last for ever.

Our Spirit and Soul

Most Christians are very clear on what their body is – one would hope! When it comes to our spirit and soul clarity dissipates quickly. Part of the reason is what's lost in translation to English from the original Hebrew or Greek in which the

Chapter 12
Who is the God of the Bible?

books were written. Let's take a look at the meanings of soul and spirit in these languages. [2]

- The word for "soul" in the Old Testament is nephesh. The meaning of nephesh's root word is "to breathe." Since those who are breathing still have "life," one of the meanings for nephesh is "life and it is used in this context 17 times in the Old Testament.

- In the New Testament the word for "soul" is psuche. Psuche is translated as life 47 times.

- The word for "spirit" in the Old Testament is either ruach or neshamah. Ruach is translated as breath 27 times and wind 94 times.

- The Greek word pnoe is used in the Septuagint (the Greek version of the Old Testament) for neshamah, but it is only used in the New Testament as in Acts 2:2 *"And suddenly there came a sound from heaven, as of a rushing mighty wind, and it filled the whole house where they were sitting."* here it is translated "wind," and in Acts 17:25 *"Nor is He worshiped with men's hands, as though He needed anything, since He gives to all life, breath, and all things."* here it is translated "breath."

- In the New Testament the word for "spirit" is pneuma. Pneuma is translated as Holy Ghost 90 times or Spirit (as in the Holy Spirit) 131 times. It is also translated as spirit (as in Man's spirit) 151 times.

The intent of the these scriptures is clear, our spirit is our life. When God created Adam, He gave him a physical body, but he was not considered "alive" until a spirit was put inside of him, referred to as the breath of life, which caused him to become a living being. Genesis 2:7 *"And the Lord God formed man of the dust of the ground, and breathed into his nostrils the breath of life; and man became a living being."*

For this reason Man is actually a spirit being living for now in a body, placed there by God. Man is a spirit being who has a soul and a body.

Our spirit very much belongs to God who gave it to us. When our body dies our spirit returns to God as we see in Ecclesiastes 12:7 *"Then the dust will return to the earth as it was, and the spirit will return to God who gave it."*

The soul while separate from our spirit is nevertheless intrinsically interconnected to it. The soul gives expression to our mind, will and emotions through feelings and empathy. This is clear when King David says in Psalm 6:3 *"My soul also is greatly troubled; but You, O Lord—how long?"* This describes the feelings and empathy as defined in Job 30:25, *"Have I not wept for him who was in trouble? Has not my soul grieved for the poor?"*

Again Man **is** a spirit being that **has** a soul and both of these are eternal. After physical death your spirit will continue to exist. When a person dies the body becomes motionless and quickly begins to decay, but the spirit doesn't skip a beat. It

Chapter 12
Who is the God of the Bible?

doesn't matter if you are good or evil – your spirit and soul will live eternally. The only question is where will your spirit and soul live?

Some people just don't care about their soul! Since they can't see it, it's easy to forget about or place little to no value on. Then death arrives, as it always does eventually, for every human being. Suddenly, people care about the soul and where it has gone!

Upon being born again the Christian's spirit becomes united and indissolubly linked to God's Spirit in an eternal bond. This linkage or union however does not automatically result in God-focused, God-honouring, God-pleasing behaviour on our part. Otherwise, Paul would not have had to say in Romans 8:16, *"The Spirit Himself bears witness with our spirit that we are children of God."* This linking of our spirit is a process as it requires us to completely surrender to the Holy Spirit and provide him with unlimited control over our hearts. He is a guardian of what God has placed in our heart 2 Timothy 1:14 *"That good thing which was committed to you, keep by the Holy Spirit who dwells in us."*

Our Soul – The Heart and Mind

Our soul contains parts with specific functions in the same way our body contains organ which have a set purpose. The heart and mind are the main components of the soul and these allow the function of will and emotions.

The "heart" describes man's true inner self. It encompasses such aspects as our desires, emotions, disposition, attitudes and capabilities. Heart (kardía in Greek) is mentioned over 800 times in Scripture, [2] but never referring to the literal physical pump that drives the blood, it is only used figuratively in both in the OT and NT.

Man's heart is the means by which he has self-consciousness; it is the medium between the spirit and the body. Who man is becomes manifests through his physical body in personality, vocation, and lifestyle as a result of;

- A heart response to what he has learned through his mind body, conscience, and emotions.
- Through what he has received from God via his spirit.
- As a result of those abilities and talents God has chosen to give him individually.

The "mind" is very much linked to the heart and encompasses aspects such as will, thoughts, motivations and goals. Man's mind is an appendage of the heart; it's his computer by which he stores information gained through his five senses – the body, spirit, soul, conscience, heart, and emotions. The mind is not the brain which is an organ or part of the body. When the body dies the brain is dead also. The heart and mind are eternal Ecclesiastes 3:11 *"He has made everything beautiful in its time.* ***Also He has put eternity in their hearts*** *except that no one can find out the work that God does from beginning to end."* [Emphasis added]

Chapter 12
Who is the God of the Bible?

The mind is the part of man which decides how he will respond to what he has learned through his spirit, soul and body, through the promptings of his conscience; and through his emotions. It is the volitional part of man, which animates the body.

Our heart is wicked in its natural state Genesis 8:21 *"And the Lord smelled a soothing aroma. Then the Lord said in His heart, "I will never again curse the ground for man's sake,* **although the imagination of man's heart is evil from his youth;** *nor will I again destroy every living thing as I have done."* [Emphasis added]. It contaminates our whole life and character and hence must be changed, regenerated, before a man can willingly obey God.

The process of salvation begins in the heart by the believing and the reception of the testimony of God, while the rejection of that testimony hardens the heart. Romans 10:10, *"For with the heart one believes unto righteousness, and with the mouth confession is made unto salvation."*

Once we believe that God's restoration begins immediately as we're told in Ezekiel 36:26; *"I will give you a new heart and put a new spirit within you; I will take the heart of stone out of your flesh and give you a heart of flesh."*

The heart is the centre not only of spiritual activity, but of all the operations of human life and is the home of the personal life, hence a man is designated, according to his heart. Matthew 12:34 *"Brood of vipers! How can you, being evil, speak* good things? For **out of the abundance of the heart, the mouth speaks.**" [Emphasis added]. Principally because of this we're told to guard our heart in Proverbs 4:23 *"Keep your heart with all diligence, for out of it spring the issues of life."* Our hearts are the source of what we speak!

Interestingly we're also told that our heart has eyes. Ephesians 1:18 *"The eyes of your understanding being enlightened; that you may know what is the hope of His calling, what are the riches of the glory of His inheritance in the saints."* We see things via our desires, emotions and attitudes independently of the physical eyes in our bodies.

From this understanding of what man is and since we're made in the likeness and image of God it becomes easier to understand the triune nature of God. The Lord our God is one God as Moses said in Deuteronomy 6:4 *"Hear, O Israel: The LORD is our God. The LORD is one."* All three facets of God work as one but each have their very own distinct characteristic and function. The following is the nature of our triune God;

- God the Father is the Soul with the will and emotions.
- Jesus is God in eternal bodily form.
- The Holy Spirit of God is the life and power.

All three are distinct but also each is fully interlinked and interdependent on each other. One considerable difference between God and Man is that God's Soul, Body and Spirit seems, to us, to function in physical separation from each other. This separation is only an apparent illusion because God

Chapter 12
Who is the God of the Bible?

is omnipresent and omnipotent. When Jesus walked on this earth as man, He was still in every way God, intrinsically connected to the Soul and Spirit of the Godhead. Let's take a closer look at the way God has revealed himself to us through His own Triune nature.

God's Body – Jesus Christ

Jesus is known to Christians as the Son of God and while this term is absolutely correct this does not mean, as some fringe Christian sects believe, that Jesus was created by God or that He was somehow inferior to God. The relationship between Jesus and God the Father is termed this way to allow our natural minds to better comprehend it. It's a straightforward term that easily allows understanding. Imagine if Jesus explained His true position in the Godhead to man at the outset of His ministry; He'd be written off by man as a lunatic. Jesus Himself did explain clearly who He was in His teaching in John 10:30 *"I and My Father are one."* Not much doubt left in that statement.

Jesus is referred to as the Son of Man and also the Son of God. Why, and what is the difference? Jesus the Son of God is His title in the Godhead, for want of a better term – as the bodily form of God. In the Old Testament Jesus physically reveals Himself in various forms; mostly these are termed as the Angel of the Lord. He appeared to many in this way such as Gideon, Manoah the father of Samson and David at the threshing floor of Araunah the Jebusite. The Lord appeared in bodily form to Abraham Genesis 18:1-2 **"Then the LORD**

appeared to him by the terebinth trees of Mamre, as he was sitting in the tent door in the heat of the day. 2So he lifted his eyes and looked, and **behold, three men were standing by him;** and when he saw them, he ran from the tent door to meet them, and bowed himself to the ground." [Emphasis added].

We're not told who the other two were in this verse but later the Lord stays behind and the other two go on to destroy Sodom, Genesis 18:22 *"Then the men turned away from there and went toward Sodom, but Abraham still stood before the Lord."* This verse names the Person who was standing talking with Abraham the LORD who is sometimes translated Yahweh. Yahweh is the Hebrew name that the children of Israel always used to refer to God. This person talking with Abraham here is God in bodily form. Man can't see Spirit or Heart but clearly Abraham could see Yahweh and talked with Him just as he would talk or react with any other man. This bodily revelation of God is Jesus Son of God. There are numerous other references to the Lord appearing to various people throughout the Old Testament.

Jesus as the Son of Man refers to Jesus taking on the form of created man. He became man born of a virgin named Mary. Mary was not God, she was just the vessel God used to bring Jesus into the world. The beatification and worshipping of Mary was never part of God's plan. Mary is just another woman of God albeit for a very important purpose. Nowhere in scripture does it ever suggest we should deify her.

Chapter 12
Who is the God of the Bible?

The way Mary became pregnant is described in Luke. Firstly God sent an angel to give her the news she would give birth to the Son of God. Luke 1:26-27 *"Now in the sixth month the angel Gabriel was sent by God to a city of Galilee named Nazareth, to a virgin betrothed to a man whose name was Joseph, of the house of David. The virgin's name was Mary."* This was an angel named Gabriel and is not the same Angel of the Lord described in the Old Testament. This angel describes exactly how the Child would come about within her, Luke 1 34-35 *"Then Mary said to the angel, "How can this be, since I do not know a man?" And the angel answered and said to her,* **"The Holy Spirit will come upon you, and the power of the Highest will overshadow you;** *therefore also the Holy One who is to be born will be called the Son of God."* [Emphasis added]. Definitely wasn't a natural conception, was it? This is how Jesus Son of God became a man, Son of Man. Colossians 1:15 *"He is the image of the invisible God, the firstborn over all creation."*

The form of the Son of Man allowed Jesus to come to earth and live as any other created person on this earth, He had all the feelings and nature of all other men except He lived a perfect life. Being born the way Luke describes it means he wasn't born of Adam's DNA and therefore wasn't born under the curse. He was born perfect and lived perfect as a man. Mark 1:11 *"Then a voice came from heaven, "You are My beloved Son, in whom I am well pleased."* This statement from God the Father is the same as what He said when He looked back after He had finished creating everything on the sixth day and saw perfection in His work, Genesis 1:31 *"Then God saw* everything that He had made, and indeed **it was very good**. So the evening and the morning were the sixth day." [Emphasis added].

Taking on this form as Son of Man allowed Jesus to suffer and to die. God cannot die and it would have been difficult for Jesus to die if He simply came among us as Son of God. As Son of Man Jesus experienced everything we undergo in our lives living in the fallen world and in that way He knows and understands everything we go thorough in our daily walk. He has complete empathy with us and for that reason we can talk to Him about anything, knowing He's fully sympathetic.

Jesus as Son of God is the physical body of God. He was the physical creator and the one who literally formed Adam out of the dust of the earth and breathed into him the breath of life. Colossians 1:15-17 *"He is the image of the invisible God, the firstborn over all creation.* **For by Him all things were created that are in heaven and that are on earth, visible and invisible, whether thrones or dominions or principalities or powers.** *All things were created through Him and for Him. And He is before all things, and in Him all things consist."* [Emphasis added].

God the Holy Spirit

The Holy Spirit is God's life force. He's God's power, breath and fire. He also encompasses God's feelings in the same was our soul does. This is first described in Genesis 1:2 *"The earth was without form, and void; and darkness was on the face of the deep.* **And the Spirit of God was hovering over the face of**

Chapter 12
Who is the God of the Bible?

the waters." [Emphasis added]. God's Spirit was feeling the emptiness and darkness of the formless earth, almost as if He was urging God the Father to do something about it.

The Holy Spirit is referenced many times in the Old Testament as the Spirit of the Lord or the Spirit of God. The Spirit of the Lord came upon various individuals endowing them with great power to prophesy, speak with authority or to carry out great exploits acting on the word of God. His actions are described well in Isaiah 11:2 *"The Spirit of the Lord shall rest upon Him, the Spirit of wisdom and understanding, the Spirit of counsel and might, the Spirit of knowledge and of the fear of the Lord."*

In the New Testament the Holy Spirit is poured out on every one of those who believed. He was promised by Jesus in John 14:26 *"But the Helper, the Holy Spirit, whom the Father will send in My name, He will teach you all things, and bring to your remembrance all things that I said to you."* John also leaves little doubt of who the Holy Spirit is and where He comes from John 15:26 *"But when the Helper comes, whom I shall send to you from the Father,* ***the Spirit of truth, who proceeds from the Father****, He will testify of me."* [Emphasis added] It is clear this is God's very own Spirit being spoken about here.

The Holy Spirit is given to every single believer; this is made clear on His initial arrival in Acts 2:1-4 *"When the Day of Pentecost had fully come, they were all with one accord in one place. And suddenly there came a sound from heaven, as of a rushing mighty wind, and it filled the whole house where they* were sitting. Then there appeared to them divided tongues, as of fire, **and one sat upon each of them. And they were all filled with the Holy Spirit** and began to speak with other tongues, as the Spirit gave them utterance." [Emphasis added] God's Holy Spirit is still here and lives within each and every Christian who truly calls Jesus Christ their Lord and Saviour.

God the Father

This term Father for God is only used in the New Testament. It describes for us in human terms the relationship that Jesus Son of Man had and also what all believers in Jesus can have. It evokes feelings of nearness, nurturing, protection and upbringing. This Father relationship is bestowed on us as described in Galatians 4:4-6 *"But when the fullness of the time had come, God sent forth His Son, born of a woman, born under the law, to redeem those who were under the law, that we might receive the adoption as sons. And because you are sons, God has sent forth the Spirit of His Son into your hearts, crying out, "Abba, Father!"* Here we are called sons of the Father and also that we can call him Abba. This word Abba is of Aramaic origin but commonly used in Hebrew. The context of its use is as a term of tender endearment by a beloved child – i.e. in an affectionate, dependent relationship with our father similar to "papa" or "daddy." These terms represent the restored relationship God originally planned for Adam before the fall. Today because of the work of our Lord Jesus Christ this relationship with God the Father is fully restored and each of us

Chapter 12
Who is the God of the Bible?

who are born again can approach the Father childlike, without any fear, confident in His overwhelming love for us.

So what are the true characteristics of The Heart and Mind of God? This following are some of the things the Bible tells us of God's Soul.

- God is Wise and Great; 1 Corinthians 1:25 *"Because the foolishness of God is wiser than men, and the weakness of God is stronger than men."*

- Love; 1 John 4:16 *"And we have known and believed the love that God has for us.* **God is love**, *and he who abides in love abides in God, and God in him."* [Emphasis added].

- God's ways are Holy; Psalm 77:13 *"O God, your ways are holy. Is there any god as mighty as you?"* (NLT)

- God is avenging and jealous; Nahum 1:2 *"God is jealous, and the Lord avenges; the Lord avenges and is furious. The Lord will take vengeance on His adversaries, and He reserves wrath for His enemies."*

- God is light; 1 John 1:5 *"This is the message which we have heard from Him and declare to you, that God is light and in Him is no darkness at all."*

- God's form is spirit; John 4:24 *"God is Spirit, and those who worship Him must worship in spirit and truth."*

- God is invisible; John 6:46 *"Not that anyone has seen the Father, except He who is from God; He has seen the Father."*

The list of God's heart attributes are endless, however it's clear from this short account that God the Father's inherent nature is the function of a Heart and Mind. They pronunciate God's desires, emotions, disposition, attitudes and capabilities together with His mind being His will, thoughts, motivations and goals.

The Bible speaks about knowing God John 17:3 *"And this is eternal life, that they may know You, the only true God, and Jesus Christ whom You have sent."* This word "know" is interesting in this context and is translated from the Hebrew word yā-da'-tî. [2] Yā-da, 'the root word of yā-da'-tî, in Hebrew, and is usually translated as knew. This word knew Yā-da' (knew) is the same word that in Hebrew describes how a man intimately knows his wife. While it can be used to describe a man making love to his wife it certainly has no sexual connotations. It infers total intimate knowledge of a person – where there are no barriers, no secrets, nothing hidden. It also assumes this knowing is achieved not through learned knowledge but through personal experience over a period of time. The knowing is also a mutual affair where both sides of the relationship fully comprehended, by experience, a comprehensive understanding of the other person.

I suspect it's going to take eternity to truly know our God in this context, however, it is also possible right now to really

Chapter 12
Who is the God of the Bible?

know God - a relationship that is developed through spending time with God in prayer, reading His word and just simply talking with Him. Of course a born-again Christian also has the Holy Spirit dwelling in them providing the means to foster this knowing relationship. The way the relationship is watered for growth is by reading of the word – the Bible, Ephesians 5:25-27 *"Husbands, love your wives, just as Christ also loved the church and gave Himself for her, that He might sanctify and cleanse her with **the washing of water by the word**, that He might present her to Himself a glorious church, not having spot or wrinkle or any such thing, but that she should be holy and without blemish."* [Emphasis added] It's interesting that the Apostle Paul in this verse uses the relationship of a man and his wife to demonstrate the cleansing result of letting God's word wash over us on a constant basis. It is that deep personal relationship with Jesus the Son of God that will result and is what God is so longing for.

So, finally what of this phrase we hear so much of today that all religions worship the same God.

The Bible gives us a very simple method to determine if this phrase is true, 1 John 4:1-3 *"Beloved, do not believe every spirit, but test the spirits, whether they are of God; because many false prophets have gone out into the world. By this you know the Spirit of God: **Every spirit that confesses that Jesus Christ has come in the flesh is of God,** and every spirit that does not confess that Jesus Christ has come in the flesh is not of God. And this is the spirit of the Antichrist, which you have heard was* *coming, and is now already in the world."* How many of these so called "other religions" confess Jesus Christ has come in the flesh? A couple I know of do acknowledge Jesus has come in the flesh but they do not confess that Jesus is the Christ, the Messiah, the anointed one of God.

Allah and God the Father are very definitely not the same God. For a start Allah is a standalone character whereas our God is Triune – The Father, the Son and the Holy Spirit.

Jesus said in John 14:6 *"Jesus said to him, "I am the way, the truth, and the life. No one comes to the Father, except through me."* No one comes to the Father except through Jesus Christ. Nobody – period!

There is no other way of salvation and eternal life. Good works or religious behaviours towards God will not do it either.

Chapter 13
Relevance Today

"I'm standing on a sea of pure gold, clear as glass, the opulence and grandeur extreme yet by no means overwhelming The walls of the city, impenetrable, the gates – what splendour! And those names inscribed above them. The foundations adorned with precious stones, each one magnificently differing from the other. The width and height of the majestic metropolis, awe-inspiring. A brilliant radiance of such a vivid white, though not blinding to the eyes, envelops the atmosphere.

I looked around enthralled at the vast multitude of people of every imaginable tongue and nation assembled for the feast. Across the crowd I see King David, there, further over, is Moses chatting with the Apostle Paul. I spot Noah recounting his ark testimony; oh look there's Luke the physician enjoying an amusing conversation with Stephen the martyr. Over to the side I catch a glimpse of my grandfather looking young and stately and incredibly there's my cousin standing beside him – he did make it here.

The conversations and laughter saturate my ears; the joy and delight provide a spectacular ambience unlike anything I had ever experienced – truly an absolute paradise of contentment. Suddenly a hush came across the gathering, a resplendent trumpet sounded and a majestic exclamation went out "behold the King of kings and the Lord of lords – the Lamb that was slain and now lives." The Glory of His presence completely encompassed the multitude, as all eyes focused upon Him and instantaneously a myriad of exquisite voices sang in unison "Hallelujah, hallelujah, glory to Jesus, Jesus." Over and over the praises reverberated throughout the imposing court.

Every heart resonated in harmony, the sensation within utterly indescribable: an exceedingly abundant and complete realisation of peace, joy and love simultaneously encompassing and welling out from each one collectively. Our eternity had begun – I am Home!"

That mouth-watering account I've pictured is the end game. That is the reason for the relevance of the Bible. Through the Word of God in the Bible we are shown clearly how to obtain eternal life and how to live a God honouring life during our remaining years on this earth. That is simply what the Bible is all about; it's not difficult for us. What the Father has laid up for those who have cleansed their hearts through the blood of Jesus by the power of the Holy Spirit is nothing short of spectacular – the half has not yet been told us.

The alternative to Heaven is outright ghastly and if truly considered no person in their right mind would ever want to spend one second there, let alone eternity. The absolute reality is that unless you have been cleansed by the blood of Jesus that

Chapter 13
Relevance Today

is exactly where you're certain to end up. Again the answer to our eternal destiny is binary – it's either Heaven or Hell.

Hell is not a popular subject and you don't hear it spoken of much, in most churches today. The reason is that unfortunately in the past there was much sermonising on the subject to the point that the fear took over and many believers became terrified that even the slightest mistake might send them there, regardless that they were already covered by the blood of Jesus. The blood of Jesus cleanses us from the curse and creates in us a new creation. Yes we can turn back to a life of sin and despise the gift of eternal life, but generally that is a deliberate, wilful act and not a momentary lapse. If a believer in Jesus falls into some sinful act then the Bible tells us that person can be restored. 1 John 2:1 *"My little children, these things I write to you, so that you may not sin. And if anyone sins, we have an Advocate with the Father, Jesus Christ the righteous."*

Regrettably the pendulum has swung too far the other way to the extent that we now hear some preachers telling us that Hell is really just a merciful death after the final judgement. Let me assure you the Bible describes Hell very clearly and it is not a merciful place.

Some ask why a tender loving God would create such a terrible place of eternal damnation for his created beings. The answer is He didn't create it for man. Jesus talked about this in Matthew 25:41 *"Then He will also say to those on the left hand, 'Depart from Me, you cursed, into the everlasting fire **prepared***

for the devil and his angels;" [Emphasis added] It was prepared for the devil and his angels, not for man. However all those that remain aligned with the devil – Satan – that have not surrendered to our Lord Jesus Christ will be dispatched to this eternal fire. God gave man a choice; do you want to live with me in Heaven or do you want to go into the eternal fire of Hell? We have a choice and the Bible clearly tells us how to receive eternal life. Now that is relevant.

So what about this merciful death in Hell that some claim is true? We get that answered in Revelation 14:11 *"And the smoke of their torment ascends forever and ever;* **and they have no rest day and night***, who worship the beast and his image, and whoever receives the mark of his name."* [Emphasis added] Later in the same book were told of the fate of Satan and his devils which further describes Hell and the Lake of Fire. Revelation 20:10 *"The devil, who deceived them, was cast into the lake of fire and brimstone where the beast and the false prophet are.* **And they will be tormented day and night forever and ever.***"* [Emphasis added]. The chapter continues Revelation 20:15 *"And anyone not found written in the Book of Life was cast into the lake of fire."* This is not a pretty place and everyone there is still very much alive. Eternity is a very, very long time to be tormented day and night. Why would anyone in their right mind ever choose to go there? Every single person on this earth has a choice to make before it's too late. Choose life!

Chapter 13
Relevance Today

For those who accept Jesus as their Lord and Saviour the future is so incredible. The amazing thing is that even though we won't experience Heaven fully until we're physically in the presence of Jesus in our glorified bodies, we can experience a remarkable walk with God in the meantime. The way to fully enjoy this great relationship now is to become sanctified. I know, *"sanctified"*; that's a word not much used in every language these days but it certainly means a lot in God's world.

The word sanctification is related to the word saint; both words have to do with holiness. [1] To "sanctify" something is to set it apart for special use; to "sanctify" a person is to make him holy.

Jesus had a lot to say about sanctification in John 17:16-19 *"They are not of the world, just as I am not of the world. Sanctify them by Your truth. Your word is truth. As You sent Me into the world, I also have sent them into the world. And for their sakes I sanctify Myself, that they also may be sanctified by the truth."* This tells us that sanctification relates to the word – the word of God in the Bible.

In Christian theology sanctification is a state of separation unto God; all believers enter into this state when they are born of God: 1 Corinthians 1:30 *"But of Him you are in Christ Jesus, who became for us wisdom from God—and righteousness and sanctification and redemption."* The sanctification mentioned in this verse is a once-for-ever separation of believers unto God. It is a work God performs, an intricate part of our salvation and our connection with Christ Theologians sometimes refer to this state of holiness before God as "positional" sanctification; it is the same as justification.

While we are positionally holy, "set free from every sin" by the blood of Christ, we know that we still sin. (Acts 13:39, *"and by Him everyone who believes is justified from all things from which you could not be justified by the law of Moses."*) That's why the Bible also refers to sanctification as a practical experience of our separation unto God. "Progressive" sanctification, as it is sometimes called, is the effect of obedience to the Word of God in one's life. It is the same as growing in the Lord or spiritual maturity, 2 Peter 3:18 *"but grow in the grace and knowledge of our Lord and Savior Jesus Christ. To Him be the glory both now and forever. Amen."* This type of sanctification is to be pursued by the believer earnestly Hebrews 12:14-15 *"Pursue peace with all people, and holiness, without which no one will see the Lord: 15looking carefully lest anyone fall short of the grace of God; lest any root of bitterness springing up cause trouble, and by this many become defiled."* As we saw in John 17:17 above this progressive growth in sanctification is given effect by the application of the Word of God. Little by little, every day, those who are being sanctified or "made holy" are becoming more like Christ. Hebrews 10:14, *"For by one offering He has perfected forever **those who are being sanctified**."* [Emphasis added]

There is a further sense in which the word sanctification is used in Scripture – a "complete" or "ultimate" sanctification. This is the same as glorification. Paul prays in 1 Thessalonians

Chapter 13
Relevance Today

5:23, *"Now may the God of peace Himself sanctify you completely; and may your whole spirit, soul, and body be preserved blameless at the coming of our Lord Jesus Christ."* When Christ returns we will also appear with Him in glory and be like Him, 1 John 3:2 *"Beloved, now we are children of God; and it has not yet been revealed what we shall be, but we know that when He is revealed, we shall be like Him, for we shall see Him as He is."* Our sanctification is made complete when we receive our glorified bodies at Christ's return.

What these verses make clear is that sanctification – our personal progressive growth in holiness – is directly related to us reading and understanding the word of God; yet further relevance for habitually reading the Bible.

So what is it that God sees in us while we're working through this progressive sanctification? Does He see us as some sort of half-baked work in progress, while hopeful of a successful outcome? Thankfully that is far from the truth. We all literally still live in an evil fallen world influenced by Satan. We were all very much a part of it but when we repent and turn to Jesus Christ the power of the world is broken over us and we're called out to become separate. 2 Corinthians 6:15, *"And what accord has Christ with Belial? Or what part has a believer with an unbeliever?"* 2 Corinthians 6:17 *"Therefore come out from among them and be separate, says the Lord. Do not touch what is unclean, and I will receive you."* This verse is actually a call to the unbeliever, come out, remove yourself from those about to perish. This does not mean we isolate ourselves in special collective communities. No, this separating is a removal from unclean environments, no longer taking pleasure from things which entangled us in our old life.

When we act upon this call and surrender our lives completely to Jesus Christ, making Him Lord of our life, then some remarkable things happen. He, Jesus, becomes our sanctification, righteousness and redemption, 1 Corinthians 1:30 *"But of Him you are in Christ Jesus, who became for us wisdom from God—and righteousness and sanctification and redemption."* We become cloaked in Christ, Galatians 3:27 *"For as many of you as were baptized into Christ have put on Christ."* Once we are fully immersed (baptised) in Christ Jesus this verse tells us that we have put on Christ – as in putting on new clothes. There may still be mountains of work progressively maturing underneath but our outward appearance is Jesus and that is what God sees when He looks upon us. He no longer sees our old self but a reflection of His beloved Son. It's not just our outward appearance, we also take on his fragrance, 2 Corinthians 2:15 ***"For we are to God the fragrance of Christ*** *among those who are being saved and among those who are perishing."* [Emphasis added]. When the Father looks upon one of His adopted sons He is explicitly delighted in what He see and smells, it must bring Him such joy.

In fact the transformation within us through redemption in Jesus is astounding. What literally occurs at that moment is not apparent for all to see but the effect soon becomes obvious to

Chapter 13
Relevance Today

the recipient. This conversion affects our spirit heart and body dramatically and it truly is being born again.

First the Father endows us with power by giving us His Holy Spirit who comes to live within each believer. Ephesians 1:13-14 *"In Him you also trusted, after you heard the word of truth, the gospel of your salvation; in whom also, having believed,* **you were sealed with the Holy Spirit of promise,** *who is the guarantee of our inheritance until the redemption of the purchased possession, to the praise of His glory."* [Emphasis added]. This Holy Spirit is God's own Spirit and not only is the Spirit a promise of our eternal future He enlightens us greatly. 1 Corinthians 2:12-13 *"Now we have received, not the spirit of the world, but the Spirit who is from God, that we might know the things that have been freely given to us by God. These things we also speak, not in words which man's wisdom teaches but which the Holy Spirit teaches, comparing spiritual things with spiritual."* The Holy Spirit – a gift from the Father - teaches us how to live for God and reveals to us all the things that the Father has freely given us.

We discussed previously that our heart is eternal. To go through into eternal life after being polluted by this filthy world the heart requires cleansing. We're told how this occurs in Ezekiel 36:26 *"I will give you a new heart and put a new spirit within you; I will take the heart of stone out of your flesh and give you a heart of flesh."* The Father removes our old stony heart and gives us a new soft malleable heart, something that can accept development. He then goes further in Hebrews

10:16 *"This is the covenant that I will make with them after those days, says the Lord: I will put My laws into their hearts, and in their minds I will write them."* The Lord actually places His laws in our hearts and writes them on our minds. We become fully equipped and have total recall of all God's laws. Notice these are God's laws, not the laws given to man such as the Ten Commandments. These laws delineate the basis on which God operates, what evokes His love, passion, anger. In reality God is imparting his DNA to us at that point as the base to establish our Christian walk. Incredible!

We have already mentioned that we've *"put on Christ, like putting on new clothes"* (Galatians 3:27 (NLT)). For this reason when God looks upon us He doesn't see our old selves but He see a clear image of his Son Jesus.

So let's put this all together. First we're gifted the Holy Spirit — God's own Spirit — to dwell in us permanently. Second God takes away our old stony heart and gives us a brand new one pre-coded with His DNA (laws). We're then shrouded in Christ Jesus as a covering of our dying bodies. What else is left? The transformation of salvation is truly a rebirth and is very rightly named "born again."

Considering the complete redemption that takes place when we're born again we are therefore totally without excuse when it comes to living for God. We are fully armed and equipped from that moment on to live for God. Naturally we have little experience in how to use all this newly acquired equipment within us and that's where sanctification comes in.

Chapter 13
Relevance Today

We read the Word, spend time talking with God in prayer and praise and allowing the Holy Spirit free reign within us. That is how we grow, that is how we mature in Christ. It's not difficult; we have all the tools necessary, we just have to use them.

So what about my mind, I hear you ask? What mechanism has the Father provided us with to control that? In a way the mind becomes the battleground over the things that our old natural self wants to repeat and what will develop us in God. The first thing to comprehend is that our mind is not our brain. Thoughts feelings and ideas first spring from our mind, which if you remember is a part of our heart. These impulses can result from external forces, our environment or what is already retained in our hearts. They can be wonderful, developmental or evil and downright deadly. The question is what to do with them.

Our brain is the centre where any thought or idea, originating in the mind, is processed. The brain's function is to turn that thought into action. This action could be physical or it could be emotional. For instance, if my mind tells my brain to go over and greet someone, the brain effortlessly provides all the necessary processing to allow that to happen. If perhaps while I'm talking with that person they say something that offends me, again the brain is the place where that offence is turned into action in whatever form that may take.

The brain is not at fault if, say, we respond with an angry outburst, no more than your hand is at fault if you lash out and hit someone. It's not the part of the body that did wrong it's the mind that allowed the thought of anger to mature enough to send a violent reaction command to your brain to carry out. I appreciate this is a very simplified description of the process but it's the concept I'm demonstrating here. Your brain will only react on input, so guarding the input is absolutely paramount.

The Holy Spirit is the filter between our minds and brains. He is the one whom we use to guard our hearts, 1 Corinthians 2:14-16 *"But the natural man does not receive the things of the Spirit of God, for they are foolishness to him; nor can he know them, because they are spiritually discerned.* **But he who is spiritual judges all things,** *yet he himself is rightly judged by no one. For "who has known the mind of the Lord that he may instruct Him?" But we have the mind of Christ."* [Emphasis added] "One who is spiritual" is one who is controlled by or more correctly, relinquishes control to the Holy Spirit. Using the Holy Spirit in this way will allow us to filter everything going to the brain. The result will be that we have the mind of Christ.

This process is not easy; some thoughts are very deep rooted in our minds and need to be dealt with drastically. The apostle Paul calls it warfare in need of special weapons in 2 Corinthians 10:4-5 *"For the weapons of our warfare are not carnal but mighty in God for pulling down strongholds, casting down arguments and every high thing that exalts itself against the knowledge of God, bringing every thought into captivity to the obedience of Christ."* The very important point in this verse is that we don't fight this battle on our own, our weapons are

Chapter 13
Relevance Today

supernatural using divine power. It's not a retraining exercise, this is a demolition job.

We're told in Romans 12:2 *"And do not be conformed to this world, but be transformed by the renewing of your mind, that you may prove what is that good and acceptable and perfect will of God."* This renewing mentioned here is anakainósis in the original Greek. The meaning of anakainósis suggests a renewing as a process rather like a renovation. A renovation requires first the complete stripping back of all that is old to provide a solid base on which to build the new. Once these renovations are underway we begin to perceive the reality of God and His true nature is allowed to be revealed. This nature of God cannot be obtained through understanding or knowledge. It operates outside that and is part of God's law which He wrote on our minds when He placed them in our hearts as we saw in the verse above from Hebrews 10:16.

Once we begin to let these things operate in us then we allow God's full protection to come upon us and God provides us with His virus catcher, to coin a computer phase. Philippians 4:7 *"And the peace of God, which surpasses all understanding, will guard your hearts and minds through Christ Jesus."* The final result of this renovation is perfection – the mind of Christ.

Again, as we touched on above, this purification and sanctification is an on-going process while we're still in these earthly bodies. Ephesians 5:26 *"that He might sanctify and cleanse her with the washing of water by the word."* This confirms that there is a washing process going on. This washing is through the Word – the reading of the Bible. When you read the Word, especially when reading several chapters at one sitting it's impossible for most of us to retain everything we read. My guess would be a retention rate of about 10%. [2] But this washing effect is fascinating as it causes all the surplus word that has washed over us seemingly un-retained, (the other 90%) to be soaked up somewhere. Many times in my own personal experience, when faced with a certain situation, a scripture I had read and long forgotten unexpectedly pops into my mind. Amazingly when that happens the verse that springs to mind is so very apt for the situation at hand. Of course we shouldn't be surprised at this because we're told that this is part of the work of the Holy Spirit within us, John 14:26 *"But the Helper, the Holy Spirit, whom the Father will send in My name, He will teach you all things, and bring to your remembrance all things that I said to you."* The significant fact is that this washing of the Word begins with a deliberate action on our part to read the word. God has given us His Word through the scripture and he does expect, or even require, us to read it.

The premise for this book is to look at the truth and relevance of the Bible today. We considered what truth is, demonstrating the Bible is factual and not fiction or the people in it, characters in a fairy tale. The evidence is astounding and given the incredible amount of fulfilled prophecy it behoves us to look very closely at what is yet to be fulfilled in our age. We saw that the writing of the books was by eyewitnesses confirming what they saw and, remarkably, despite so many

Chapter 13
Relevance Today

different authors it contains no conflicting accounts. We came to an understanding of what knowledge is and its place in our hearts, together with the underlying story the combined books of the Bible tell. We discussed God's amazing redemptive plan through Jesus Christ and who God is, how He is expressed in three persons, the Father, the Son and the Holy Spirit. Finally here we're discussing relevance – will the Bible enable me today to get to know God better and live for Him now?

From the outset God gave us free will. The pleasure of being selected is of no comparison to forced acceptance. I lay before you the evidence and say – you choose. Days before the Children were to cross the Jordon to take possession of the land, we read in Joshua 24:15 *"And if it seems evil to you to serve the Lord, choose for yourselves this day whom you will serve, whether the gods which your fathers served that were on the other side of the River, or the gods of the Amorites, in whose land you dwell. But as for me and my house, we will serve the Lord."* Who are you going to believe; evolutionist man or a God who cannot lie? Peter put it well when many of Jesus' disciples found His words hard to take in John 6:68 *"But Simon Peter answered Him, "Lord, to whom shall we go? You have the words of eternal life."* That is the end game; it's not about having a fantastic life on this earth during our few years here, it's about all those billions of years yet to be experienced living with God in eternity. That's not to say we don't enjoy life now. Of course we can but we must always remember our time here is very short when compared to eternity.

It makes no difference if you're a brand new Christian or have been serving Him for a lifetime; His Word enshrined in the Bible is the cornerstone to understanding God the Father, the Son and the Holy Spirit. Every word in the Bible is absolute truth and you can stake your life on it – literally. Moses says of God's word in Deuteronomy 11:18-20 *"Therefore you shall lay up these words of mine in your heart and in your soul, and bind them as a sign on your hand, and they shall be as frontlets between your eyes. You shall teach them to your children, speaking of them when you sit in your house, when you walk by the way, when you lie down, and when you rise up. And you shall write them on the doorposts of your house and on your gates."* Now that's serious attention. The only way the Word can be fixed in our hearts and minds is if they enter there through our eyes or ears.

Choose you today these words of eternal life! Jesus said in, John 14:6 *"I am the way, the truth, and the life. No one comes to the Father, except through me."* There absolutely is no other way.

> *"Heaven is for everyone but you must RSVP."*

Chapter 14
How to Read It

We're told in Psalm 119:105 *"Your word is a lamp to my feet, and a light to my path."* God's word allows movement, direction and light. Conversely, therefore, without God's Word we're stumbling around in the dark with no idea where we're going or why. Obviously physically reading the word of God is very important. However it is an enormous book containing about three quarters of a million words – how do I go about reading it?

Understanding the Bible can be daunting, especially to someone not able to read well but also for to those with excellent reading skills. First up, you have to have a reason to study it and that reason should not be just because we're told to – although if that's all you have, do it anyway.

Psalm 119 is a very long Psalm but it's filled with copious descriptions for the desire and hunger for God's Word. Here's a sample; Psalm 119:9-16

"How can a young man cleanse his way?
By taking heed according to Your word.

With my whole heart I have sought You;
Oh, let me not wander from Your commandments!
Your word I have hidden in my heart,
That I might not sin against You.
Blessed are You, O Lord!
Teach me Your statutes.
With my lips I have declared
All the judgments of Your mouth.
I have rejoiced in the way of Your testimonies,
As much as in all riches.
I will meditate on Your precepts,
And contemplate Your ways.
I will delight myself in Your statutes;
I will not forget Your word.

What wonderful oratory and expressions of passion for the Word of God. Living for God begins with seeking Him with all our heart – a deliberate act. The main excuse I hear from those I speak with about reading their Bibles is that they would love too, but they just don't have time. Life is too busy. Seems strange though that these same people always find time to grab a cup of coffee or eat some food every day. What is your priority?

We'll never develop a reading pattern without making a conscious step to do so. When I was young my parents, "encouraged" by their religious church leaders, forced me to read my Bible every day in the evening before I went to sleep. I had to go to my room, say my prayers then read a chapter of my Bible, then I could relax in sleep. I absolutely hated it. To a

Chapter 14
How to Read It

young nine year old with poorly practised reading skills a single chapter seemingly went on for a hundred pages. Many a tearful evening was spent and more than once a completion lie was spoken. However as time went on things changed; the chapters miraculously became much shorter and the task morphed into a necessary ritual to complete before finding peaceful sleep. Sleep would certainly be deprived if I didn't read my Bible chapter, or so I believed. Unfortunately it was only an empty ruse, yes I was being obedient and reading my allotted chapter each night but I gained very little from my reading. I had no delight in the Word and nor was I seeking it with all my heart.

Looking back on that time in my life it certainly was hard but today I thank my parents so much for doing that as it formed a habit. Yes, for many years it was just a ritual but eventually I learned of the person of the Holy Spirit and I asked Him to give me understanding. My view of God turned from obscure black and white to vibrant clear colour. My Bible reading, no longer a chore, became a delight like delving into a box of exciting new treasures every day. My Bible reading went from a modest one chapter a day to multiple chapters each morning and night and often a few sneak Word studies in-between.

The Holy Spirit is the key to understanding. There is little point in reading your Bible just for the sake of reading it, as then it's just information. Information stored is subject to human interpretation and that's dangerous ground. Your natural mind is very clever and will readily twist God's Word to suit any situation. So-called church leaders in the past have used isolated verses of scripture, generally out of context, to justify all sorts of religious piety. God's word is not for private interpretation. The Apostle Paul makes it clear where our understanding comes from when he was writing in Colossians 1:9 *"For this reason we also, since the day we heard it, do not cease to pray for you, and to ask that you may be **filled with the knowledge of his will** in all wisdom and spiritual understanding; that you may walk worthy of the Lord, fully pleasing Him, **being fruitful in every good work and increasing in the knowledge of God.**"* [Emphasis added]. We do the reading; the Holy Spirit gives the understanding and thereby we grow and bear fruit. Each one individually has a responsibility to read God's Word as that develops our personal relationship with God and that's how I learn, to know who God is and how I can relate to Him.

If you have children it's imperative to set them an example. Let them see from a young age you reading your Bible so it becomes a common everyday event and not just used to add reverence at say Christmas or Easter. Perhaps during meal times or family moments have mini Bible studies, constantly portraying the Bible in positive terms. Waiting until they're teenagers to encourage them to read is difficult. It starts much earlier. Reading aloud to them even before they acquire the skills to read is great. I recall my Mother reciting verses from the Gospels about the miracles that Jesus performed. Those seeds matured during my teenage years allowing me to more fully comprehend that Jesus truly was the Son of God.

Chapter 14
How to Read It

Have the Word of God as a central point in our families and treat it not as something extra special. Use is as an ordinary way to learn about our wonderful Lord and Saviour. This will instil a curiosity about God, into our children, which will later develop to seeking and eventually hunger. The most important impartation any parent can give their child is a hunger for seeking the Lord and an understanding of where to feed that hunger.

Genesis 2:7 *"And the Lord God formed man of the dust of the ground, and breathed into his nostrils the breath of life; and man became a living being."* The direct breath of God into man brought about real life – Man became a living soul or being, as other translations term it. The breath of God is life. The scriptures also say in 2 Timothy 3:16 *"All Scripture is given by inspiration of God, and is profitable for doctrine, for reproof, for correction, for instruction in righteousness."* So, let's take these two verses together in context. God breathed into natural man Adam and it sparked life within him and he became a living soul. In the same way every Scripture is God breathed – the very breath of God. Imagine the life that will result as we inhale these God-breathed scriptures. A mighty unstoppable fire will erupt within you, fuelled by every word of God leaping from the pages as you read or listen. The result will be an infectious, contagious life bubbling up within you, maturing your understanding of God as you daily experience walking with Him.

If we surrender our lives to Jesus and live out our days for Him but without reading a single verse of the Bible we are definitely saved and will end up in Heaven but our life will be devoid of so much understanding and enjoyment. When negative things happen – and they will – how do we cope, what do we do? Lacking understanding of what God says in His Word dramatically limits our ability to fight off these attacks. The Apostle Paul tells us in Ephesians 6:17 *"And take the helmet of salvation, and the sword of the Spirit, which is the word of God."* The word of God is the sword of the Spirit. You can do a lot of damage to your negative circumstances by wielding this very powerful weapon.

There are simply so many reasons to read our Bibles frequently and thoroughly. In Revelation it tells us there is a blessing for reading it aloud and taking it into our heart, Revelation 1:3 *"Blessed is he who reads and those who hear the words of this prophecy, and keep those things which are written in it; for the time is near."* I believe this verse is specifically referring to the book of Revelation but it can also be taken to mean the whole Bible. The fact is there is a blessing and the method of obtaining it is far from arduous.

So how do you read a book containing over 700,000 words? Someone once plainly answered that by saying; "By starting with the first word and continuing!" [1] Yes, but not quite what I was meaning. What reading plan is best?

There are numerous Bible reading plans available for free. Google "Bible reading Plans" and you'll find a huge array of

Chapter 14
How to Read It

different ones to suit your current Christian development, age or reading goal. Many provide a plan to read your Bible in one year and, while this is noble, it's not imperative to read your whole Bible every year. That said, it certainly is an excellent goal. There are other guides which follow particular subjects and they can be helpful if you're going through specific events in your life. Reading all the books in the Bible is very useful, as how else will you discover the hidden gems in the Old Testament prophets or the encouragement found in a colourful Psalm? In addition to web-based plans most Christian book shops carry a reasonable range of hard copy plans which some find easier to complete.

Personally I have a simpler method. I divide the number of pages in my Bible, which is 1218, by 365, the number of days in the year. This tells me that if I read only three and a third pages every day of the year I will easily read it through in a year. It's not difficult in those terms, as that's only one and a third pages over breakfast in the morning and another couple in bed at night before sleep. I find I often read much more than my allotted 3 pages to such an extent that I've read right through it more than twice in a year.

In addition to daily reading of the scripture, which is the starting point, is Bible study. This can be done collectively, individually or both. Usually a specific subject is selected and you search the scriptures to see all that it says about that subject, actually much like we've done in many parts of this book. This is very useful as it allows you to more clearly understand what God says specifically about something particular you're going through in your life or just have a curiosity about. I personally love doing these as I find it absolutely amazing the detail and clarity on such a vast assortment of subjects that the Bible expounds upon from a Godly perspective. In our electronic age today searching for a particular phase of subject in the Bible has become stress-free. Websites such as www.biblehub.com is an excellent resource. This site, in additional to search, provides parallel comparisons to several translations and access to the original Greek and Hebrew wording which provides greater understanding of various translated words from their native source. Not only does it have various word studies it also has Bible resources for free download and a number of good reading plans. There are a number of such Bible resource sites but I personally find Biblehub one of the better ones.

Another important reason to search your Bible is to make sure what you hear or are told is actually the Word of God. How do you know, for instance, that the Pastor at your Church is actually telling you the truth? Thank the Lord that very few Pastors fall into the untruthful category but it does happen. When it does it's rarely blatant but very subtle – the thin edge of the wedge, to coin a phrase. Pastors and teachers are men and women just like the rest of us. Most are very able orators and conveyors of God's Word and have a particular calling and gifting on their lives. Apart from that they are all exactly the same as the rest of us, growing in their experience, knowledge and understanding of God on a daily basis. They can get it

Chapter 14
How to Read It

wrong. I recall my own personal experience of the occasional occurrence of parishioners approaching me after I'd spoken from the pulpt to explain things to me more exactly, which I greatly appreciated. Sometimes they were not accurate in their loving correction and the base I always used as the foundation to settle any difference is what the Bible says. Any other basis simply becomes a difference of opinion and the one whom is the best debater usually wins. With God Word as the foundation there is no room for private opinions.

You would think that someone like the Apostle Paul could be relied on if he happened to drop by your Church one Sunday. I think I probably would tend to agree with everything he said, but not the Christian Jews in Berean as we read in Acts 17:11 *"And the people of Berea were more open-minded than those in Thessalonica, and they listened eagerly to Paul's message. They searched the Scriptures day after day to see if Paul and Silas were teaching the truth."* (NLT) They had no hesitation in checking up on the Apostle Paul and we also should all check our Pastor's words. Not as religious police but to personally ensure everything we're told conforms to scripture. If it doesn't then plainly it is not of God. Again Paul tells us in Galatians 1:8 *"But even though we, or an angel from heaven, should preach to you any "good news" other than that which we preached to you, let him be cursed."*

It's abundantly clear that only God's Word is acceptable, regardless of where it comes from. Even if an angel from Heaven comes with a message that differs from the Bible the word of the Bible has precedence. It is the ultimate and it cannot be broken or changed. It behoves us to completely accept and understand it. Read it every day ask the Holy Spirit to give you understanding, it's unequivocally essential for your walk and growth with God.

Most importantly every single word in the Bible is true. It is God's Word and it's impossible for God to lie. From The first word in Genesis to the last word in Revelation not one thing is false. You can, and must, stake your very life on it. Read it, read it, read it and gain life.

About the Author

Robert (Bob) Cottle has been a scholar of the Bible for over 60 years having read, studied and analyzed God's word extensively during his lifetime. The discipline of reading his Bible was instilled in him at an early age. At first, this was a burdensome chore but later it developed into a perfunctory habit. As the years progressed, however, the habit matured into a pleasurable pastime exploring the detail of the God he loves and serves.

Bob has been actively involved in church life from a young age and served as a lay preacher for several years and also as a church elder for a time.

Married for 40 years Bob and his wife Julie live in Nelson, New Zealand and have three adult children and three grandchildren — to date. In his secular life Bob trained and worked in professional engineering then later in senior business management but is now retired from full-time employment and enjoys writing Christian books.

Blessed with a natural aptitude to portray verbal and/or written word pictures. In retirement Bob has focused his abundant free time to the study and understanding of God's Word in the Bible which combined with his previous writing skills has enabled him to develop and author his interesting books.

Bob has five books commercially published, and he is confident with the subject matter particularly given his extensive knowledge of the Bible. His desire is to pass on a little of this understanding for the aid of other fellow Christians for the furtherance of God's work.

Feel free to follow or contact Robert (Bob) on;

- Robert J Cottle Author,
- @bobcottle,
- robertjcottle@gmail.com

Notes:

Introduction – What is it about the Bible?

1. Bible Statistics – 2016 Statistic Brain Research Institute, publishing as Statistic Brain. Date research was conducted: August 28, 2016
   http://www.statisticbrain.com/bibles-printed/

2. Extract from the print edition of The Economist "The battle of the books" Dec 19th 2007 WASHINGTON, DC
   http://www.economist.com/node/10311317 .

3. Extract from "Why The Bible Is The True Best Seller" June 24, 2012 by Ennis P.
   http://nowthinkaboutit.com/2012/06/why-the-bible-is-the-true-best-seller/

4. Extract from the Ponce Foundation "Christians Don't Read Their Bible" 1999.
   http://poncefoundation.com/project/christians-dont-read-their-bible/

5. Extract from LifeWay Research study on Transformational Discipleship 2016
   http://www.lifeway.com/Article/research-survey-bible-engagement-churchgoers

6. Quoted from article at LightSource.com,
   http://www.lightsource.com/devotionals/live-it/so-

many-christians-have-no-idea-how-to-read-the-bible-do-you-11739007.html

7. Extract from Gallup Poll – Three in Four in U.S. Still See the Bible as Word of God June 4, 2014 http://www.gallup.com/poll/170834/three-four-bible-word-god.aspx

8. The State of American Theology Study 2016 - American views on Christian theology from Nashville-based LifeWay Research http://lifewayresearch.com/wp-content/uploads/2016/09/Ligonier-State-of-American-Theology-2016-Final-Report.pdf

9. Extract from posting by John Macarthur, CP guest contributor June 9, 2014 Christian Post http://www.christianpost.com/news/recent-gallup-poll-on-americans-view-of-bible-reveals-utter-chaos-regarding-nature-and-authority-of-scripture-121204/

Chapter 1 - Truth

1. Simple Definition of truth. Source: Merriam-Webster's Learner's Dictionary

2. From the Jewish Virtual Library – Joseph Goebbels: On the "Big Lie" www.jewishvirtuallibrary.org/jsource/Holocaust/goebbelslie.html

Notes:

3. From Wikipedia, the free encyclopaedia "Big Lie:" Holocaust, Jeffrey Herf
   https://en.wikipedia.org/wiki/Big_lie

4. Anonymous, November 2013 - http://philosophy.stackexchange.com/questions/8053/what-is-the-difference-between-fact-and-truth

5. NPNF1-02. St. Augustine's City of God and Christian Doctrine Chapter 9. — Whether we are to Believe in the Antipodes. Page 315.

6. Extract from Farhana Qazi article 72 Virgins in Heaven: Fact or Fiction? February 2015
   http://farhanaqazi.com/72-virgins-in-heaven-fact-or-fiction/

Chapter 2 – Fact or Fiction

1. Simple Definition of fact. Source: Merriam-Webster Dictionary.

2. Clear Evidence, Truth Versus Fact Blog, July 2006
   http://clearevidence.blogspot.co.nz/2006/07/truth-versus-fact.html

3. Creation Ministries International – Catastrophic plate tectonics: the geophysical context of the Genesis Flood

4. by John Baumgardner, April 2002
   http://creation.com/catastrophic-plate-tectonics-the-geophysical-context-of-the-genesis-flood

5. Free Google Images - https://www.google.co.nz/search?q=fossilised+fish+eating+another+fish&tbm=isch&tbo=u&source=univ&sa=X&ved=0ahUKEwiC6t62nYvQAhUEGJQKHR_LACAQ7AkIJw&biw=1493&bih=791&dpr=1.13

6. No 24 WA21946, The Babylonian Chronicles, The British Museum – From Wikipedia, Nebuchadnezzar Chronicle, Siege of Jerusalem https://en.wikipedia.org/wiki/Nebuchadnezzar_Chronicle

7. Awesome Stories – Daiva Inscription - Xerxes Celebrates His Victories, https://www.awesomestories.com/asset/view/Daiva-Inscription-Xerxes-Celebrates-His-Victories

8. Extract from Bible Believer's Archaeology - Volume 3: Behold the Man! By John Argubright Pages 93 – 94.

9. From Wikipedia - Tomb of Daniel Susa, Iran https://en.wikipedia.org/wiki/Tomb_of_Daniel

10. From Wikipedia - Pilate stone https://en.wikipedia.org/wiki/Pilate_stone

11. From Wikipedia – Josephus https://en.wikipedia.org/wiki/Josephus

12. Extract from Flavius Josephus: Antiquities of the Jews, Book 18, Chapter 3, 3

Notes:

> https://en.wikipedia.org/wiki/Josephus_on_Jesus#Testimonium_Flavianum

13. Extract from Flavius Josephus: Antiquities of the Jews Book 20, Chapter 9
    https://en.wikipedia.org/wiki/Josephus_on_Jesus

14. The Annals of Tacitus published in Vol. V of the Loeb Classical Library edition of Tacitus, 1937 chapter 44.
    http://penelope.uchicago.edu/Thayer/e/roman/texts/tacitus/annals/15b*.html

15. Pliny, Letters 10.96-97 Pliny to the Emperor Trajan
    http://faculty.georgetown.edu/jod/texts/pliny.html

16. Pliny, Letters 10.96-97 Trajan to Pliny
    http://faculty.georgetown.edu/jod/texts/pliny.html

17. The Monster of Cameroon and Gabon by Genesis Park
    http://www.genesispark.com/exhibits/evidence/cryptozoological/apatosaurs/cameroon/

18. Dragons of the Deep by Carl Wieland, chapter on Sarcosuchus. – Creation Ministries International
    http://creation.com/was-leviathan-a-parasaurolophus

Chapter 3 – Fairy Tales

1. Free Google Images
   https://www.google.co.nz/search?q=evolutionary+ascent+of+man+icon&biw=1493&bih=791&tbm=isch&tbo=u&source=univ&sa=X&ved=0ahUKEwjZ2NTU24vQAhXGk

5QKHQNEDV8QsAQIGA&dpr=1.13#imgrc=1GjjDMAoM4XFyM%3A

2. Simple Definition of miracle. Source: Merriam-Webster Dictionary.

Chapter 4 - Evidence

1. Israel Antiquities Authority – The Leon Levy Dead Sea Scrolls Digital Library, Discovery and Publication http://iaa-dss.appspot.com/learn-about-the-scrolls/discovery-and-publication?locale=en_US
2. Israel Antiquities Authority – The Leon Levy Dead Sea Scrolls Digital Library, Scrolls Content http://iaa-dss.appspot.com/learn-about-the-scrolls/scrolls-content
3. From Wikipedia - Shrine of the Book https://en.wikipedia.org/wiki/Shrine_of_the_Book
4. The chart was adapted from three sources: 1) Christian Apologetics, by Norman Geisler, 1976, p. 307; 2) the article "Archaeology and History attest to the Reliability of the Bible," by Richard M. Fales, Ph.D., in The Evidence Bible, Compiled by Ray Comfort, Bridge-Logos Publishers, Gainesville, FL, 2001, p. 163; and 3) A Ready Defence, by Josh McDowell, 1993, p. 45.
5. Defending Your Faith: Reliable Answers for a New Generation of Seekers and Sceptics by Dan Story, P 42 & 43.

Notes:

6. Don't check your brains at the door" by Josh McDowell and Bob Hostetler p39.

7. Adapted from Faith Facts Archaeological and External Evidence for the Bible: An Outline - Archaeology and the Old Testament http://www.faithfacts.org/search-for-truth/maps/archaeological-and-external-evidence

8. Adapted from Faith Facts Archaeological and External Evidence for the Bible: An Outline - Archaeology and the New Testament http://www.faithfacts.org/search-for-truth/maps/archaeological-and-external-evidence

9. Adapted from "The RZIM Zacharias Trust" – Why trust the Bible? The External Test http://www.rzim.eu/why-trust-the-bible

10. Millar Burrows, What Mean These Stones? New York: Meridian Books, 1956, p.1.

Chapter 5 – Prophecy

1. Extract from Fulfilled Prophecy: Evidence for the Reliability of the Bible, by Dr. Hugh Ross, 2003. Reasons to Believe Ministries. http://www.reasons.org/articles/articles/fulfilled-prophecy-evidence-for-the-reliability-of-the-bible

2. Based on information from article titled Daniel 11: The Most Detailed Prophecy in the Bible by David Treybig at Church of God, a Worldwide Association, Inc. website.

http://lifehopeandtruth.com/prophecy/understanding-the-book-of-daniel/daniel-11/

3. Information derived from Prophecies of Jesus Fulfilled table of 44 Prophecies of the Messiah Fulfilled in Jesus Christ at About Religion & Spirituality website. http://christianity.about.com/od/biblefactsandlists/a/Prophecies-Jesus.htm

4. Extract from article "What are the odds surrounding Jesus Christ? Who was this child really?" At ChristianAnswers.Net. http://www.christiananswers.net/q-aiia/jesus-odds.html

5. Based on information from article titled 10 Prophecies Fulfilled in 1948 at Watchman Bible Study website http://watchmanbiblestudy.com/articles/1948ProphesiesFulfilled.html.

6. Extract from Israel's rebirth in 1948 foretold by Ezekiel by Grant Jeffrey - JeffBIBLE-EzekVision2.pdf, The Third Captivity (Worldwide) – 2520 years. http://www.grantjeffrey.com/pdf/JeffBIBLE-EzekVision2.pdf

Chapter 6 – History in the Bible

1. http://www.thefreedictionary.com/predestined

Notes:

2. From Wikipedia, Predestination in Calvinism,
   https://en.wikipedia.org/wiki/Predestination_in_Calvinism
3. From Wikipedia, Predestination
   https://en.wikipedia.org/wiki/Predestination
4. Rev. A. B. Simpson writings on The Days of Heaven - August 1, Page 220.
5. Lead on Purpose by Daniel Blakeslee P11.
6. Merriam-Webster on-line dictionary
   http://www.merriam-webster.com/dictionary/history
7. From 37 Common English Sayings (From the Bible) by Kevin Halloran 2012. At Unlocking the Bible.
   http://unlockingthebible.org/common-english-sayings-bible/

Chapter 7 – Writing of the Bible

1. Extract from The Invention of Writing, by Joshua J. Mark 28 April 2011, on the Ancient History Encyclopaedia
   http://www.ancient.eu/writing/
2. Wieland, C., Living for 900 years, Creation 20(4):10–13, 1998; www.creation.com/living-for-900-years
3. Developed from, "Who were the authors of the books of the Bible?" At https://gotquestions.org/Bible-authors.html

Chapter 8 – Conflicts within the Bible

1. Refer to "Why is The Message (Bible) not safe?" By Justin Peters 2011. https://fortheloveofhistruth.com/2011/10/07/why-is-the-message-bible-not-safe/
2. Source www.biblehub.com

Chapter 9 – History of the Bible

1. Information from Wikipedia, Nevi'im https://en.wikipedia.org/wiki/Nevi%27im
2. Information from Wikipedia, Ketuvim https://en.wikipedia.org/wiki/Ketuvim
3. Information from Wikipedia, Septuagint https://en.wikipedia.org/wiki/SeptuagintInformation
4. Information from Wikipedia, Old Testament https://en.wikipedia.org/wiki/Old_Testament
5. Information from Wikipedia, New Testament https://en.wikipedia.org/wiki/Bible
3. English Bible History Article & Timeline by John L. Jeffcoat III. At www.greatsite.com. Used by permission. http://www.greatsite.com/timeline-english-bible-history/

Notes:

Chapter 10 - Knowledge

1. From English Oxford Living Dictionaries, Definition of knowledge in English https://en.oxforddictionaries.com/definition/knowledge
4. From Wikipedia, Friedrich Immanuel Niethammer, https://en.wikipedia.org/wiki/Friedrich_Immanuel_Niethammer

Chapter 11 – What is the real story?

1. The Bible Story, Bible Society New Zealand, http://www.biblesociety.org.nz/get-resources/for-individuals/the-bible-story/the-bible-story-web?showall=1
2. NPNF1-05. St. Augustine: Anti-Pelagian Writings, - Grace, Concealed in the Old Testament, is Revealed in the New. Chapter 27 [XV.] – Public domain.

Chapter 12 – Who is the God of the Bible?

1. Based on the characteristics of God in the Bible from the book, "Knowledge of The Holy", by A.W. Tozer 1961 – Public domain.
2. Source www.biblehub.com

Chapter 13 – Relevance today

1. Based on information in article "What is sanctification? What is the definition of Christian sanctification?" at Got Questions? Org. https://gotquestions.org/sanctification.html.

2. Original research done by Edgar Dale on Learning Retention Rate
http://www.tenouk.com/learningretentionrate.html

Chapter 14 – How to read it

1. Adaption of quote by Lao Tzu an ancient Chinese philosopher from 6th century BC "The journey of a thousand miles begins with one step."

Other books by Robert J Cottle

- The Bible, True, Relevant or a Fairy Tale. (Non-fiction)

- Fifty Shades of White, one man's quest for righteousness. (A novel, fiction)

- The Gospel of the Kingdom, not the Gospel of the Church. (Non-fiction)

- Not Many Fathers, why Othniel became a Judge. (A novel, fiction.)

- Eschatology 101, What the Bible says about the end of time. (Non-fiction)

www.ingramcontent.com/pod-product-compliance
Lightning Source LLC
Chambersburg PA
CBHW071215080526
44587CB00013BA/1388